Llewellyn's 1996

Organic Gardening Almanac

Edited by Cynthia Ahlquist

Contributors:

Susan Wittig Albert, Harriet Amar, Peter Bahouth, Bernyce Barlow, Mary Brown, Candia Lea Cole, Dr. Walter Crinnion, N.D., Kristine M. Distel-Bennett, Deborah Duchon, Roald Gundersen, Penny Kelly, Tim King, Jack Kittredge, Phil Klein, Janet LaBarre, Harry MacCormack, Steven McFadden, John Navazio, Leslie P. Nielsen, Sharon Parker, Roslyn Reid, Gilbert Schoenstein, Pamela Spence, Michael VeSeart, Carly Wall, Monica Wallace, Susun Weed, Jude Williams, and Betty Wold.

Llewellyn's Organic Gardening Almanac

Book Design and Layout:	Cynthia Ahlquist
Cover Design:	Lynne Menturweck
Cover Art:	Brian Jensen
Clip Art:	Dover Publications
Photo, page 8:	Paul Peterson
Photos, pages 70, 72:	Harry MacCormack
Photo, page 203:	Gilbert Schoenstein
Drawings, pages 44, 47:	Penny Kelly
Drawing, page 84:	Harriet Amar
Drawing, page 113:	Leslie Nielsen
Drawings, pages 177, 178, 179:	Tom Grewe, from original sketches by Janice King
Drawings, pages 198, 199:	Anne Marie Garrison
Drawings, pages 3, 4, 289:	Tom Grewe

ISBN 1-56718-915-6

Llewellyn Publications
A Division of Llewellyn Worldwide, Ltd.
P.O. Box 64383-915
St. Paul, MN 55164-0383

Table of Contents

Why Organic Gardening?

Saving Seeds

Building the Soil

Pests and Disease

Practical Application

The Lawn

Herbs

Flowers

Specialty Gardens

Hi-Tech Gardening and Building

Health and Alternative Medicine

From Garden to Kitchen

Conservation and Ecology

Gardening Tables

Directory of Products and Services

1995

JANUARY
S	M	T	W	T	F	S
1	2	3	4	5	6	7
8	9	10	11	12	13	14
15	16	17	18	19	20	21
22	23	24	25	26	27	28
29	30	31				

FEBRUARY
S	M	T	W	T	F	S
			1	2	3	4
5	6	7	8	9	10	11
12	13	14	15	16	17	18
19	20	21	22	23	24	25
26	27	28				

MARCH
S	M	T	W	T	F	S
			1	2	3	4
5	6	7	8	9	10	11
12	13	14	15	16	17	18
19	20	21	22	23	24	25
26	27	28	29	30	31	

APRIL
S	M	T	W	T	F	S
						1
2	3	4	5	6	7	8
9	10	11	12	13	14	15
16	17	18	19	20	21	22
23	24	25	26	27	28	29
30						

MAY
S	M	T	W	T	F	S
	1	2	3	4	5	6
7	8	9	10	11	12	13
14	15	16	17	18	19	20
21	22	23	24	25	26	27
28	29	30	31			

JUNE
S	M	T	W	T	F	S
				1	2	3
4	5	6	7	8	9	10
11	12	13	14	15	16	17
18	19	20	21	22	23	24
25	26	27	28	29	30	

JULY
S	M	T	W	T	F	S
						1
2	3	4	5	6	7	8
9	10	11	12	13	14	15
16	17	18	19	20	21	22
23	24	25	26	27	28	29
30	31					

AUGUST
S	M	T	W	T	F	S
		1	2	3	4	5
6	7	8	9	10	11	12
13	14	15	16	17	18	19
20	21	22	23	24	25	26
27	28	29	30	31		

SEPTEMBER
S	M	T	W	T	F	S
					1	2
3	4	5	6	7	8	9
10	11	12	13	14	15	16
17	18	19	20	21	22	23
24	25	26	27	28	29	30

OCTOBER
S	M	T	W	T	F	S
1	2	3	4	5	6	7
8	9	10	11	12	13	14
15	16	17	18	19	20	21
22	23	24	25	26	27	28
29	30	31				

NOVEMBER
S	M	T	W	T	F	S
			1	2	3	4
5	6	7	8	9	10	11
12	13	14	15	16	17	18
19	20	21	22	23	24	25
26	27	28	29	30		

DECEMBER
S	M	T	W	T	F	S
					1	2
3	4	5	6	7	8	9
10	11	12	13	14	15	16
17	18	19	20	21	22	23
24	25	26	27	28	29	30
31						

1996

JANUARY
S	M	T	W	T	F	S
	1	2	3	4	5	6
7	8	9	10	11	12	13
14	15	16	17	18	19	20
21	22	23	24	25	26	27
28	29	30	31			

FEBRUARY
S	M	T	W	T	F	S
				1	2	3
4	5	6	7	8	9	10
11	12	13	14	15	16	17
18	19	20	21	22	23	24
25	26	27	28	29		

MARCH
S	M	T	W	T	F	S
					1	2
3	4	5	6	7	8	9
10	11	12	13	14	15	16
17	18	19	20	21	22	23
24	25	26	27	28	29	30
31						

APRIL
S	M	T	W	T	F	S
	1	2	3	4	5	6
7	8	9	10	11	12	13
14	15	16	17	18	19	20
21	22	23	24	25	26	27
28	29	30				

MAY
S	M	T	W	T	F	S
			1	2	3	4
5	6	7	8	9	10	11
12	13	14	15	16	17	18
19	20	21	22	23	24	25
26	27	28	29	30	31	

JUNE
S	M	T	W	T	F	S
						1
2	3	4	5	6	7	8
9	10	11	12	13	14	15
16	17	18	19	20	21	22
23	24	25	26	27	28	29
30						

JULY
S	M	T	W	T	F	S
	1	2	3	4	5	6
7	8	9	10	11	12	13
14	15	16	17	18	19	20
21	22	23	24	25	26	27
28	29	30	31			

AUGUST
S	M	T	W	T	F	S
				1	2	3
4	5	6	7	8	9	10
11	12	13	14	15	16	17
18	19	20	21	22	23	24
25	26	27	28	29	30	31

SEPTEMBER
S	M	T	W	T	F	S
1	2	3	4	5	6	7
8	9	10	11	12	13	14
15	16	17	18	19	20	21
22	23	24	25	26	27	28
29	30					

OCTOBER
S	M	T	W	T	F	S
		1	2	3	4	5
6	7	8	9	10	11	12
13	14	15	16	17	18	19
20	21	22	23	24	25	26
27	28	29	30	31		

NOVEMBER
S	M	T	W	T	F	S
					1	2
3	4	5	6	7	8	9
10	11	12	13	14	15	16
17	18	19	20	21	22	23
24	25	26	27	28	29	30

DECEMBER
S	M	T	W	T	F	S
1	2	3	4	5	6	7
8	9	10	11	12	13	14
15	16	17	18	19	20	21
22	23	24	25	26	27	28
29	30	31				

1997

JANUARY
S	M	T	W	T	F	S
			1	2	3	4
5	6	7	8	9	10	11
12	13	14	15	16	17	18
19	20	21	22	23	24	25
26	27	28	29	30	31	

FEBRUARY
S	M	T	W	T	F	S
						1
2	3	4	5	6	7	8
9	10	11	12	13	14	15
16	17	18	19	20	21	22
23	24	25	26	27	28	

MARCH
S	M	T	W	T	F	S
						1
2	3	4	5	6	7	8
9	10	11	12	13	14	15
16	17	18	19	20	21	22
23	24	25	26	27	28	29
30	31					

APRIL
S	M	T	W	T	F	S
		1	2	3	4	5
6	7	8	9	10	11	12
13	14	15	16	17	18	19
20	21	22	23	24	25	26
27	28	29	30			

MAY
S	M	T	W	T	F	S
				1	2	3
4	5	6	7	8	9	10
11	12	13	14	15	16	17
18	19	20	21	22	23	24
25	26	27	28	29	30	31

JUNE
S	M	T	W	T	F	S
1	2	3	4	5	6	7
8	9	10	11	12	13	14
15	16	17	18	19	20	21
22	23	24	25	26	27	28
29	30					

JULY
S	M	T	W	T	F	S
		1	2	3	4	5
6	7	8	9	10	11	12
13	14	15	16	17	18	19
20	21	22	23	24	25	26
27	28	29	30	31		

AUGUST
S	M	T	W	T	F	S
					1	2
3	4	5	6	7	8	9
10	11	12	13	14	15	16
17	18	19	20	21	22	23
24	25	26	27	28	29	30
31						

SEPTEMBER
S	M	T	W	T	F	S
	1	2	3	4	5	6
7	8	9	10	11	12	13
14	15	16	17	18	19	20
21	22	23	24	25	26	27
28	29	30				

OCTOBER
S	M	T	W	T	F	S
			1	2	3	4
5	6	7	8	9	10	11
12	13	14	15	16	17	18
19	20	21	22	23	24	25
26	27	28	29	30	31	

NOVEMBER
S	M	T	W	T	F	S
						1
2	3	4	5	6	7	8
9	10	11	12	13	14	15
16	17	18	19	20	21	22
23	24	25	26	27	28	29
30						

DECEMBER
S	M	T	W	T	F	S
	1	2	3	4	5	6
7	8	9	10	11	12	13
14	15	16	17	18	19	20
21	22	23	24	25	26	27
28	29	30	31			

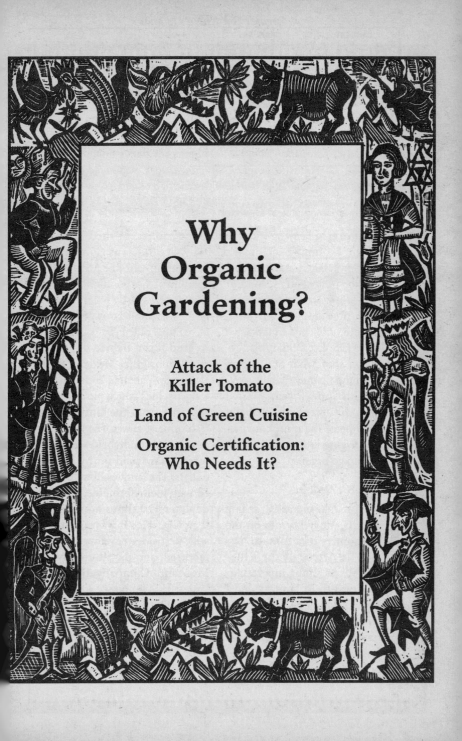

Why Organic Gardening?

**Attack of the
Killer Tomato**

Land of Green Cuisine

**Organic Certification:
Who Needs It?**

Attack of the Killer Tomato

By Peter Bahouth

Excerpted with permission from the 1994 Seeds of Change Catalog. *Seeds of Change sells 100% certified organically-grown, open–pollinated seeds—including hybrid, regional, and heirloom varieties. To obtain a copy of the current* Seeds of Change Catalog, *call 1-800-95-SEEDS.*

EDITOR'S NOTE: In keeping with the tradition of beginning each year's *Organic Gardening Almanac* with a piece on the philosophy behind or benefits of organic gardening, I have excerpted this article from a longer piece published in the *Seeds of Change Catalog.* While this segment takes somewhat of a departure from the themes we have covered in this spot in years past, I think you will agree with me that it presents one of the most convincing (and frightening) reasons for a gardener to go organic.

I want to take a crack at telling you the story I wrote on the economics of a tomato. It's called "The Attack of the Killer Tomato." I was sitting in a restaurant in Toronto in January and I ordered a salad. The salad came with a tomato on it, and I looked at it and asked, "Where did this tomato come from?" So I tracked it. This tomato's story begins on land acquired by the U.S.–based Jolly Green Giant Company, in partnership with the Mexican Development Corporation. The land was once used by local Mexican farmers as publicly-owned cooperative farms called *ejidos.* The tomato seed was a hybrid developed from an original Mexican strain, but is now patented and owned by Calgene, Inc., which purchased the research from the University of California at Davis. The University developed the hybrid with a research grant paid for by U.S. tax dollars. The land was first fumigated with methylbromide, an ozone depleter 120 times more potent than CFC-111. It was also treated with pesticides developed, manufactured, and distributed by the Monsanto Company, one of the largest U.S. polluters. Production waste was shipped to the world's largest hazardous waste landfill in Emelle, Alabama, a predominately poor African-American community. The Mexican farm workers formerly of the *ejidos* cooperatives have been given no protection from the pesticides used: no gloves, masks, or safety instructions. They make approximately $2.50 a day and have no access to health care.

Once harvested, the tomato itself is first placed on a plastic tray covered in plastic wrap, then packed in cardboard boxes. The plastic is manufactured with chlorine manufactured by the Formosa company of Point Comfort, Texas. Workers and citizens of Point Comfort face a potentially significant rise in cancer, immune suppression, and developmental effects due to exposure to high levels of dioxin. The cardboard comes from 300-year-old trees from British Columbia, and is then processed in the Great Lakes pulp mills, where residents are warned against eating dioxin-contaminated fish. The cardboard is then shipped by the United Trucking Company to Latin American farms.

The boxed tomatoes—reddened by ether, tasteless, with no nutritional value—are sent via refrigerated trucks throughout North America. Both trucks and distribution centers are equipped with CFC cooling equipment made by DuPont of Wilmington, Delaware. If, however, the tomatoes come to the border at a time of competition from U.S. tomato production, delivery may be

stopped under the pretense that they are contaminated by pesticides. Once at their destination in Toronto, the plastic packaging is thrown away, where it is picked up, shipped back into the U.S., and burned in an incinerator in Detroit, Michigan.

Throughout the process, fossil fuels drive the tomato's trip. Fueling the trucks and warming the climate is oil drilled for in the Gulf of Comanche, Mexico, extracted by Chevron and processed by Pemex. This fuel, which makes the tomato's trip possible, is then shipped via tanker, dodging 3,800 existing oil rigs in the Gulf of Mexico to refineries on the U.S. Gulf Coast which are uniquely responsible for the death of that region's environment and economy. The fuel is then distributed to the plastic-makers, pesticide-pushers, packaging-barons, and vehicles that make this tomato's 3,000 mile attack possible.

This tomato probably cost $0.50 in Toronto. As you can see, if we really look at the true economics of an everyday item like a tomato, we are not folding in the social costs of this type of production. When you know that that's what's really driving this type of economic system, you realize that having your own garden and growing your own tomatoes can be a very subversive and radical act. And it makes the fruit taste that much sweeter.

❧⊂⊃❧

PETER BAHOUTH acted as director of Greenpeace before joining the Turner Foundation, whose founder, Ted Turner, is an ardent conservationist. Peter has turned his formidable organizing talents to forestry and the conservation of ancient forests.

Land of Green Cuisine

An interview with Meg Anderson and David Washburn of Red Cardinal Farm

By Candia Lea Cole

EDITOR'S NOTE: Red Cardinal Farm is a Community Supported Agriculture (CSA) farm in Stillwater, Minnesota. For those not familiar with the concept of CSA, here is a simplified explanation: CSA farms sell "shares" to members of their communities. The money earned from the sale of shares is used to run the farm, which in turn provides the shareholders/members with a weekly supply of fresh produce during the growing season. CSA farms usually use organic and sustainable agriculture methods.

❖C❧❖

A midst a sweet stretch of country on a rural highway less traveled, an artistically rendered sign reaches out from behind a thick green curtain of Minnesotan trees and foliage. To the curious passers-by, it signals the roots growing in a community where green thumbs and a thriving interest in green cuisine mingle.

To Meg Anderson and David Washburn, it is known fondly as "Red Cardinal," a sanctuary for

their life's work. Signs forbidding pesticide use are posted on the front gates of the thirty-acre property on which they reside, where visitors can—should they possess the gumption—enter a brave new world of agriculture. A short walk along the dirt-paved driveway and a whispering cathedral of birch and pines ends with a dramatic panorama. Those of us who stop here regularly during the summer to pick up baskets of produce are often greeted by the freckled faces that belong not only to Meg and Dave, but their extended "farm family" as well.

Bustling in and out of an on-site refrigerated trailer (buff with the Red Cardinal logo), a college-aged woman and man lend hands to the delivery of baskets and sacks of food. By all appearances, they are serious stewards of the Earth, mastering the early stretch of an organic farming apprenticeship. Everett Myers, a neighbor and the third partner-in-chief of the farming operation, is the only one whose background comes directly from farming experience. If Red Cardinal members are lucky, they might have the chance to mingle with Dave, Meg, or Everett, who together have a wealth of insight about the land.

From the raft of cars that arrive with children, teenagers, adults, and senior citizens, Red Cardinal shareholders/members are invited to congregate among flowery sights, chirping sounds, and enjoy a complimentary cup of fresh-brewed coffee and a scone. The Red Cardinal members' weekly food share is generous. Throughout the season it includes two varieties each of fresh tomatoes, cucumbers, melons, beets, potatoes, onions, kohlrabi, broccoli, cauliflower, sweet corn, and zucchini, as well as a variety of peppers, green beans, cabbage, squash, chard, and spinach. Last but not least, there are mesclun field greens. Considered by French chefs to be the fragrant balm of a salad bistro, they're the delicacy said to have built this farm's early reputation. Also helping to build its reputation are the recipe suggestions that Meg passes along with every basket of food.

In addition to our shares of produce, we're always invited to help ourselves to bins of freshly-cut herbs in a neighboring green outbuilding. Inside the modest, farmers' market-like corridors, the rustic ambiance reflects productivity and abundance. Crates strewn about and fresh-cut flowers in water-filled buckets suggest to us that the local markets and restaurants will also partake of the bounty here.

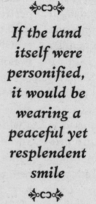

If the land itself were personified, it would be wearing a peaceful yet resplendent smile

The food and flowers grown at Red Cardinal Farm have an unmistakable aliveness—uncharacteristic of commercially-grown produce. Recalling my first tour of the place, I understand why on this farm, one path seems to flow in unity with the rest. A rare and mystifying energy seems to hover over the earthen beds of life below, as if to communicate the spirit of people working in intimate and loving cooperation with the miraculous forces of nature. One might gather, as I did, that if the land itself were personified, it would be wearing a peaceful yet resplendent smile.

With at least two tractors in plain sight, I know that life here is not maintained by some kind of magical meditation alone. All of the chancy elements of nature appear to be resting in the hands of three individuals. Something tells me the hand of faith is keeping their dream alive and their shovels down to Earth.

Q: Meg and David, how long had it been in your minds and hearts to create this place before you actually settled here?

MEG: Thinking back to my childhood, I think I always had sort of a hankering to be on a farm someday. But I don't really know where that desire came from because I didn't grow up on one, or actually have a memorable visit to one. The opportunity to settle on some land and create a small farming enterprise didn't really border on reality until after David and I met in September, 1988. Prior to this time, I was pursuing an art history degree and making homes in Colorado and Seattle, Washington. After moving to Minnesota in 1980, I worked as a fashion and image consultant at a well-known department store for eight years.

During this time, I was committed to the work because it seemed to be a stabilizing piece of my life. But as time passed, I became increasingly dissatisfied with my work, my lifestyle, and even the townhouse I was living in, which, although it was comfortable, was also a hermetically-sealed environment, surrounded by city lights and freeways. The feeling that somehow it didn't represent all of what I really valued and believed in began creeping into my thoughts more and more while nudging me to make a change. Yet I felt overwhelmed by the prospect of uprooting. I guess the winds of change were in my favor, because it wasn't long afterward that the opportunity arose to work in a friend's gardening business. It was organic for the most part, so I got the full breadth of experience—including hand-pitching manure into the truck used for plant mulch. It really got me in touch with my instinctive love for gardening and I began to sense the purpose for getting my hands into the Earth.

DAVID: I think I was also yearning to do something more real and gratifying with my life before, and especially after Meg and I were introduced in 1988. At the time, I was applying my background in psychology and business to the management of a popular workout club and fitness gear shop. Later, I became the owner of a large, successful health club which I bought in 1989 and eventually relinquished my stock in. I wanted the freedom to "walk" in a new direction. I saw a lot of people who were dedicated to their health, but also many who were in pain and addicted to exercise. It struck me

Red Cardinal Farmers Everett Myers, Meg Anderson, and
David Washburn, photographed by Paul Peterson

that they were not truly living what you would call a healthy, balanced lifestyle. While thinking about the fact that I was earning a living in their company, I found myself reevaluating my motives. I was feeling the urge to create a different kind of wholeness for myself. That's when we hit upon the idea for growing gourmet salad greens. We acted pretty boldly that next season when the greens shot through the soil in the lettuce patch. One day, we filled up about twenty crates with our spicy, colorful greens and dashed off, unannounced, to a number of local restaurants. It wasn't long before chefs were calling and asking us what else we could grow for them.

Q: Did you have help with your farm work that year?

DAVID: My sister and a good friend of ours helped out and developed that early sense of community with us. During the course of the same year, we also met our neighbor, who owned 200 acres of land. She told us about her son, Everett, who along with his wife, had just come back from Ecuador, where they had been farming in the Peace Corps. After meeting them, it seemed more than probable that we would form a loose partnership and explore ways to maximize our potential as farmers.

MEG: Part of Everett's job in the Corps was introducing different foods to the villagers and working to help farmers diversify crops. Having been exposed to the vast and indiscriminate use of pesticides, he was adamant about resuming organic farming methods when he returned home.

Q: Was there a turn of events that led to your expanded partnership?

MEG: Yes. In 1991, while researching different farming methods and visiting several farms, we ran across an article in *Veggie Life* magazine which told about CSA. It succinctly described the plan we were going forward with.

Q: For those who have not been exposed to CSA, can you explain what it is?

DAVID: CSA stands for community supported agriculture. It's a system of farming where the consumer (in this case, the community) and the farmer understand that agriculture is a partnership with each other and the land.

MEG: In other words, the farmer grows food directly for people and not only for a market, where there is no end contact with the user. A more ethical and humane approach is used in producing the food, one that considers ways to sustain the land, and one that encourages people who are buying the food to do the same.

DAVID: The first CSA movement began during the sixties in Japan and Europe, and caught on in the states of Vermont, Massachusetts, and Pennsylvania in the eighties.

Q: What is CSA doing to change the way we approach food and agriculture?

MEG: I think it is filling both a spiritual and practical need. More and more people are looking at the land as a precious resource that cannot be taken for granted. They're beginning to realize that not every tract of land can be used for a housing development. Food is essential to our lives, but how will we eat, if we choose not to rely on the commercial manufacturers of this food? Community supported agriculture is giving us the opportunity to forge ahead and take a new kind of responsibility for our health and survival.

DAVID: Before the Great Depression, a majority of our country farmed. Now, it's down to 2 percent. Out of that low percent, the farms are mostly large, commercial operations with only 5 percent of landowners owning more than half of the farmland. On these farms, there is less biodiversity and more dangerous use of pesticides and herbicides. By choosing to go the route of community supported agriculture, we are hoping to educate people about aspects of food production that can more favorably impact their health, the economy, and the environment. The time has come when we have to stop buying food from the standpoint of how much it costs. As Americans, we're interested in getting a bargain. By comparison to the portion of income Europeans spend on food, Americans spend half the amount. There is not the same kind of appreciation for food here. American food is produced and sold too cheaply.

MEG: For one thing, the cost of using chemicals on the environment is not included in the price. The cost to health insurance companies (should we become sick from chemicals) is not built into the cost of food either. There are also hidden costs to the taxpayer, including billions in federal subsidies, as well as costs for pesticide regulations, hazardous waste disposal, and groundwater cleanup.

DAVID: We pay with our lives, and yet we have been slow to see the value of paying a little more out of our pocketbooks up front for quality food and eco-preservation.

Q: Please clarify the term *organic*.

DAVID: Well, the proof is in the dirt. Organic food should not contain synthetically-compounded nourishment (i.e., fertilizers) or pesticides, fungicides, or herbicides. These things kill the soil. Basically, there are natural chemicals and synthetic ones. Our aim is to do away with chemicals altogether in favor of soil building so that the plant can take in what it needs. The plants are secondary to the soil itself. Organic farming is a carbon- and nitrogen-based mineralized farming system.

MEG: We add wood chips to the soil for carbon, and green alfalfa for nitrogen. We also compost a variety of cow and horse manures for up to a year in advance of incorporating them into the soil.

DAVID: The pile heats up to about 160°F and becomes almost sweet smelling in the process. We have big red earthworms excavating our soil. Of course, the rich soil base continues the decomposition process, whereby it naturally releases all of the nutrients that the plants thrive on. Organic foods do, in fact, have significantly higher nutritional content than non-organic.

MEG: We find that our plants have a healthy resistance to disease and bugs due in part, we assume, to the quality of the soil. We do rotate our plants as well, and use hay mulches or plastic covers to conserve moisture and prevent sunstroke on some plants.

Q: Are you ever at a loss as to what a plant needs?

DAVID: It's a different game every year, but we are getting a pretty good feel for our gardens and plants. Between the knowledge we've gained from personal experience, coupled with information from books and perhaps an intuitive sense, we are figuring things out as we go along.

Q: What was it that united you in the decision to buy land together, and how did you find the place?

MEG: After almost a year of great friendship, David and I decided to spend our Thanksgiving holiday in Hawaii on a two-week sailing trip. Needless to say, it was pure paradise. We couldn't escape the lushness of nature and we found ourselves talking about finding land in Hawaii to farm.

DAVID: The last five days of the trip turned the table in terms of solidifying our desire to farm and work the Earth together. Sitting in the tranquillity of nature made the prospect even more profound.

MEG: When we first began looking for land, we checked out Northfield, which was a relatively slow-growing community in southern Minnesota with a lot of wide-open space. But after considering its long distance to our marketing and delivery destination, we started our search around Stillwater. The first time we looked at the property we

are now living on, we weren't sure it had everything we wanted. It took exposure to other properties and another tour of the grounds to make us realize its true potential. We ended up buying the property in the spring of 1990, although we didn't live there right away. David, who is also a master carpenter, used the first several months to renovate the house.

American food is produced and sold too cheaply

Q: Since you haven't mentioned special training in the area of organic farming, how did you prepare for your roles as organic farmers?

DAVID: Our first year on the property, we spent most of our time getting settled and preparing to have our own personal kitchen garden. We bought seeds from companies such as Johnny's and Shepard Seeds, and planted a little of everything on a small plot close to the homestead. We probably purchased enough seeds to plant twenty acres. In fact, we still have leftover seeds from that experiment! In the beginning, wherever Meg had her hands in the Earth, I was close at hand, with the likes of Eliot Coleman's organic gardening book. Nature was awfully gracious that year. We had very good luck our first season. It gave us confidence to start thinking bigger.

MEG: In preparation for the following spring planting season of 1992, we began to discuss the idea for growing and pricing a food we could sell to small restaurants or the farmers' market. We did have the opportunity in 1993 to travel to Monterey, California, where we attended the Asimilar Eco-Farming Conference. We also visited a handful of organic farms and farmers who were very open to sharing what made their farms successful. It was a wonderful experience.

Q: Is it necessary for the beginning farmer to start out with a lot of equipment? Also, what kind of capital is needed to get a CSA started?

DAVID: Initially, we started out simple, using a rototiller on the land and an extra refrigerator for keeping flowers and greens fresh. And, we purchased some gardening tools and totes. We found that we could feed 15–30 members on only one acre of food. We pur-

chased the other farm machinery as we went along, but found that we didn't actually use some of it right away.

MEG: We did invest some of our savings on items such as our logo, refrigerated trailer, and farm equipment, but our costs for producing the food each season are recovered through the sale of shares.

Q: How do you determine the cost of a share?

DAVID: We sit down together and determine our operating expenses together for the season. Presently, our full share comes in at $395.00 for our sixteen-week season. Some of our members find that one share is more than they can eat each week, so they ask a neighbor or friend to split it with them.

MEG: It's important not to undersell yourself. You must remember that the CSA is not about how to provide food cheap. It's about food reflecting the true costs of bringing it from sustainable ground to the dining table. In essence, we are providing not only high-quality food to members, but other services as well. A lot of care and research goes into selecting and planning, farming without chemicals, providing recipe sheets, and being present to serve them in whatever capacity is called for.

Q: Is there anything about the nature of this work that has surprised you along your way?

MEG: I knew it would be a lot of work, but when it's something you want, you sort of have an endless reserve within yourself.

DAVID: Nevertheless, we thank God that we didn't decide to farm in Hawaii where there's no off-season! We have great help with our summer live-in apprentices. And, we have discovered that producing crops for more people is a matter of getting systems down. We have become more and more organized, which makes the work seem easier in many regards, even though the demands on our time are increasing. We will, I'm sure, hire more hands as the farming load increases, giving ourselves a more managerial role.

Q: This place seems to me to be a haven of peace, beauty, and harmony. There seems to be such a pure intentionality to everything you're doing, and a real relationship between yourselves and the land.

DAVID: There is an intentionality about what we're trying to create. We have set a direction for ourselves, and in the "doingness" of the work, I imagine we are becoming more and more connected in spirit to the land.

MEG: There's an osmosis that occurs when you're out amidst the pine trees and oak forests. And although you're in "production mode," you can feel that nature is with you, supporting who you are.

DAVID: If everybody would adopt a favorite farm as they do a favorite restaurant, they would get a taste of how satisfying our work is. And, how good it feels to work for Mother Nature.

CANDIA LEA COLE lives in Mahtomedi, Minnesota with her family. She refers to herself as a "nutritional artist and culinary shaman." She is the author of three whole-foods cookbooks available through Woodbridge Press of Santa Barbara, CA. Tel. 1-800-237-6053. Meg Anderson and David Washburn can be contacted at (612) 653-1485 for membership inquiries.

Organic Certification: Who Needs It?

By Jack Kittredge

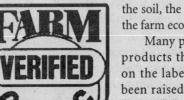

Increasingly, consumers who buy organic foods are finding the words "certified organic" on the box label or on the sign hanging over the produce case. Even at farmers' markets, a carefully handwritten notice is often on display, giving the name of a certifying organization. What does it mean to be certified? Is it really a guarantee of quality? Who pays for it, and is it worth the price?

What is Organic Certification?

As the term implies, certification is a third-party assurance to the consumer. It is not, as many believe, a guarantee that the food is residue-free. Nothing short of tissue-testing every bite could assure that. It is, instead, an assurance that the food was grown or produced according to certain methods that not only minimize the likeliness of harmful residues but are also environmentally sound and build the health of the soil, the crop, and the farm ecosystem.

Many people see products that claim on the label to have been raised by some "organic" standard (such as the California Organic Food Act of 1990). Such a claim may be true, but a farm making it does not submit documents to, or undergo regular inspections by, any third-party organization. Rather than having, like a certified farm, to prove that it is "organic," such a farm leaves the burden of proof on the consumer to prove that it is not. Increasingly, the growers' industry is uncomfortable with label claims and is insisting on third-party certification.

Who Certifies Farms as Organic?

Obviously, certification is only as reliable as the group doing the certifying. That's why any reputable certifying organization requires that its name be displayed with the food it certifies. The words "certified organic" without the name of the certifying group should be a red warning flag. At best, the seller doesn't understand what the term means.

You need to know the certifying groups because they 1) establish the standards by which certification is granted; and 2) administer the application and inspection process itself. If the standards are too weak, even rigid adherence is meaningless. But tough standards without adequate enforcement are also of no value to the consumer.

Fortunately, most certification groups in the United States use similar, strong standards and have reasonable enforcement procedures, including on-farm inspections, documentation of farm purchases and sales, and provisions for soil, water, or tissue-testing, when necessary. A list of reputable certification programs follows this article, with addresses and phone numbers. If you have any questions about particular programs, contact them and find out how they work. Most will be happy to send you their standards, application, and enforcement procedures for a nominal fee.

The existence of so many different certification groups is understandably confusing to consumers. But consider farming itself. It is uniquely local. Each part of the country has its own climate,

soil types, growing period or "season," population density, and myriad other factors that make a particular kind of farming, cropping, and marketing appropriate. In New England we don't raise much corn or soy for wholesale markets. Land is too valuable; fresh fruits and vegetables return far more income per acre, and our demographics mean the consumer can be enjoying them the same day they are picked.

Certification groups grew up to supply various needs. Some of the earliest were set up by processors who wanted to be able to assure buyers that the snack chips, noodles, and packaged flours they produced were composed of organic ingredients. These "processor-driven" programs aren't interested in fresh produce and have no geographical limits. Their inspectors may fly to, and spend several days checking out, a faraway farm

or plantation that is under contract to the processor.

As a result of increasing demand for organic food in Europe and Japan, as well as upscale North American markets, many large growers wanted to be able to sell to whomever they pleased. Processor-driven certification would be a nightmare to these free agents, so some programs evolved that cater to certifying for sale into global markets. Still other programs were initiated by wholesalers and retailers who wanted an increased supply of local organic produce, but felt certification fees were out of the reach of small growers. Finally, some state legislatures have established certification programs for their own farmers as a way of helping them command higher incomes while staying on the land.

Virtually all these programs agree about prohibiting synthetic pesticides and chemical fertilizers from organic production, with most requiring that the land be free of such inputs for three years before an organic harvest can take place. In place of depending on "cures," organic farmers stress prevention through proper management practices, such as crop rotation and soil building. Natural inputs like manure, compost, rock powders, and biological and botanical controls are used instead of synthetic chemical ones. Different programs may quibble about the amount of phosphoric acid allowed as a stabilizer in fish emulsion, but on 95 percent of the questions, all agree.

How Much Does Certification Cost?

Obviously, to certify an organic farm costs money. A professional inspector must visit once or more during the season. A committee must evaluate the inspector's report and all the paperwork and decide upon a range of certification issues. There must be phone calls, letters, and copies of documents. In most cases, those costs are somewhat proportional to the size of the farming operation, so farms are charged a fee based upon their acreage or gross income.

Some certifiers are private firms, which hope to make a profit. They usually work with the larger farms and plantations, which can afford fees of up to several thousand dollars. Other groups, perhaps the majority, are non-profit associations. They must meet their costs of operation, but often members donate many hours of labor by serving on committees, writing standards, researching farm inputs, and reviewing applications to spot questionable practices. Thus non-profit groups, by subsidizing the full costs, are able to certify smaller farms and often charge as little as $50.00 or $100.00 for the service. Finally, state programs, which are tax-supported, can certify a farm for nominal amounts or even for no charge.

How is the System Regulated?

Whether their fees are large or small, certification programs impose a lot of restrictions on participating farms: detailed records must be kept from year to year, documents must be properly filled out and notarized, soil must be regularly sampled and tested, purchased inputs must be checked out and approved before use. Some organic farmers find all this oppressive and never even apply for certification. These farms primarily sell to local buyers at roadside stands, in farmers' markets, and via Community Supported Agriculture projects—a relatively new idea which involves consumers buying a yearly "share" of a farm's produce and receiving it on a weekly basis throughout the season. Such local buyers have access to the farm, know the farmer, and often feel that their relationship of personal trust is a better guarantee of organic practices than certification by an outside organization.

Organic food now accounts for about 2 percent of all food purchased in the U.S. While this seems tiny on a percentage basis, it still represents a lot of money. There have been instances where sellers, attracted by the higher price, have misrepresented conventionally-grown produce as organic. Although isolated, such cases, com-

bined with the obvious growing public demand for organic food, moved Congress to pass the Organic Food Production Act (OFPA).

Although the government is still writing the final regulations and OFPA has not been implemented yet, this law will fundamentally change organic certification. Food, to be labeled "organic," will have to meet strict minimum production standards pertaining to how it was grown, harvested, stored, and processed. The law also will require that any food labeled "organic" be certified by an accredited certification program. (An exception will allow backyard growers—anyone grossing less than $5,000 annually—to sell without being certified so long as they meet the production standards.)

Many small certification groups are worried that government accreditation of their programs will involve high costs which neither they nor their farmers can absorb. Historically, regulation has been accompanied by the disappearance of small producers who cannot afford to modernize. If high costs of accreditation under OFPA mean that small farmers will no longer be able to sell their produce as "organic" without violating the law, some will go out of business, but others will probably just drop the name and use another. Already words like "biological," "ecological," and "Earthwise" are being bandied about as potential replacements.

Whatever the future of small, local growers, it is clear that organic food is an increasingly important part of our national food supply. Certification has become vital to large growers and processors who need a system of quality assurance in a constantly changing marketplace. It is also a tool that intelligent consumers can use to demand value in their own food purchase decisions. By doing so, they will not only secure the highest quality food for their own families, they will also benefit those of us who are trying to raise healthy crops in a manner that preserves clean soil and water and assures that our children may continue to do so a hundred years hence.

Certification Programs

CALIFORNIA CERTIFIED ORGANIC FARMERS (CCOF)

1115 Mission St.
Santa Cruz, CA 95060
(408) 423-2263

CCOF has chapters throughout California, and certifies both growers and processors.

CAROLINA FARM STEWARDSHIP ASSOCIATION

> 115 West Main St.
> Carrboro, NC 27510
> (919) 968-1030

This is a private, non-profit group organized to further organic practices and sustainable agriculture in the Carolinas.

COLORADO DEPARTMENT OF AGRICULTURE

> Division of Plant Industry
> 700 Kipling St., Suite 4000
> Lakewood, CO 80215-5894
> (303) 239-4140

FARM VERIFIED ORGANIC
> RR1, Box 40A
> Medina, ND 58467
> (701) 486-3578

The FVO program is set up to certify ingredients used by Mercantile Development, Incorporated, a Connecticut-based processor.

GEORGIA ORGANIC GROWERS ASSOCIATION

> P. O. Box 567661
> Atlanta, GA 30356
> (404) 621-4642

GOGA is a non-profit association to encourage organic growing.

IDAHO DEPARTMENT OF AGRICULTURE

> P. O. Box 790
> Boise, ID 83701
> (208) 334-2623

MAINE ORGANIC FARMERS & GARDENERS ASSOCIATION

> P. O. Box 2176
> Augusta, ME 04338
> (207) 622-3118

This is one of the oldest private non-profit certification groups.

NEW MEXICO ORGANIC COMMODITY COMMISSION

> 118 Amherst Drive NE
> Albuquerque, NM 87106
> (505) 266-9849

This is New Mexico's state certification program.

NORTHEAST ORGANIC FARMING ASSOCIATION (NOFA)

> 411 Sheldon Rd.
> Barre, MA 01005
> (508) 355-2853

NOFA is a private, non-profit association with chapters in New York, New Jersey, Massachusetts, Connecticut, Rhode Island, Vermont, and New Hampshire.

OHIO ECOLOGICAL FOOD & FARM ASSOCIATION

> P. O. Box 02234
> Columbus, OH 43202
> (614) 294-3663

This is a non-profit group.

OREGON TILTH CERTIFIED ORGANIC
> P. O. Box 218
> Tualatin, OR 97062
> (503) 692-4877

This is the certification program of the non-profit group Oregon Tilth.

ORGANIC CROP IMPROVEMENT
ASSOCIATION (OCIA)

> 3185 Twp. Rd. 179
> Bellefontaine, OH 43311
> (513) 592-4983

OCIA is a non-profit group working with Midwestern grain farms.

ORGANIC GROWERS AND BUYERS
ASSOCIATION (OGBA)

> 1405 Silver Lake Rd.
> New Brighton, MN 55112
> (612) 636-7933

OGBA is a certification agency particularly active in the Midwest.

TEXAS DEPARTMENT OF
AGRICULTURE

> P. O. Box 12847
> Austin, TX 78711
> (512) 463-7602

This is Texas' state certification program.

WASHINGTON STATE DEPARTMENT
OF AGRICULTURE

> P. O. Box 42560
> Olympia, WA 98504
> (360) 902-1885

This is the state of Washington's organic certification agency.

JACK KITTREDGE owns a small NOFA-certified organic family farm in central Massachusetts, serves on his local Certification Committee, and is the editor of *The Natural Farmer*, a quarterly newspaper about organic farming in the northeastern U.S.

Saving Seeds

Seed Saving
Fundamentals

A Step into the Past to
Save the Future

Seed Saving Fundamentals

By John Navazio

In the history of agriculture, until quite recently, all who tilled the Earth were responsible for the development and improvement of the crop plants from which humanity obtained its sustenance. The wealth of genetic diversity that exists today in our modern crop plants is due to the ingenuity and perseverance of our agricultural ancestors.

The domesticated crop plants that grace our tables daily are all derived from a much larger number of plants that were found to be edible and were used extensively by hunter-gatherer societies. While natural selection had already shaped these wild plants, the selection pressure of the people who grew them under cultivation changed them to better suit humanity's needs. These farmers worked in concert with natural selection, and sometimes acted contrary to it by preserving variants they deemed useful which would not have survived outside of cultivation.

While some of these early domesticates flourished during the beginnings of agriculture, other potential crops were abandoned. The most promising crop plants spread across the countryside via trade and migration. This dissemination placed these crops into many diverse environments under the stewardship of the hands and minds of people who often had quite different goals in their selection criteria. Selected strains of the same crop with various favorable traits were eventually grown in close enough proximity to one another to cross and produce offspring with new combinations of these traits. Coupled with occasional "sports," or spontaneous mutations, there was an outwardly spiraling, ever-increasing pool of inherited traits as long as there was a large number of farmers saving seeds under a variety of conditions year in and year out.

Why Save Seeds?

With the advent of an increasingly specialized agriculture during this past century, more and more farmers and gardeners alike have relied on seed companies to supply all of their seed needs. This is unfortunate, because until recently, seed saving has served as an unbroken chain by which uniquely

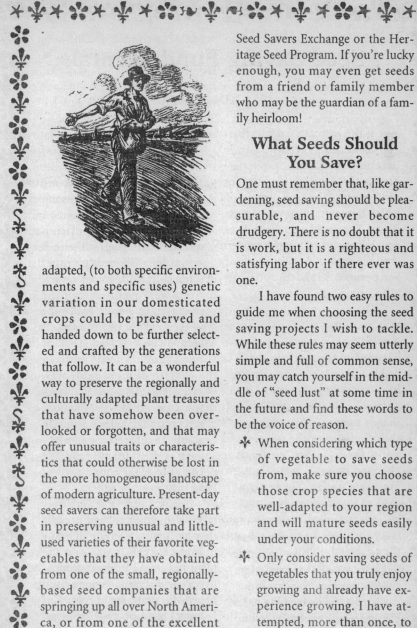

Seed Savers Exchange or the Heritage Seed Program. If you're lucky enough, you may even get seeds from a friend or family member who may be the guardian of a family heirloom!

What Seeds Should You Save?

One must remember that, like gardening, seed saving should be pleasurable, and never become drudgery. There is no doubt that it is work, but it is a righteous and satisfying labor if there ever was one.

I have found two easy rules to guide me when choosing the seed saving projects I wish to tackle. While these rules may seem utterly simple and full of common sense, you may catch yourself in the middle of "seed lust" at some time in the future and find these words to be the voice of reason.

- ❧ When considering which type of vegetable to save seeds from, make sure you choose those crop species that are well-adapted to your region and will mature seeds easily under your conditions.

- ❧ Only consider saving seeds of vegetables that you truly enjoy growing and already have experience growing. I have attempted, more than once, to save seeds on crops that didn't

adapted, (to both specific environments and specific uses) genetic variation in our domesticated crops could be preserved and handed down to be further selected and crafted by the generations that follow. It can be a wonderful way to preserve the regionally and culturally adapted plant treasures that have somehow been overlooked or forgotten, and that may offer unusual traits or characteristics that could otherwise be lost in the more homogeneous landscape of modern agriculture. Present-day seed savers can therefore take part in preserving unusual and little-used varieties of their favorite vegetables that they have obtained from one of the small, regionally-based seed companies that are springing up all over North America, or from one of the excellent seed saving organizations like the really "turn me on," only to not follow through on all of the vital steps necessary to properly save them. I was left with little or nothing to show for my efforts.

In order to successfully save seeds, gardeners need a basic understanding of the entire life cycle of the particular crop plant they wish to maintain, as well as knowledge of when it bears seed, the type of flower that it has, and the pollination system that it uses.

Life Cycles

In some common garden vegetables—beans, peas, or corn, for example—seed is what we actually eat. But in many cases, the seed-producing phase of the reproductive cycle is only rarely seen, and is then avoided or even held in disdain. For proof of this we need go no further than our language. When I grew my hair long in the 1960s I can remember my grandmother commenting that I looked as if I was "going to seed." Clearly, it was not a positive image for her. Nowadays, whenever I observe my crops "going to seed," I get a deep sense of satisfaction as I glimpse life's cycles moving to completion.

Most garden crops are either annuals, completing their life cycles at the end of one season, or biennials, completing their life cycles after two seasons. Very few perennial vegetable crops exist, and the ones that we are most familiar with in North America—asparagus, rhubarb, and horseradish—do not reproduce true to type from seed. Therefore, perennials will not be considered in this article.

As mentioned, the seeds of some annual crops are in fact the part we eat, and therefore saving their seeds is a natural outgrowth of growing these garden plants. Another group of annual crop plants are routinely grown to seed maturity, but their seeds are either ignored (tomatoes, for example), or are a minor nuisance in the preparation or enjoyment of the crop (i.e., melon, watermelon, or winter squash). A third group of annuals produce seeds much to the chagrin of most gardeners, who don't want the loss in quality that accompanies reproduction. When crops like lettuce, spinach, broccoli, cucumbers, or summer squash start to form seeds, the palatability of the edible parts of these plants usually suffers.

Biennial vegetables are only rarely seen going to seed because they are almost always utilized by humans for the "food" that the plant has stored for its reproductive phase during its second season of growth. Examples of commonly-grown biennial crops are beets, cabbage, carrots, onions, and Swiss chard. Biennial crops may have occasional plants that "bolt," or form seed heads, in their first season of vegetative growth. Many gardeners believe that by picking off the flowering structures that appear under these circumstances, that they can help revert the plant to strictly vegetative growth. Unfortunately, there is little or no chance of reversing the physiological flowering response once it begins. Also, seeds from these prematurly-bolting plants should never be saved, because you will then be selecting toward annual seed bearing and against the big, luscious vegetables that should be produced during the first season of growth.

Flower Structure

Flowering plants produce seeds via the sexual union of male gametes, or sex cells, which are carried by the pollen, and female gametes, which are part of the embryo sac that is within every ovule of the plant's ovary. After fertilization, the plant's ovaries become the developing fruit.

The female flower parts are known collectively as the pistil. At the base of the pistil is the ovary, which may hold anywhere from one (peach or avocado) to hundreds (tomatoes or squash) of ovules. Each of these ovules contains an embryo sac with an egg cell, which, if fertilized, has the po-tential of becoming a seed. Above the ovary is a long, stem-like structure, the style, which holds the stigma at its tip. The stigma is receptive to pollen from the male flowers. When a pollen grain comes in contact with the stigma it germinates, forming a pollen tube that grows down the style in an attempt to fertilize the egg cell in one of the ovules. Needless to say, conditions must be right for this to happen. Pollen must reach the stigma by wind or insect, temperatures must be in the right range (not too hot or too cold) for the pollen to germinate and grow down through the style, and the stigma, style, and ovary must be sound.

The mode of pollen transfer unique to the crop whose seeds you plan to save will determine the methods you use in the actual raising of the seed crop.

Self-Pollinated Crops

Self-pollinated species all have "perfect" flowers (male and female flower parts in the same flower). In self-pollinated crops, the stigma of a particular flower is usually only pollinated by the pollen from that same flower, thereby ensuring "self-pollination." Most self-pollinated species are pollinated and fertilized inside a flower that never opens (i.e., many legumes) or before the flower opens (i.e., tomatoes). Because of this, different varieties of the same crop species require minimal isolation distances when increasing seed. However,

Like gardening, seed saving should be pleasurable, and never become drudgery

due to certain environmental conditions, or the presence of several very "effective" pollinizing insects, it is possible for many self-pollinated crops to "out-cross" 1–2 percent per generation, and a few crops can exceed 5 percent outcrossing. Therefore, it is always a good idea to plant a tall-growing barrier crop between the different varieties of the species that you are reproducing, to minimize the chances of either physically mixing seed or of having an errant outcross occur.

Cross-Pollinated Crops

Cross-pollinated crops are naturally crossed by either insect- or wind-borne pollen. While crossing between different varieties of the same crop is undesirable when saving seeds, cross-pollinated species require a healthy, active interchange of genes within a popula-

tion of plants (a population can be a variety) to avoid the potentially deleterious effects of inbreeding depression. "Crossers" have several built-in mechanisms to ensure this "out-crossing," and should therefore be allowed, and even encouraged, to "cross" freely within the confines of the variety that you wish to increase.

Cross-pollinated species use several strategies to ensure that a large number of progeny in any generation arise from a "cross" between two individuals, thus avoiding inbreeding, and in fact creating new genetic combinations that may prove to be "better adapted" to the environmental conditions in which they are grown. An effective strategy used by "crossers" to ensure cross-pollination between individuals in a population is to have a physical separation between the male and female flower parts. This is achieved by the plant characteristics of monoecy or dioecy, which are found in a number of crops.

Monoecious crops like corn, cucumbers, and squash produce separate male and female flowers on different parts of the same plant. Corn is a dramatic example. Corn's tassel contains the male flowers and is on the top of the plant's stalk, whereas the ear, which is the female flower, is borne further down the stalk in a leaf axil. Hence, when corn's pollen is shed and carried by the wind, the chances of it being carried to another plant and therefore "crossing" are greatly increased. In cucumbers and squash, the male and female flowers are often separated by only one or two nodes on the plant and may occasionally occur at the same node. Because the vines of different plants of these insect-pollinated crops usually intertwine when grown in the field, the chances of bees randomly going from male to female flowers of different plants and thus promoting "crossing" are great.

The surest plant mechanism for promoting cross-pollination between plants is dioecy. Dioecious crop plants, like asparagus and spinach, have separate plants that have either male or female flowers exclusively. Therefore, reproduction is absolutely dependent on cross-pollination, and seed is only gathered from female plants.

Lastly, there are cross-pollinated species that have perfect flowers but are still largely "out-crossing" in their reproduction. This is accomplished by way of differential maturity of male and female flower parts within the same blossom. In other words, some species of plants have perfect flowers that shed pollen several days before the maturity and receptiveness of the stig-

matic surface of the female part of the flower. The reverse order of events may also occur, and this mismatch of male and female maturity thus insures a high degree of cross-pollination in a number of vegetable crops that have perfect flowers, including carrots, onions, and leeks.

To produce seed of any of the cross-pollinated species and maintain varietal purity, it is very important to isolate the variety whose seeds you wish to save from the pollen of any other variety within that same species. This requires physical isolation, which can be achieved through the use of either space, time, or a barrier (i.e., caging with special netting) that can stop insects or wind-borne pollen. Caging and hand-pollination are advanced techniques requiring equipment and "know-how" beyond the scope of this article, but if you are interested in these methods, you may consider joining an organization like the Seed Savers Exchange or the Heritage Seed Program (addresses listed below). The easiest way to achieve physical isolation for the beginning seed saver is with physical distances. This means that not only can you only grow one variety of a certain cross-pollinated crop per season, but you must be certain that none of your neighbors are growing that crop either. Insect-pollinated species should be separated by one half mile if seed purity is desired. Different varieties of wind-pollinated crops require a minimum separation of one mile for purity (see the chart at the end of this article for a listing of wind-pollinated crops).

Selection

Seed savers need to be concerned with selecting the healthiest, most vigorous plants of any variety that they are maintaining. "Roguing," or discarding of any off-type plants that can be identified by gross morphological differences of the plant or fruit is recommended. Genetic changes invariably occur in all organisms over time due to mutation, natural selection, and, in the case of domesticated plants, selection at the hands of humans. By saving seed you will be a part of this process, thereby becoming a "manager" of the population of plants. Geneticists define population as "a community of sexually interbreeding individuals." A population of individuals comprises a gene pool. Selection within any population that you are managing deserves some forethought.

Seed savers should ask themselves two questions before practicing any selection on a crop variety:

✤ Do I want to save the variety as "true-to-type" as possible,

or do I want to adapt the variety to my own preferences, possibly changing its characteristics in the process?

✤ Is the variety that I intend to save an older, more variable "farmer variety" (these veritable storehouses of genetic traits are often consciously maintained with lots of variation intact for genetic resiliency), or is it a more modern, non-hybrid vegetable variety that is quite uniform in its characteristics?

It is necessary to consider the uniqueness of the varieties that you are "managing." If in fact a variety you are keeping has a unique trait not often found in that crop, or the variety is historically significant, it follows that maintaining the variety as true-to-type as possible is important. However, people often save seeds of a modern non-hybrid vegetable variety that "just plain" performs well for them. In this situation, it seems that molding a variety through selection toward something quite different than what you started with is certainly acceptable and in fact is more akin to what our agricultural ancestors practiced when developing our present-day crops.

Another important consideration comes up when saving seed

of a variable "farmer variety" (sometimes called a "land race"). In this case it is important to leave as much of the natural heterogeneity in the population as possible, thereby maintaining it, much as the farmers who deliberately kept it variable to withstand the erratic temperament of the natural world. Plant breeders have often been successful picking plants out of a heterogeneous population like this, fashioning them into something new, but meanwhile still maintaining the farmer variety through the years as a genetic repository.

Population Size

To maintain the genetic diversity inherent in a population, it is important to grow an adequate number of individuals to ensure "getting all the genes" that are in the population each time you reproduce its seed. Information concerning the minimal number of plants needed in a population to maintain genetic diversity is sorely lacking in the seed saving literature. While specific numbers for many crops are hard to come by, it is possible to give general guidelines on the minimum number of plants that should be grown for each variety that you wish to maintain. Self-pollinated crops have evolved to tolerate inbreeding, and therefore can be perpetuated with

population sizes of approximately twenty plants and remain genetically healthy. An exception to this in self-pollinated crops is the heterogeneous "farmer variety," that exhibits a lot of variation. To preserve all of the genetic variation in cases like this, it is important to grow at least fifty individuals or more, depending on the extent of the variation.

Cross-pollinated crops have evolved to avoid inbreeding depression with the mechanisms previously described that promote out-crossing. All cross-pollinated species are therefore prone to some degree of inbreeding depression, and should be grown in sufficient numbers to avoid this condition. At least three categories exist for consideration when reproducing a cross-pollinated species:

- Corn. Extensive genetic research on this crop gives us some hard numbers! Be sure to grow 200 corn plants whenever increasing any corn variety. Then be sure to save seed from each of the 200 plants. Mix this seed well, using it for your next planting.

- Cucurbits. While cucumbers, squash, melons, and watermelons are all highly outcrossing species, many cucurbit breeders have reported little inbreeding depression

when self-pollinations of these crops are made. Nevertheless, to maintain diversity in these crops, it is best to grow at least 20 plants of each variety each time you reproduce the seed. While this may not be possible for many gardeners, considering the size of squash vines, seed savers should strive for a bare minimum of 8–10 of any of these vine crops to avoid the loss of genetic diversity.

❧ Opinions are quite varied regarding the minimum population size for other cross-pollinated species. However, it is safe to say that retaining genetic resiliency among most other "crossers" requires at least 40–50 plants be grown per increase. This number should climb to at least 80–100 plants if there is the inherent variation associated with an older variety.

Listed below are several crops and numbers. The numbers correspond to the crop list key, which lists factors to take into consideration when saving seeds from the plants on these lists.

Crop Lists

SELF-POLLINATED	CROSS-POLLINATED	CROSS-POLLINATED
chicory	beet 2, 3, 4, 5	mangel-wurzel 2, 3, 5
common bean	broccoli 6, 10	melon
eggplant 1	Brussels sprouts 3, 6	onion 3
endive	cabbage 3, 6	parsnip 3
fava bean 1	cauliflower 6, 10	pumpkin 11
lettuce	celeriac 3, 7	radish 4, 9
lima bean	celery 3, 7	rutabaga 3
okra	cabbage 8	spinach 2, 4
pea	corn 2	squash 11
peanut	cucumber	sunflower
pepper 1	kale 3, 6	Swiss chard 2, 3, 5
runner bean	kohlrabi 3, 6	turnip 8
soybean	leeks 3	winter radish 3, 9
tomato	lettuce 4	

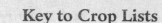

Key to Crop Lists

1. Outcrossing (greater than 5 percent) may occur due to environment or presence of certain insects.

2. Species pollinated due to wind-borne pollen; all other cross-pollinated species are pollinated predominantly by insects.

3. Biennial species; seed produced in second year after exposure to cold treatment.

4. Flower initiation is dependent on long daylength (greater than twelve hours).

5. Beet, mangel-wurzel, Swiss chard, and sugar beets will cross with each other.

6. All *Brassica oleracea* crops will cross with each other.

7. Celeriac will cross with celery.

8. Chinese cabbage will cross with turnip.

9. Radish will cross with all types of winter radish (includes daikon, black Spanish, and Chinese radishes).

10. Most modern forms of these vegetables are annuals; however, there are older "overwintering" biennial forms that require a period of cold treatment to flower.

11. Constitutes types from the four major species of *Cucurbi-ta* grown in North America. For a list of which varieties belong to which species, see *Seed to Seed*, p.114-119.

Conclusions

Seed saving is currently undergoing a resurgence with groups supplying specific information on many of the crops that you may want to maintain by saving their seed. For many gardeners, seed saving is an empowering process, enabling them to rub shoulders with their ancestors by passing on a heritage of valuable genetic resources that may otherwise be lost.

Seed Saving Groups

SEED SAVERS EXCHANGE
    3076 North Winn Rd.
    Decorah, Iowa 52101

The flagship of grassroots seed saving organizations. Seed Savers publishes three informationals a year, full of both philosophical and "how-to" articles. If you become a member you are entitled to "exchange" seed of heirloom and other hard-to-find varieties with other members. Write for details.

HERITAGE SEED PROGRAM
    Rural Route #3
    Uxbridge, Ontario L9P 1R3

The Canadian version of the Seed Savers Exchange offers many of the same benefits of its American counterpart. Its magazine is very informative and its "exchange" always has jewels for northern gardeners. Write for details.

References

Ashworth, Suzanne. *Seed to Seed: Seed Saving Techniques for the Vegetable Gardener*. Decorah, Iowa: Seed Saver Publications, 1991.

The most complete text available for a crop-by-crop breakdown on how to save seeds.

Nabhan, Gary Paul. *Enduring Seeds: Native American Agriculture and Wild Plant Conservation*. San Francisco: North Point Press, 1989.

Nabhan offers philosophy gathered from native peoples on seed saving.

Welsh, J.R. *Fundamentals of Plant Genetics and Breeding*. New York: Wily and Sons, 1981.

This technical book contains an excellent section on pollination biology.

JOHN NAVAZIO is Research Director and Plant Breeder for Garden City Seeds, a company which specializes in cold-climate seeds. He received his Ph.D. in plant breeding and plant genetics from the University of Wisconsin, and spent ten years as an organic truck farmer in Oregon and Maine. His current focus at Garden City is breeding carrots, cucumbers, beets, and tomatoes for nutritional quality. To receive a catalog from Garden City Seeds, contact them at 778 Highway 93 North, Hamilton, MT 59840, tel. (406) 961-4837, or see their advertisement in the Resources section in the back of this book.

A Step into the Past to Save the Future

A Tour of Native Seeds/SEARCH

By Jude Williams

Farmers have lost the right to save, swap, or sell seeds to other farmers, except for seeds produced from a protected variety. Because of this regulation and other factors, the biodiversity of the world's crops is greatly threatened.

Currently 95 percent of all sorghum, 90 percent of all sugar beets and 99 percent of all corn are planted from seeds sold by seed companies, most of which are owned by pharmaceutical and oil companies.

Within the last twenty years, more than 1,000 seed companies have been bought by major chemical and pharmaceutical companies such as Lily, Dow, International Chemical Companies, Monsanto, and Royal Dutch Shell. These companies also are the largest producers of pesticides, agriculture chemicals, and synthetic fertilizers. These companies see the marketability of seeds that are patented or registered. In Europe, these corporations have instituted the Common Catalog, which restricts the sale of seeds to those that are patented or registered in the Common Catalog. Three-fourths of all traditional European seed varieties are under threat of extinction. Many of the old seed varieties are already gone.

Plant extinctions are now occurring at 1,000 times the natural rate. This comes to about 27,000 species a year. For each plant that is gone, thirty or more animals and insects also become extinct because they were dependent on that plant for survival. We are co-authors of such destruction, because we destroy natural habitats without thought on a daily basis. We have allowed the chemical and pharmaceutical companies to hybridize the seeds, which causes loss of biodiversity. Seed Savers Exchange has stated that 44.6 percent of all non-hybrid vegetable varieties available to us in 1984 had been dropped from mail order catalogs by 1991, and these losses appear to be escalating. This is causing massive destruction of the biodiversity of the plants.

E.D. Wilson of Harvard University stated, "Biological diversity is responsible for the maintenance of the world as we know it. This is the assembly of life that took a billion years to evolve. It has eaten the storms, folded them into its genes, and created the world that created us. It holds the world steady."

Biodiversity is the key to our survival. Witness the Irish potato famine, when over one million people died because of a blight that struck the crops, and this because only one variety of potato was planted. Three-fourths of all potatoes planted in the U.S. today are made up of four kinds of potatoes, and these are closely relatedgenetically . Only 3 percent of the plants that were left to us by our forefathers are available today. There are over 80,000 plant varieties, but we use only twenty plant varieties for 90 percent of our food.

Does all this sound like a science fiction tale? I can assure you that it is not. As of April 4, 1995, the farmers' exemption to the Plant Variety Protection Act (PVPA) has been eliminated by Congress and limited by the U.S. Supreme Court. Congress has taken the right of farmers to resell seeds harvested by them to neighboring farmers. The sale of seed will be restricted to a group of less than a dozen seed and pharmaceutical companies, which control over 70 percent of world seed trade. This effectively robs Third World farmers who, through experimentation, have developed methods of farming with seeds that they have engineered to grow in specialized areas. This act of piracy by the Transnational Companies is called "The biggest race for property since the the Great Land Rush of 1889" by the *Wall Street Journal*. Genes are the ticket to the rush. The companies stand to make billions while effectively robbing all farmers.

Three-fourths of all traditional European seed varieties are under threat of extinction

The patented seeds are being claimed as intellectual property by the transnationals because they altered perhaps one or two genes out of 23,000. The world market for medicinal products derived from medicinal plants runs around $44 billion per year. These drugs came from traditional medicine, and yet, less than .001 percent of the profits are returned to the indigenous peoples who gave the researchers access to their information regarding the plants.

Learning from the Past

Is there hope? There are organizations that are attempting to save the biodiversity of plants, and I think they deserve our support. I had the recent good fortune to visit one such place. Native Seeds/SEARCH (NS/S) is a seed conservation organization located in Tucson, Arizona, founded twelve years ago by a group of people intent on saving the biodiversity of the plants in the southwestern region of the United States and the northwestern corner of Mexico. Another goal of NS/S is to make sure that the traditional farmers before them are honored and given the respect due them. These farmers developed techniques that enabled them and future generations to farm in an environment that receives less than 12" of rain per year. This knowledge, along with seed, was handed down to successive generations.

Farmers in that area were still using traditional methods of gardening as late as the 1920s. As many as 10,000 acres were cultivated using the floodwater method that had proven effective for them. Today there are very few such farms. They developed seeds that could withstand the severe weather and insect conditions of the southwest. As the seeds disappear, so do the traditional ways of farming.

It was only about fifty years ago that Native Americans of that region began to experience a high incidence of diabetes—in fact, one of the highest in the world. This was brought about by the change from a traditional diet to a more European way of eating. Crop varieties provided by NS/S to nutritionists have proven to have more fiber, minerals, and protein, and are therefore much healthier than hybrid vegetables available in the markets.

Native Seeds/SEARCH began a research project in 1990 to promote traditional diet as a way to stop the onset of diabetes among Native Americans. Exercise and native diet are strongly encouraged and practiced, as is the use of native medicine. Medicines derived from the plants in the area have been used for centuries as preventives as well as treatments for illness.

The organization now has a conservation farm located in southern Arizona, where farmers and gardeners come to learn traditional methods of dryland planting and harvesting. The farm is open to the public, and serves many schools as an educational opportunity to learn about the past, and as encouragement to learn how to go into the future using the wisdom of the past. As Tohono O'odham farmer D. J. Blaine puts it, "How

we care for the lima bean sprout—
or the maize kernel, or the bitter
potato—may indeed forecast our
own survival."

Many of the ancient seeds are
a storehouse of genetic diversity,
and may well be the only way we
will be able to survive into the future. Global warming, along with
weather pattern changes, may
make these seeds the only answer.

Projects that Promote Seed Saving

Angelo Joaquin, Jr., now serving as
Executive Director of Native
Seeds/SEARCH, along with Jan
Waterman, Assistant Director,
most graciously took the time to
take us on a tour of the facilities. I
can only say that I was very impressed with the growth of the organization and the valuable seed
information being shared with the
thousands of people who are very
aware of the danger of the loss of
the native seeds. Mr. Joaquin is a
native O'odham and is active in
promoting such knowledge.

There are many projects recently started that are worthwhile
of our attention. One such project

is the ongoing formation of The
Sylvester House. This urban mini-
farm includes several large gardens,
trees, and perennials from around
the region, and will include more
space to store seeds and conduct
research. It will soon have library
facilities. Adobe bricks made in the
back yard are used to make additions to the existing buildings.

Many of the seeds gathered
from the Mayos and Yaquis in
western Mexico are offered for sale
in the NS/S seed catalog. The
Guarijio in the Sierra Madre
foothills contributed panicgrass
grain, once thought extinct because of the damming of the Colorado River. From the Tohona
O'odham, the most heat- and
drought-resistant seeds in existence are offered through the catalog. The tepary bean seems to be a
very important seed because of the
short growing period needed for
maturity. In fact, over 1,200 varieties of seed are offered through
the seed catalog.

Mr. Joaquin explained the
concept of waffle farming to us as
we saw the actual method in use on
the grounds. In waffle farming,
crops are planted in recessed 4' x 4'
blocks, which collect and conserve
the water that runs off of the
mountains. The blocks are divided
by narrow walkways, which give
the field its waffle-like appearance.
As Mr. Joaquin told us about this

spiritual method of farming, still in use today, it brought back many memories of my father. We were often told to plant more than was needed. This gave us plenty to share with wildlife and others, as well as ensuring that we received all we needed. The seeds were planted with a prayer, and thanksgiving was offered at harvest. We were also instructed never to spray or destroy plants or insects.

Mr. Joaquin explained that if certain "weeds" were allowed to grow along with the vegetables, that the insects would be attracted to the weeds and leave the crops we needed alone. I know this is true, because this is exactly how I garden. All of the insects have a job to do, and we do a disservice to all of nature when we use pesticides to destroy a life of which we have no-knowledge. Many of the practices that were explained brought home to me the truth and wisdom of our ancestors' farming methods.

Native Seeds/SEARCH shares its home with Tucson Botanical Gardens, located in Tucson. The demonstration gardens are open Tuesdays and Thursdays from 10:00 AM to 4:00 PM throughout the year. The public is also invited on Saturdays, from 11:00 AM to 3:00 PM during the months of January–February and October–December. Take time to tour both gardens, as there is much to see and learn.

Native Seeds/SEARCH offers many of their seeds for sale, along with items made by native farmers. The seeds come in a rainbow of colors. Just looking at the many colors helps you to realize how many years these seeds have been in existence and how important it is to support such groups. Will they too become a thing of the past, or can we offer enough help to encourage the saving of our food supply as well as the heritage of the seeds?

Principles of Preservation

The preservation of life, whether insect, animal, human, or plant, is the objective of NS/S, and their belief that all life is connected has helped to make us more aware of the responsibility we must share if we are to leave a better world for our children. Native Seeds is currently involved with a number of projects in the Sierra Madre of Chihuahua, Mexico to help traditional farmers remain farmers in their communities.

What Native Seeds/SEARCH is all about is best summed up by this forum of ideas and views. These are Native Seeds/SEARCH's principles for honoring indigenous knowledge, and their views on intellectual property rights:

1. Cultures should use, manage, or conserve their traditional medicines, foods, and ceremonial plants and animals in their own ways, according to their own culture and historical backgrounds. Orally-transmitted indigenous science has as much validity in its context as "Western" or "Eastern" sciences do in their contexts. Traditional healers, farmers, and taxonomists should be honored as intellectual equals to their Western counterparts.

2. We support the reaffirmation and restoration by indigenous peoples of their traditional ways of healing and feeding themselves. Foods and medicines from outside sources may not be culturally or economically suitable.

3. All people need to respect and refrain from abusing or intruding upon indigenous knowledge and practices regarding plants and animals. This knowledge may be restricted to a single tribe, clan, or gender, or restricted to a single season or traditionally dedicated site.

4. We encourage wider recognition of the ways in which land-based cultures conserve plant or animal resources. It is well-documented that many indigenous peoples traditionally sow, replant, and ritually encourage sacred and medicinal plants. If not harvested and cared for in the traditional ways, plants may decline or weaken in strength.

5. We encourage the emergence of a cross-cultural conservation ethic from the recognition that all peoples depend upon plants and animals for their survival and well-being, and that many traditions have developed their own ways of conserving local plants and animals.

6. Traditionally-used plants and animals currently require protection from overuse and other pressures if they are to be preserved for future generations. Everyone loses if plants or animals become extinct.

7. Because of language loss and disruption of oral traditions, indigenous knowledge about plants and animals is becoming as endangered as the plants and animals themselves. Traditional knowledge

about plants and animals needs to be passed on by experienced elders to younger generations through their own means of instruction.

8. Plants and animals retain healing power and spirit only if harvested and used properly. The abuse of this power may be dangerous to users or to the plants and animals.

9. There are other dangers and disadvantages to taking traditional medicinal ceremonial or culinary knowledge out of traditional contexts. Such dangers need to be more widely discussed among practitioners, researchers, users, commercializers, and communities, on and off reservations.

10. Cultures that gain from the traditional botanical or zoological knowledge of another culture should return to the communities from which this knowledge was derived. These benefits might include monetary or nonmonetary compensation (such as educational opportunities, material donations, and/or community development and land rights assistance), but the communities should have the say about the kinds and distribution of the compensation.

11. Tribal or non-tribal researchers who seek to work with indigenous communities or on their traditional lands need to state clearly what kinds of information or samples they seek, how they might be used, and who may benefit. They should respect the guidelines of both community leaders and traditional practitioners. For example, researchers should record and publish only information about medicinal herbs that herbalists believe necessary to keep users from being injured by the plant, while at the same time protecting the plant and indigenous rights to it. In some cases, written descriptions are intrinsically improper for recording information, and other means must be considered.

12. Native Seeds/SEARCH encourages and will provide technical assistance to any cultural communities in its region wishing to formulate, adopt, and enforce plant and wildlife protection ordinances (like those of the Gila River Indian Community) or cultural preservation ordinances (like those of the Hopi Reservation). We invite communities to stipulate their own

guidelines for collecting, interpreting, or repatriating cultural resources. We will take into account cultural-specific concerns about what is interpreted, exhibited, or recorded

through our programs, events, and publications, and will involve community representatives in the formulations and review of future programs.

Addresses for Seed Saving Organizations

NATIVE SEEDS/SEARCH
2509 N. Campbell #325
Tucson, AZ 85719
(520) 327-9123

SEEDS OF CHANGE
P.O. Box 15700
Santa Fe, NM 87506-5700
(505) 438-8080

Further Reading

Seeds of Change: The Living Treasure. The Passionate Story Of The Growing Movement To Restore Biodiversity and Revolutionize The Way We Think About Food. The book was written by Kenny Ausubel and can be ordered through Seeds Of Change.

JUDE WILLIAMS is a Master Herbalist, having received her degree from Dominion Herbal College. She believes the growing interest in simple living will guide us to work with nature so that healing for ourselves and our Earth can take place.

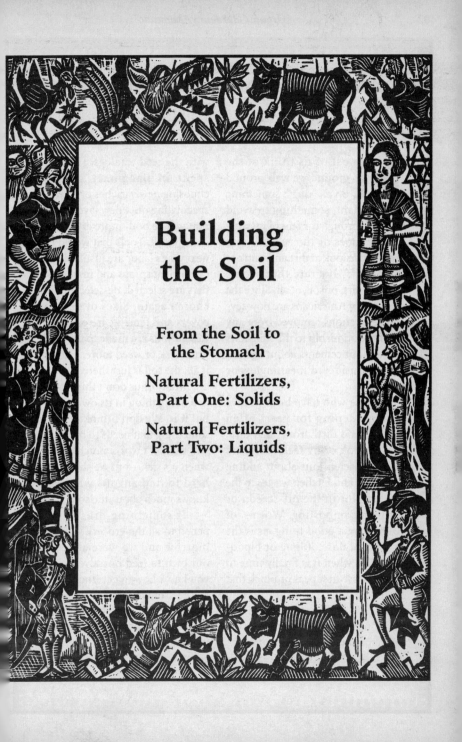

Building the Soil

From the Soil to the Stomach

Natural Fertilizers, Part One: Solids

Natural Fertilizers, Part Two: Liquids

From the Soil to the Stomach

By Penny Kelly

Most of us think of the ground we walk around on as "dirt"; something unimportant, something to avoid walking through for fear of messing up our shoes or the rug. It's rare that people look at dirt and think of it as "soil." It's rare that people think of dirt, or soil, at all. Since the majority of Americans are now several generations removed from any sort of relationship to the soil, news and announcements about soil are either considered meaningless or ignored.

Those who have been in love with gardening for years often know "good dirt" from "bad dirt" just by look or by feel. Many are quite conscientious about adding old leaves and kitchen wastes to the garden plot in the off-season or through composting. Worms, of course, are a good thing, as is the occasional dose of lime or blood-meal. But when it is finally time to gather those first peas or pluck that sweet Early Girl tomato, any awareness of the soil and what it might need is often eclipsed by the excitement of ripening vegetables.

When the growing season is over, snowy layers of winter arrive with the seed catalogs. Hours are spent in imaginary gardens, choosing new varieties of seeds, or speculating on a new layout—one that will be both more artistic and easier to till. Tools that would ease next year's labor are justified. Fancy nutrient sprays and insect powders are selected, de-selected, then chosen again. Sizes of new row covers and fencing are estimated. Resolutions are made to do better, waste less, or weed more. Through it all, the soil is just there.

Many of us don't think of soil as a living thing in its own right— but it is. We don't think of soil as something that needs to be healthy and we don't worry much about it when it's sick—but we should. It's hard to find anyone who really knows much about the soil.

If something drastic happened to all the grocery stores tomorrow and we were all left on our own to feed ourselves, would you know how to get from the soil to the stomach and end up with something to eat? Knowing that food was the bottom line in staying healthy and alive, could you grow what you needed? Could you do it year after year? If there was trouble in the garden patch, would you panic and run for chemical fertilizers, weed killers, and insecticides? Would you know enough to realize that sickly plants, invading insects, and weeds that outgrow your vegetables no matter what you do are the results of sick soil?

A Recipe for Healthy Soil

Good soil is a combination of particles of sand, silt, clay, minerals, and decaying matter—the bodies of millions of living, highly-active fungi, bacteria, and other microorganisms. Healthy soil also has structure to it—a crumb structure! This structure is only made possible by the presence of these tiny living creatures.

Fungi growing in the soil put out fine, hair-like arms called *mycelia* that wrap themselves around a miscellaneous group of particles, creating a small, individual crumb made up of sand, silt, minerals, compost matter, and trace elements. As microorganisms and bacteria go through the process of living, they excrete sticky substances, and as they die they deteriorate into gooey globs. This sticky, gooey material then acts like a glue that cements the mycelial arms in place, binding particles together in their crumb formation even more firmly. These crumbs, like marbles in a vase,

form a complex honeycomb of passages through which the roots of plants move in a constant search for water and nutrients.[1]

As plant roots move through the soil, they also put out fine root-hairs that wrap themselves tightly around these crumbs. Once firmly entwined, the root-hairs emit weak acids called humic acids. These acids react chemically with soil in two ways. One is with the glue-like elements excreted by the microorganisms, causing the glue to break down into its original elements and making these elements available for use by the growing plants. The other reaction is with the particles of the crumbs themselves, dissolving parts of them, releasing needed minerals and making them available for uptake into the plant.[2]

If the plant is able to find and take in all of the nutrients it needs, it will be healthy, and it will produce the vegetable, grain, or fruit it was genetically destined to produce. It will emit a vibrating electromagnetic field that will keep bugs and insects from attacking and devouring it, and it will resist a number of diseases and blight. It will be able to endure drought periods, and it will produce vegetables and fruits with much higher levels of proteins, carbohydrates, enzymes, vitamins, minerals, and other necessary nutrients,[3] sometimes 200–300 percent higher.[4]

Soil gradually changes from a healthy state with good structure to an unhealthy condition in two main ways. One is the continuous use of the land to grow food, over and over, without taking the time, effort, or money needed to replenish what was used. The other is the use of chemical fertilizers, pesticides, herbicides, and fungicides.

We have already pointed out the three main factors to consider when working with soil: a balanced mix of decaying matter (called carbon), clay, sand, minerals, and silt; a healthy population of bacteria and microorganisms; and good crumb structure. Healthy topsoil is the soil that is characterized by these three factors. The deeper this layer of matter, crumbs, and organisms, the deeper your topsoil is.

To keep your topsoil healthy, it is necessary to feed your microorganisms and bacteria! That is what you do when you add manures, composts, kitchen wastes, old leaves, and other carbon-based materials to your soil.[5] These materials are broken down and digested by the millions of bacteria and microorganisms which reprocess the nutrients already taken out of the soil and return them to a condition in which they can be reused by plants.

The Path to Collapse

By putting your garden in the same spot every year, the minerals and carbon matter used by your fruits, flowers, berries, and especially your vegetables may begin to decrease. If you do not add compost or other carbonaceous materials to the soil, your microorganisms and bacteria begin to go hungry and die off. After only one or two years, the nutrients reprocessed and released by these organisms will be used up faster than they are being replaced. When the microorganisms and bacteria are dead and gone, there will be no more mycelial arms to scoop soil particles into its crumb structure, and no excretions to glue the crumbs firmly together.

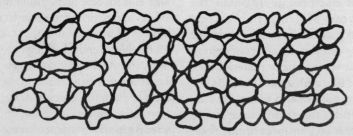

Healthy soil crumb structure

Gradually the soil will collapse. Insecticides, herbicides, and fungicides are all poisons, usually in a heavy metal base. Spraying these chemicals on your garden or field simply kills the microorganisms and bacteria outright. The soil collapses quickly.

Once the soil has collapsed, adding the wrong chemical fertilizers can cause it to turn into a hardened mass called hardpan. Hardpan is much like cement, and roots have a very difficult time working their way through it. Delicate roothairs have no soil crumbs to encircle in their search for minerals and other elements which, when found, trigger the plant into releasing appropriate humic acids that allow the plant to dissolve and sip the elemental solutions. Indeed, collapsed soil is often deficient in some of the most important compounds and minerals because what has been used by previous crops has not been replaced. If minerals are present, the roots may simply be unable to get to them because of the absence of other elements that act as catalysts.

Rainwater falls noisily onto dead soil, puddles immediately, and splashes muddy droplets in every direction, unable to sink into the myriad passages formed by the crumb structure. The combination of dead soil and water makes a pasty mud that sticks to everything it touches, and in a very short time the rainwater begins to run off the hardened, collapsed soil.[6] The result is flash floods that are dangerous and do us the disservice of carrying off whatever is left of the topsoil, depositing it in streams, lakes, rivers, and sometimes the houses of those who have unwittingly bought homes on land that was so thoroughly destroyed by chemical farming that it would no longer grow anything profitably.

Rainwater falls silently onto healthy soil, sinking into it quickly, sliding through the honeycomb of tunnels formed by the crumbs. Excess water is carried deeply into the ground, diluting the humic acids as they pass through and preventing stunted plants burned by an overdose of nutrients. As the water works its way toward the deeper layers of the soil, the decaying leaves, manure, and other carbonaceous materials soak it up.[7] Healthy soil with a good supply of carbon-based materials will hold up to four times its original weight in water, (sometimes more) and will not stick to shoes and boots.[8]

Feeding Your Soil

Food needs healthy soil with good structure and plenty of minerals and nutrients. When the list of basic soil ingredients is incomplete, you may get plants that are green and good-looking, but produce no flowers, fruits, grains, or vegetables. More likely, you will get plants that look nice at first but, since they are basically unhealthy, they are quickly attacked by insects or taken over by blight and fungus.

Insects that attack and devour your precious lettuce, mildews that cause your cucumbers and cantaloupe to collapse, or worms that invade your radishes and onions are signs of sick soil, and therefore sick plants.

Running out to get an insecticide, a fungus spray, or a quick application of chemical fertilizer to prop up the sagging health of your plants might help you save this year's crop, but it will create even graver troubles at the soil level for next year.

Research over the past decades has shown that biological systems are fundamentally energetic. This means that the basic mechanism driving the growth and chemistry of plants and animals is light energy. Ultraviolet photons are the medium of biological communication, and any change in chemical or physical properties is immediately preceded by a conversion of the biophotons associated with the chemicals or the matter.[9]

For those of us raising grains or growing vegetables, it works like this: the soil is the source of the nutrients for plants. Good soil should have an ample supply of things like nitrogen, phosphorus, and potassium, the standard ingredients in any N-P-K fertilizer, but plants have a critical need for more than fifty other minerals if they are going to be healthy and produce nutritious food. Elements like copper, boron, manganese, selenium, and others are essential.

Every element of the periodic table, every molecule and even every kind of matter is surrounded by a vibrating field of electromagnetic energy. The pattern of this energy field is different for every element, each as unique as a fingerprint, and by using a device called a spectrometer, we can study this energy field to determine if an element is present in a compound or a living system.

When a plant has absorbed a particular mineral element, the frequency pattern of the mineral will affect the frequency pattern of the plant. The mineral thus becomes a contributor to the total pattern of the plant's electromagnetic field frequency. All of the frequencies of the various minerals and nutrients combine to form a particular pattern for each kind of plant, and when complete, this vibrating pattern becomes a healthy plant's electromagnetic signature.

With this in mind, it should then come as no surprise that the antennae on insects and bugs are exactly that—antennae! When a

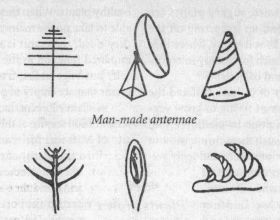

Man-made antennae

Insect antennae

plant is deficient in nutrients and minerals, insects using the infrared band of the electromagnetic spectrum can pick up alterations in the electromagnetic signal of the plant. Using their antennae as a built-in radar system, they zero in on and attack diseased, dysfunctional, and deficient plant systems. After all, that is their job. Insects and fungi are nature's way of cleaning up the landscape! Even when healthy and unhealthy plants are placed right next to each other and their stems and leaves are intermingled, the insects will only go after the leaves of the unhealthy specimen.[10]

Now, if you were an insect searching for lunch and found a plot of unhealthy vegetables with all the wrong signals mixed in with healthy veggies that had all the right signals, what would keep you from munching on either or both of them? Since both are rather handy and equally tasty, what would be the difference?

The difference is that healthy plants not only give off a different frequency, they maintain a very high level of natural carbohydrates (simple plant sugars) in their stems, leaves, and fruits. Of course, you might think that the insects would be anxious to get their mandibles into the sweetest, juiciest plants. That's what most *people* would do. But insects that go after plants with high sugar levels quickly get a serious, even paralyzing, stomach ache. The sugar combines with the internal chemistry of most bugs to create an alcohol that leaves the bugs intoxicated, uncoordinated, and unable to manage themselves. Bugs that insist on eating the sweet, sugary plants are likely to end up staggering off the leaf into the soil below, where they become lunch for hungry microorganisms and bacteria! [11]

Many of us have suffered the frustration of trying to grow vegetables in poor-to-mediocre soil. First we watch them shrink without plenty of water, then suddenly collapse into a mound of mildews when it rains. One day we smother them in sprays and "dusts" to keep insects at arm's length, and the next day the rain washes our chemical protection away, polluting the soil. We have struggled with monster weeds and aching backs, never appreciating the fact that a particular variety of weed (perhaps chickweed) will grow best in an unbalanced soil (perhaps one with too much potassium and sulfur) and do us the favor of using up some of those excesses, thus helping return the soil to a healthy balance. Worst of all, we never really recognize the obvious—that plants grown in failing soil are not healthy enough to withstand an untimely cold snap, intense heat, lengthy periods without rain, competition with weeds, or insects, fungi and viruses.

Plants grown in depleted, deficient soils become deficient, un-

Plants grown in depleted, deficient soils become deficient, unhealthy plants

healthy plants. When they are unable to take up the many nutrients they need, the result is not only impaired function in the plant itself, but vegetables, fruits, and grains that are empty of nutrients.

William Albrecht, famed professor of soil science at the University of Missouri for many years, described the plant's struggle as one "to synthesize proteins, and then living tissue, to support growth, provide self-protection, and reproduction." He pointed out that humans were also struggling for adequate proteins. "Proteins are synthesized from the elements only by plants and microbes; hence the soil, its microbes, and its crops, are the quality control of man's nutrition and the nutrition of all the animals supporting him."[12]

Shortly after the start of this century, samples of soils were taken from all over the world and studied to find out what their average viable protein output was. The minimum necessary for animal and human health is 25 percent viable protein. Disturbingly, it turned out that the samples taken had an average of 12 percent viable protein output. In the United States, the samples averaged only 6 percent. During the late 1960s and early 1970s, follow-up studies were done and the U.S. Department of Agriculture released figures showing that the viable protein output of U.S. soil had slipped to somewhere between 1.5 percent and 3 percent.[13]

Says Dan Skow, a soil consultant and veterinarian, "Protein contains nitrogen, and nitrogen is essential to the construction of a new cell. A deficiency of protein, and thus of nitrogen, will short-circuit new cell construction and thus signal the beginning of disease. In humans, this wasting away of health is called degenerative metabolic disease."[14]

Bad Soil Makes People Sick

The reality of this is now hitting home. There are two basic forms of human illness. One form is infectious disease, and the other is degenerative disease. Degenerative disease is rampant in this country. There are nine-year-olds with arthritis, twenty-year-olds with heart disease, forty-year-olds who need hip and knee replacements, and millions who suffer from allergies. Each generation is displaying degenerative symptoms at earlier and earlier ages. Viruses abound, and new ones are regularly announced. It would be more accurate to announce that the gene that activates our systems to resist many infections and viruses has degenerated into inactivity because the nutrition that would trigger it into action is insufficient.[15] Almost every family I know has someone seriously sick, overweight, or even terminally ill. Even those who are health-conscious get sick because our soils are, for all practical purposes, dead, and we are eating nutritionally-deficient foods.

Over the thousands of years that people have been on Earth, whenever we have overworked or neglected our soils, we simply picked up and moved on. Droughts, attacks by hordes of locusts, or the failure of a group's staple crop, such as potatoes—these have been the driving factors in the continuous westward migration of human beings over the past several thousand years. Now we are at the end of the trail. We have encircled the globe, filling the planet almost beyond capacity with sick and degenerating people, polluted water, and poisoned soil. There is nowhere left to run.

It is time to recognize that dead soils produce seriously deficient foods. Deficient foods result in sick and degenerating people. When the deficient foods are also laced with pesticides, herbicides, fungicides, and heavy metals, the degeneration process accelerates.

The time, money, and effort needed to practice organic farming cannot be any more than the time, money, and effort demanded by the medical industry. It certainly cannot be more than the expenses of chemical agriculture.

For a serious turn-around of the health problems in this country, we may all have to return to gardening for awhile, or at least until those who produce our food have understood that we cannot survive on deficient produce laced with poisonous chemicals.

Before we have lost our way entirely, we need first to understand our connection to the soil. We need to understand and honor the way that takes us from the soil to the stomach.

Endnotes

1 Martin, Deborah and Grace Gershuny, ed. *The Rodale Book of Composting.* Emmaus, PA: Rodale Press, p. 13-18.

2 Ibid.

3 Skow, Dan, D.V.M., and Charles Walters, Jr. *Mainline Farming for Century 21.*

Kansas City, MO: Acres USA Publishers, 1991, p. 92, 108, 144, 163.

4 Thompkins, Peter, and Christopher Bird. *Secrets of the Soil.* New York: Harper and Row, 1989, p. 29-33.

5 Skow, *Mainline Farming,* p. 9, 27.

6 Ibid., p. 39-40.

7 Martin, *Book of Composting,* p. 15-18.

8 Skow, *Mainline Farming,* p. 35-40.

9 Anderson, Arden. *Science in Agriculture.* Kansas City, MO: Acres U.S.A. Publishers, 1992, p. 4.

10 Thompkins, *Secrets of the Soil,* p. 256-277.

11 Anderson, *Science in Agriculture.*

12 Ibid.

13 Ibid. p. xi

14 Skow, *Mainline Farming,* p. 3.

15 Anderson, *Science in Agriculture,* p. 49.

❖c❖

PENNY KELLY is a writer, gardener, and small farmer raising Concord grapes for Welch Foods Corporation. She has been a tool and process engineer for Chrysler Corporation, and was an educational consultant specializing in brain-compatible and accelerative learning techniques for more than thirteen years. She was recently awarded a degree as Doctor of Naturopathy and is currently working on a Ph.D. in nutrition.

Natural Fertilizers, Part One: Solids

By Roslyn Reid

Chemical fertilizers are neat, available just about everywhere, and fairly cheap. So why use organic fertilizers, which can be messy to make, heavy to haul around, smelly, and sometimes expensive?

Because of the soil. Chemical fertilizers will not build up nutrients in a poor soil. Even the richest soil in the world will become depleted of nutrients after a few seasons of intensive gardening.

Garden vegetables draw their nutrition from minerals in the soil. When we eat the vegetables, we also absorb nutrition from those minerals. This act of generosity on the part of the soil deserves to be repaid. Nourishing the soil is the best investment one can make in a garden, and the best way to nourish it is by copying nature—using natural fertilizers.

Because of environmental problems associated with the use of chemical fertilizers, many gardeners are returning to this ancient, effective, and safe means of fertilization for their crops. Natural fertilizers are low in toxins, thus keeping these poisons out of your veggies. Also, natural fertilizers can provide a balanced source of nutrients for plants.

What Is NPK?

Both organic and non-organic fertilizers have varying combinations of plant growth nutrients. The most important of these nutrients are known by the shorthand designation of NPK. N stands for nitrogen (necessary for growing leafy plants), P for phosphorus, and K for potash (both necessary for growing root crops). In commercially-available fertilizers such as bonemeal, the amount of NPK will be stated on the label in numeric form. For instance, a rating of 10-5-0 indicated on its label shows that this particular fertilizer contains twice as much nitrogen as it does phosphorus, and that it contains no potash at all. Therefore, this fertilizer is more suitable for a leafy plant like lettuce than for a root crop such as potatoes.

The highest number an NPK rating can reach is 15. If you see a fertilizer label reading 15-5-5, this means that the material inside contains the maximum amount of nitrogen any fertilizer can have.

In addition to NPK, some natural fertilizers contain substances known as trace minerals. This designation refers to small quantities of minerals such as manganese and selenium. While generally not as important as NPK, trace minerals are important to the growth of some crops which prefer them. It's best to experiment with several different fertilizers when trying to determine if trace minerals are important to your garden.

Types of Solid Fertilizers

There are many different kinds of natural fertilizers in solid form—in fact, entire books have been written on this subject. However, because this article is intended as an introduction to the matter, we shall narrow our discussion to five of the most common: compost, manure, and three types of powders (bloodmeal, bonemeal, and wood ashes).

Compost

As Mother Nature's preferred method of fertilization, compost is one of the best and most widely-found soil builders around. Composting is cheap and easy—I began composting right in my kitchen over a decade ago (see Llewellyn's

1995 Organic Gardening Almanac for details on this simple method which anyone can do). Kitchen scraps, yard waste—almost any non-meat substance can be tossed into the compost heap. In fact, it's a great place to dispose of autumn leaves, instead of bagging them and hauling them down to the dump.

During the winter, you can also add fireplace ashes to the heap, because they are a good source of acidity, which most vegetables love. But it's very important to make sure the ashes are cool first—I once burned up my compost heap by not checking ashes thoroughly! Although my heap was not near any buildings, and the fire was not serious, it caused several problems: because all my compost burned up, I had to start from scratch again—including building a new bin! Also, due to the loss of the compost, it was necessary to find another fertilizer for my garden. So be careful of what you put into your heap.

If you wish to construct a compost pile, plans are available in books and magazines (see "resources," at the end of this article), or even from friends who have assembled their own piles. Commercially-available compost bins usually contain instructions for their use. A compost pile can be as simple as a chicken wire bin, a plastic trash can with holes punched in the sides and bottom, or even a hole in the ground. However, if you don't have room for these, you may be able to locate a neighbor from whom you can obtain compost in return for contributions to the pile.

Compost is one of the only fertilizers which can be placed into freshly-dug holes for fruit trees or shrubs without concern for harming the young plants. Compost should be tilled into garden soil before spring planting, and again at the end of the season to nourish the soil for next year's crop. For best results, apply it to growing plants about once a month. Because compost usually has a well-balanced NPK, there is no danger of "burning" plants by over-fertilization with this substance. It is also a good source of trace minerals.

Of course, this miracle natural fertilizer has a few disadvantages as well. It is truly a home-grown substance; it cannot be purchased at the garden store. Furthermore, making it is a slow process—even with a compost accelerator, available in many catalogs and garden stores, you need to wait at least three weeks before your compost is ready to use. Compost is not particularly light to shovel or to haul around, even if your heap is close to the garden (which is the ideal place for it).

But if you can live with these few drawbacks, compost is the solid fertilizer of preference. Just ask your plants!

Manure

What if you can't obtain compost? Then manure is probably the next best thing to use. Many people think of manure as a balanced nutrient, but actually, its NPK composition varies according to the diet of the animals that produce it.

Take guano, for instance, which is another term for bat or bird manure. The *Pinetree Garden Seeds Catalog* (see "Catalogs," below) offers two different types of bat guano—desert bat and island bat—as well as fossilized seabird guano. All these substances vary in their amounts of NPK: desert bat guano has an NPK listing of 8-4-1 (good for leafy plants), island bat guano consists of 5-5-1 NPK (also good for leafy plants, but pretty good for root crops, too), and seabird guano has an NPK of 1-15-1 (excellent for root crops). As you can see, if you wish to go with guano, you must choose the variety carefully, to suit the type of crops you want to grow.

A variety of fresh manures may be available in your area—with the exception of dogs and cats, manure from any animal may be used on a vegetable garden. However, there are two drawbacks to fresh manures: their NPK content cannot be precisely determined; and all manures must be composted before they can be used. Many people think they can

❧C❧

During the summer, worms may be dug up from the ground and added to the compost heap as a means of enriching it

❧C❧

just toss fresh manure into their garden as is, but actually, fresh manure is much too strong for the garden, and applying it directly to crops will "burn" them, causing the plants to wilt and die.

If you are able to handle these drawbacks, manure can be your primary natural fertilizer. Furthermore, if you have a truck to haul it in, frequently you can obtain all the fresh manure you want for free!

One way to circumvent the problem of having to process manure is by using compressed manure pellets instead. These handy little devices are sold by Gardener's Supply Company (see "Catalogs," below) and are packaged in a smell-proof plastic bucket. They may be "broadcast" (tossed) over the garden once a month—an old coffee

scoop is ideal for this job. In addition, they store neatly, taking up little space in a cabinet or garden shed; and I think they are one of the best inventions since sliced bread. With an NPK rating of 3-4-3, they provide a well-balanced set of nutrients for the plants.

Ready-to-use manure is available in bags from garden centers or catalogs. Already aged enough to be safe, this substance can be placed right on the garden. (For the correct amount, follow the instructions on the label.) One particularly intriguing brand is called "Zoo Doo," because it is collected from animals at the Bronx Zoo.

Finally, there is a fertilizer known as worm castings. This term refers to the actual soil bed where the worms live, as well as the worm byproducts (such as manure) which the bed contains. Worm castings are wonderfully rich in nutrients, which seems apparent from the dark color of this material. However, unless you wish to raise worms, castings are best bought from a catalog or garden store.

Although raising the little wigglers may seem easy, they require an environment which is strictly temperature-controlled. If you can't conveniently raise worms in your greenhouse or basement, sometimes an attached garage will be adequate if its temperature doesn't drop below 40°F. During the summer, worms may be dug up from the ground and added to the compost heap as a means of enriching it. However, they are not likely to survive the winter in a compost heap unless you keep it warm by adding to it regularly, covering it, and using a thermometer to check its temperature. For the dedicated gardener, this is no trouble at all; but for weekend gardeners, the task of looking after worms may be overwhelming.

Like compost, manure is another good source for trace minerals. Commercially-available manures such as compressed pellets and worm castings should list the trace minerals they contain on their labels. Bagged manure might also have a listing. Fresh manure contains trace minerals, too; but due to variation in the diets of the animals, there is no way to determine just which minerals are in it.

Powders

Powdered forms of solid fertilizer may be used singly; but due to their lack of a balanced NPK, they are best used in combination with each other or with another type of fertilizer. Also, powders do not contain trace minerals. If you wish to use powders but think your crops prefer trace minerals, then be sure to add another substance

containing them, such as a liquid fertilizer (see Part Two: Liquids). At the end of this section on powders is a recipe for a fertilizer mix of several substances—but be aware that despite being a mixture, this fertilizer still contains no trace minerals.

You may have seen meal powders in a garden store or catalog. Bloodmeal is one of the most popular of these, and it is widely available. As you might conclude from its name, bloodmeal consists of dried animal blood. Because of its composition, it can also be used as a pesticide—but that's a subject for another article. As a fertilizer, bloodmeal contains high nitrogen

❖C❖

Powders are best used in combination with each other or with another type of fertilizer

❖C❖

(N), but low phosphorus (P) and potash (K), so when used on its own, bloodmeal is best suited for leafy vegetables.

Bonemeal, derived from ground animal bones, is another commonly used powder which can be found in catalogs and garden centers. This substance is popular for bulb plants such as tulips, because it can be sprinkled into the hole before the bulb is planted. Unlike most other fertilizers, this practice will not cause any harm to the growing plant. However, the biggest drawback I've noticed when using this particular fertilizer is that it seems to draw predators who like to eat the bonemeal, as well as the plants it's applied to. Also, as with any other powder, bonemeal does not contain a balanced NPK. Best suited for root crops, its nitrogen (N) level is quite low, but both its phosphorus and potash (P and K) levels are high.

Common wood ashes can be a relatively free source of the high acidity that most vegetables love. If you have a fireplace or use hardwood to barbecue—and DO NOT use starting fluid—you may put ashes into your compost heap (see the previous discussion in the "compost" section about the importance of cooling them first). In fact, you can even put them right into the garden. My loofahs were the only plants I've ever seen which loved to have ashes sprinkled all over them—and, as well as feeding them, the ashes seemed to keep the pests down, too! Almost all other plants prefer the ashes to be placed on the ground. Like other powders, ashes are not a balanced source of NPK and should not be used alone.

The above powders can be combined into a natural fertilizer which contains a well-balanced amount of NPK and trace minerals by using a recipe found in the book *Square Foot Gardening* by Mel Bartholomew (see "Books," below), Mix these ingredients in the following proportions:

1 cup bloodmeal

2 cups bonemeal

3 cups ashes

4 cups compost

The amounts can be adjusted according to the type of crops grown and how they respond to the mix. You can keep this mixture in a small trash can and broadcast it over the garden once a month, using a coffee can. In fact, this recipe may be made in large quantities, because it will keep for years.

Conclusion

It's always a good idea to test several different fertilizers on your particular soil and garden before deciding on which ones to use. Not every fertilizer works well everywhere—it took me several years to discover that compost, compressed manure pellets, and liquid foliar feed (see Part Two of this series) worked best on my plants.

One suggested plan for testing various fertilizers on your garden can be found in a book called

Where There Is No Doctor (see "Books," below). The author developed some simple instructions for experimenting with garden fertilizers by adjusting all the different conditions present. This approach was part of a holistic health program which included nutrition; and because resources are meager in these areas, it was important to know what worked.

The book also includes graphics illustrating the results of using various amounts of manure, including what happens when too much manure is applied to the crops. This is a good demonstration for those who mistakenly think that more is better. Finally, there is information on crop rotation, which is another way to keep the land fertile and healthy.

Resources

Books

Bartholomew, Mel. *Square Foot Gardening.* Emmaus, PA: Rodale Press, 1981. How to grow a large organic garden in a small space.

Kains, M. G. *Five Acres and Independence.* New York: Dover Publications, 1973. Originally published in 1935 as a guide for the small farmer, much of this material predates the chemical fertilizer era.

Readers Digest Illustrated Guide to Gardening. Pleasantville, NY: Readers Digest Assoc. Inc., 1978. A comprehensive guide to gardening, with color pictures of plant diseases and pests.

Werner, David. *Where There Is No Doctor* (revised). Published by the Hesperian Foundation, P.O. Box 1692, Palo Alto, CA 94302. While this book consists mostly of medical and health advice for populations in isolated places, it also contains a section on organic soil building and crop raising.

Magazines

Back Home. P.O. Box 370, Mountain Home, NC 27858. A group of former *Mother Earth News* staffers started this magazine, which is full of advice on organic gardening.

Mother Earth News. P.O. Box 70, Hendersonville, NC 28793. This magazine offers pertinent articles for homesteaders and organic gardeners.

Catalogs

ECOLOGY ACTION, 5798 Ridgewood Road, Willits, CA 95490. This organic gardening group offers a catalog called *Organic Gardening with Bountiful Gardens.*

GARDENS ALIVE! 5100 Schenley Place, Lawrenceburg, IN 47025. A good place to find materials for the totally organic garden

GARDENERS SUPPLY CO., 128 Intervale Road, Burlington, VT 05401. A sourcebook for bat and seabird guano, as well as many other items for the organic gardener.

JOHNNY'S SELECTED SEEDS, Foss Hill Road, Albion, ME 04910-9731. More than just a seed catalog. But if seeds are what you want, this company offers both treated (for fungus) and untreated versions.

PINETREE GARDEN SEEDS, Box 300, New Gloucester, ME 04260. A good selection of guanos and other natural fertilizers.

Miscellaneous

If you own a computer, there is an on-line forum sponsored by *National Gardening Magazine* on CompuServe. To access it, sign onto CompuServe and type GO GARDENING. (Kits for obtaining a CompuServe account are available from software dealers.)

One excellent resource is your County Extension Agent, who will have a great deal of information about the soil and weather conditions specific to your area. Your local agent will be glad to answer your questions and can be found under the "County" listing in the blue pages of the phone book, or at a state university.

Last, but not by any means least, you can always turn to your local reference librarian for any other information on organic gardening which you might need.

ROSLYN REID has been a gardener since the early 1980s. She also reads and teaches tarot, and is a practicing Druid. Roslyn's favorite garden treat is fresh corn right off the stalk.

Natural Fertilizers, Part Two: Liquids

By Roslyn Reid

As mentioned in "Natural Fertilizers, Part One: Solids" (the companion article on natural fertilizers in solid form), nourishing the soil is the best investment one can make in a garden, and the best way to do this is by imitating Nature in the use of natural rather than chemical fertilizers. This article, which is part two of the series, will introduce the different forms of some popular natural liquid fertilizers and show how to use them.

Nourishing the soil is the best investment one can make in a garden

Some types of liquid fertilizers are applied to the leaves of plants, and some are poured directly onto the soil. When applied to the leaves, liquid fertilizer only incidentally replenishes nutrients taken from the soil by the plants. Therefore, if you wish to build a good, healthy soil, it is best to use a combination of both solid and liquid natural fertilizers on your garden.

Because fewer liquid than solid forms of natural fertilizer exist, very little information on the use of liquid fertilizers is available. However, all natural liquid fertilizers are made by mixing some solid or liquid substance with water. Even if your method for spreading liquid fertilizer is by using a bottle attached to a garden hose, you must first mix the fertilizing substance with water before pouring it into the bottle.

The practice of producing liquid fertilizers with water means this type of fertilizer is fairly inexpensive, which is one of its biggest advantages. In fact, some liquid fertilizers are nearly impossible to find in commercial form, and have to be made by the gardener.

Now, mixing liquid fertilizers is too messy and time consuming for some folks to undertake. Furthermore, several of these liquid fertilizers do not keep very well after they are mixed, requiring the gardener to make a fresh batch for each use (although this means they require less storage space). However, if mixing is not a concern for you, these substances can be a very easy way to nourish your plants.

Liquid fertilizers are quite versatile and may be used on almost all kinds of vegetation, including houseplants. Some of the most commonly available liquid fertilizers are compost tea, fish emulsion, gelatin, and foliar feed.

NPK—What Is It?

Like natural solid fertilizers, liquids also provide the three major plant nutrients known as NPK—nitrogen (N) for leafy plants, and phosphorus (P) and potash (K) for root crops. However, because liquid fertilizers are usually homemade, their NPK ratings can vary considerably, even within the same category of liquid. (For a complete discussion of the numeric NPK ratings of fertilizers, please see Part One on solid fertilizers.)

On the other hand, due to their homemade nature, almost all natural liquid fertilizers contain trace minerals such as selenium. So if you notice that your garden seems to grow better when you fertilize it with a substance containing trace minerals, then liquid fertilizers may be the way to go.

Compost Tea

Compost tea is another term for the runoff from a compost heap. This natural liquid fertilizer is just as good for plants as solid compost. Now, a compost heap can be a fairly simple affair to build. However, if you wish to use compost tea as a liquid fertilizer, you must carefully plan the construction of your compost heap with the intention of collecting the runoff.

This isn't as easy as it sounds. Most compost piles are collections of yard waste and kitchen scraps which are placed upon the ground and surrounded by some kind of enclosure—chicken wire, wood slats, or whatever the gardener has available. While this arrangement is fine for regular composting, collecting compost tea from such a setup is virtually impossible. To capture the runoff from a compost heap, it is necessary to place a basin-type formation or some kind of drainage pipe underneath the pile. As you can see, this is why you need to plan before you start a heap—retrofitting an existing heap is not easy.

Probably the simplest pile specifically designed for catching compost tea is a plastic trash can with holes punched in its sides and bottom. When used with this device, a stiff plastic kiddie pool makes an excellent basin for catching the runoff. Simply place the trash can into the pool, wait until the can is filled with compost, and water the pile. Or, if you're too

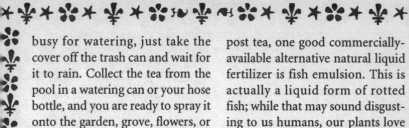

busy for watering, just take the cover off the trash can and wait for it to rain. Collect the tea from the pool in a watering can or your hose bottle, and you are ready to spray it onto the garden, grove, flowers, or berry patch.

Collecting compost tea from a traditional compost heap—that is, one enclosed by chicken wire or wood—is more difficult and likely to involve trenching under the pile before the heap is begun. Although composting directly in the garden makes use of the tea in soil building, this method renders compost tea unavailable for spraying on the plants. However, it is still a good way to maximize use of the compost.

One other disadvantage in the use of compost tea is the necessity for a mature compost heap from which the tea can be collected. Just as you cannot start a compost heap and expect to have great compost the next day, the same goes for the tea—both require the same amount of time to ripen. As in solid compost, the NPK composition of compost tea varies according to the materials used in the pile.

Fish Emulsion

If you don't have a compost pile, or the inclination to gather com-

post tea, one good commercially-available alternative natural liquid fertilizer is fish emulsion. This is actually a liquid form of rotted fish; while that may sound disgusting to us humans, our plants love it! Even houseplants respond well to it. In fact, this versatile food may be used on every kind of plant.

❧cɔ❧

Almost all natural liquid fertilizers contain trace minerals such as selenium

❧cɔ❧

Fish emulsion may be purchased as a bottled concentrate. After being mixed with water, the resultant natural liquid fertilizer is poured onto the soil around the plants just like water; in fact, a watering can is probably best for applying it. (With houseplants, some people use a system which waters them from the bottom of the pot. Fish emulsion may be used in the same way as water for these bottom-watering systems.) Fish emulsion may be applied with every watering.

Probably the biggest drawback to fish emulsion is its strong smell. Some of the older formulas could kindly have been described thusly: "Revolting—not only did they smell bad while being mixed, but the smell transferred to the plants, too!" As you might imagine, fish emulsion was fairly unpopular for house plants at that time.

Newer fish emulsions such as Squanto's Secret are considered

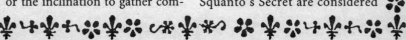

odorless. They are indeed odorless, if mixed fresh and the entire batch is completely used. If the mix sits stored in a bottle for awhile, however, it does develop an odor. Still, the odorless type does not emit nearly as strong a smell as previous fish emulsions did.

Another disadvantage to this substance is that it must be purchased at a garden center or from a catalog. Most people don't like the idea of keeping rotting fish around just to collect fertilizer from them. However, because it is a concentrate, fish emulsion is fairly inexpensive. (See "Catalogs" at the end of this article, for a listing of gardening catalogs, or visit your local garden store.)

As an animal product, fish emulsion has a fairly balanced NPK. In addition, it contains several trace minerals, such as magnesium and selenium, which are an added bonus for some plants.

Gelatin

Found in every grocery store, ordinary, unflavored gelatin is a much-overlooked source of natural liquid fertilizer. If you are squeamish, you may not want to know the origin of this colorless jelly—it is made by thoroughly boiling the skin (in-cluding hooves), bones, and connective tissue of animals. As such, it can be a good organic source of protein for humans; but plants seem to appreciate a helping of gelatin too.

Although a box of gelatin sometimes offers a drink recipe for strengthening your nails, it usually does not include similar information for making plant food from this substance. Fortunately, this is a fairly simple procedure: dissolve one envelope of gelatin in a gallon of warm water, stir, and apply it as if you were watering the plant. (Use the unflavored, unsweetened type—NOT Jello!) This natural liquid fertilizer is best if used about once a month.

Gelatin is a much-overlooked source of natural liquid fertilizer

However, like most organic products, gelatin tends to become smelly when stored for a short period after mixing with water. For this reason, storage of the liquid is inadvisable; like fish emulsion, you should not make more gelatin fertilizer than you can completely use at one time.

Another disadvantage to gelatin is that it must be purchased—grinding up hooves and boiling them is a difficult undertaking these days! Also, as you can deduce from the amount which

must be used, gelatin is far more expensive than fish emulsion, the other store-bought liquid fertilizer mentioned above. You can see that although gelatin is popular for use on houseplants, one of those little supermarket boxes will not go very far in a garden. But if you need fertilizer in a pinch, gelatin is a good product to use, because storage of the dry product does not require much room.

Like fish emulsion, gelatin is an animal product. Therefore, it contains a fairly balanced amount of NPK, and plants which are fertilized with this substance will receive all three of these major nutrients. Also, because it is common for house plants to show signs of nitrogen deficiency (brown leaves may be one indication of this), fertilizing them with gelatin will supply the important N nutrient.

Foliar Feed

Foliar feed is one of Nature's wonder plant foods. By using foliar feed, I've managed to grow loofahs as long as my arm, a single summer squash plant which took over half my garden and exploded into at least three dozen squash, raspberry vines which bent under the weight of the fruit, and a very happy orchard of six dwarf fruit trees. I was truly impressed with the results.

So where can you get some of this miracle substance? Well, here's the *good* news—foliar feed is almost impossible to find. This is probably because it's ridiculously easy to make, so hardly anyone would dream of buying it.

Foliar feed is a natural liquid fertilizer made with one of three perennials: comfrey, nettle (stinging or stingless), or thistle. You can even use all three of them in the mixture together.

Comfrey is an herb which does not grow wild, and must be cultivated. However, the other two plants are considered by most folks to be weeds. As such, they can be found almost everywhere, free for the picking; in fact, people are likely to be thrilled if you offer to harvest any nettle or thistle which is growing in their yards. And one really big plant (around 4' tall) may be all you need.

The only problem in using these plants might be the picking itself—thistle and stinging nettle are warrior plants, with a nasty bite! Rose-pruning gloves are probably the best protection for your hands and arms when gathering or handling either of these plants. And in the unlikely event that you cannot find any of these plants growing somewhere, dried versions of them may be used, although this drives up the price of the foliar feed.

As mentioned, making foliar feed is simple. First, find a large plastic bucket—if it was previously used, make sure it did not contain toxic chemicals. Wash it carefully, fill it with the plants you have harvested or bought, cover them completely with water, and let the bucket sit for a month. You may keep your bucket outside in any weather if you cover it to prevent dilution of the feed by rain.

After a month of fermenting, your foliar feed is ready to use. Strain and apply to plants with a hose sprayer or watering can. That's all there is to it. In fact, sometimes you don't even have to strain! Furthermore, a gallon bucket of foliar feed will last and last. I spray my garden, fruit trees, berry patch, and ornamental shrubs about once a month, and I've been using the same bucket of foliar feed for several years.

Sounds ideal? It is. Ever notice how much happier plants look after a rainstorm? I used to think it was because they were getting a lot of moisture; but they didn't seem to look that happy after I watered them myself, no matter how much water I used. Then I realized that all the dew sitting on decaying plant material all over the world is drawn up into the air by evaporation every day, taking minute particles of this natural compost with it. These par-

ticles condense in the atmosphere; and when it rains, they return to the plants, giving the vegetation a natural foliar feeding. A gardener who uses foliar feed on crops is doing the same thing.

Does this put acid rain into a new perspective for you?

Foliar feed may be used on almost any type of plant—vegetables, fruit trees, flowers, etc. You can even put it into a spray bottle and use it on house plants.

❖ᴄᴐ❖

Foliar feed may be used on almost any type of plant

❖ᴄᴐ❖

So does this wonder food have any disadvantages? Yes, a few. For one thing, it should have an airtight lid if you store it indoors—being composed of decayed organic material, foliar feed can develop a smell. Also, this natural liquid fertilizer requires thirty days to ferment; and, as mentioned, it usually must be made by the gardener.

Although I have seen foliar feed for sale in at least one garden catalog, I prefer to make my own. This enables me to know just what ingredients are in it and where they came from. For instance, when buying foliar feed from a catalog, you may be unable to determine whether or not the ingredients are organic. If you buy dried herbs for making foliar feed, you need to exercise the same caution.

The NPK composition of foliar feed varies, but this liquid tends to be high in potash (K) and fairly low in the other two nutrients, nitrogen (N) and potassium (P). Being made from real plants, it contains many trace minerals important to plants, which respond very well to its application.

Conclusion

As always, it's a good idea to test fertilizers on your crops and soil to find one which ones work best for you. Some plants, such as squash, become disease-prone if their leaves are wet, which means foliar feed would not be right for them. But this may not be true in all cases, so try a technique of "mix and match" until you strike the right balance for your garden. For instance, suppose your plants respond well to foliar feed, but you think that the presence of some nitrogen in the mix would suit them even better. In that case, just add the recommended amount of fish emulsion to your home brew to increase its N content.

Sometimes plants respond better to a new fertilizer just because they enjoy a change. Experiment with your garden and have lots of fun!

Resources

For further reading, the following are recommended:

Books

Familiar Flowers of North America (Eastern Region). Audubon Society Pocket Guides. New York: Alfred A. Knopf, 1986. An excellent book for identifying nettle and thistle in the field.

Lust, John. *The Herb Book.* New York: Bantam Books, 1974. Useful for identifying not only wild, but also cultivated herbs, such as comfrey.

Weed, Susun S. *Healing Wise.* Woodstock, NY: Ash Tree Publications, 1989. Although mostly medicinal recipes are found in this book, there are a few for foliar feed.

Magazines

Back Home. P.O. Box 70, Henderson, NC 28793. Published by a group of former *Mother Earth News* staffers, with the same theme of organic and natural living.

Mother Earth News. 49 W. 21st Street, 11th Floor, New York, NY 10010. Aimed at homesteaders and organic farmers, this magazine is where I found my first recipe for foliar feed.

Organic Gardening. Rodale Press, 33 E. Minor St., Emmaus, PA 18908-0001. The granddaddy of organic gardening magazines. Rodale Press also pub-

lishes many books on organic gardening.

Catalogs

To obtain material mentioned in this article, here is a list of catalogs for your convenience:

ECOLOGY ACTION 5798 Ridgewood Road, Willits, CA 95490. The catalog issued by this organic gardening group is actually called *Organic Gardening with Bountiful Gardens.*

GARDENS ALIVE! 5100 Schenley Place, Lawrenceburg, IN 47025. Products for the totally organic gardener.

JOHNNY'S SELECTED SEEDS Foss Hill Road, Albion, ME 04910-9731

Herb Resources

GREEN TERRESTRIAL PO Box 266, Milton, NY 12547 Proprietor Pam Montgomery sells some of the finest quality dried organic herbs available, including comfrey.

TATRA HERB CO., PO Box 60, Morrisville, PA 19067. A large, reasonably priced selection of herbs from around the world.

As mentioned in part one of this series, you can also call your County Extension Agent if you have questions about weather and soil conditions specific to your area. Finally, further information on natural fertilizers can be obtained at your local library. The reference librarians will be glad to help you.

ROSLYN REID has been a gardener since the 1980s. She also reads and teaches tarot, and is a practicing Druid. Roslyn's favorite treat is fresh corn right off the stalk.

Pests and Disease

Soil Fertility and Pests

Beneficial Nematodes

Mistletoe Endangers Valuable Trees

Cutworm Collars: The Natural Deterrent

Dealing With Damping Off

Soil Fertility and Pests

By Harry MacCormack

Albert Einstein's work convinced many of us that life is energy. All living organisms are related. All elements are alive. Nitrogen fills our atmosphere. Phosphorus lives in rocks, sands, and clays. Calcium gives structure to plant stems and bones, and remains behind as those bodies decompose. All elements are charged energy, ions positive and negative, exchanging at sub-atomic wave levels. All our kin are common ancestors, be they *monera, eubacteria, archaebacteria, protocitists,* fungi, plants, or animals. Over the 4.6 billion years of Earth history, only humans have organized and disrupted the always interacting flows of wave energy. Only humans practice agriculture. It is we who have a 5,000 year history of gardens. It is our species which uses up fertility and leaves behind deserts and chemically polluted land, water, and air.

Ironically, we people of agriculture spend a great deal of our time focused on "pests." Maybe that is because in the natural scheme of free energy interactions, we are the primary pest. It is we who rip open topsoil to plant and harvest annual crops. It is we who have promoted monocultures as we wipe out fantastically complex diverse energy interactions among all species. So, when we look into our fears of pests, just whom are we looking at? Are we looking at other creatures, or are we looking into a mirror of our practices as growers?

In the agriculture literature and around land grant universities, pests are identified as any other species that actively gets in the way of producing what we humansexpect to produce in a garden or farm operation. In other words, all of nature is potentially a pest! How arrogant can we get? But look at it: in most people's conceptions, insects, plant life (weeds), basic life forms of bacteria, fungi, molds, and algae are all pests. To fight these pests we have invented myriads of insecticides, herbicides, fungicides, antibiotics. We spend lots of energy on traps for slugs, snails, gophers, moles, mice, etc.

Meanwhile, we take our tools of disruption into the garden or field, open up the topsoil over and over, and in the majority of cases put in bags of synthetically formulated foods, as if nature could survive on supermarket convenience. Since the 1950s, more and more chemicals fuel our food production systems. I've given seminars where almost no one in the audience "knows how to farm." All they know is pour on some plant food, spray for pests, harvest, process, and ship cheaply, with the largest profit possible.

Always, as growers, we must go back to basics. Basics include balanced soil, stimulation of the microorganisms that create life, stimulation of ionic exchanges (the fire within the soil), and resource-conscious water usage.

Balanced Soil Nutrition

Most modern-day growers understand a little bit about nitrogen, phosphorus, and potassium as basic foods for gardening or farming. How many of us learned how these elements function in complex interactive soils while we were in school? Almost no one. Yet our lives depend upon healthy soil. They do not depend upon knowledge of high-tech electronic equipment. Our priorities have been, and continue to be, backward. Balanced soil nutrition is the key for living healthy lives on this planet.

The best way to learn the balancing of soil is to do it. Begin with a soil test. There are many labs that do such tests. The basic soil test will tell you the mineral contents of your soil. Because of how we have treated soils, many are mineral deficient. Backyard gardeners might be trying to garden on soils pushed around by a bulldozer while a house was being built. Farmers may have inherited farmed-out soil where minerals were only taken and rarely, if ever, added. Mineral-deficient soils will produce mineral-deficient plants, if they grow them at all.

Mineral-deficient plants, like mineral-deficient animals (including humans), are sick. They are not vibrant. They attract insects, fungus, and bacteria just as weaker members of animal herds attract predators like coyotes, wolves, cougars, etc.

Soil tests give a rough analysis of several important factors that can act as guides to balancing soil and prompting health. PH is a complex assessment of available calcium (CaO). Calcium should be

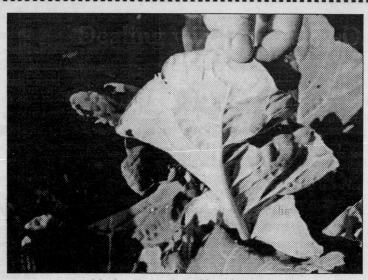

Healthy leaves resisting cabbage looper damage

thought of as an essential element in growing any plant. It is calcium that builds cell walls and regulates the availability of other mineral nutrients. Also remember that calcium additions to your soil in the form of limestone are really additions of decomposed organic matter, namely the bones of our ancestors. If your soil has a pH of less than 6.0, you should apply agricultural limestone or dolomite (calcium-magnesium limestone) to raise the pH. Available calcium can also be added in the form of sea shells, crab meal, or shrimp meal. A pH of around 6.5 is just about right for most microorganisms to function in high activity, and for the mineral and other nutrient exchanges that are the keys of healthy growth. If you live on an alkaline soil, where the pH is above 7.0, you can adjust down to 6.5 with agricultural gypsum or sulphur. As you make these adjustments, picture your soil as a living organism. It contains billions of organisms per square foot. You are feeding this microherd. You need calcium as a balance in your system, and so do they.

Many soils show low to adequate levels of phosphorus and potash, yet these can remain unavailable, locked up, if the pH is too low or too high. While adding lime or gypsum, I recommend the addition of rock phosphate. Phosphate comes in several forms. It is most often placed in commercial formulas as super phosphate. This acid-treated form of phosphate is almost immediately available for soil. The problem is that immediate availability may be too much, to quick. Immediacy itself can contribute to imbalance, and superphosphates do not stimulate slow microbial mining of solid phosphates present in the background structure.

Longer-lasting rock phosphate forms place available phosphate in the soil structure in a manner that can remain available for several years. In acid soils, some of that phosphate will be available in the season when it is added. My colleague, Dr. Alan Kapuler, is fond of reminding us that "phosphate is the biochemical connector in making all cellular energy. Nothing grows without phosphate."

Recently, much has been made of our need to remineralize Earth, particularly where we have done agriculture, but also in forested areas where pollutants rain down from the atmosphere as a result of industrialization. Rock dusts contain many minerals. They are usually good sources of phosphorous, which microherd activity makes into available phosphate. I recommend adding rock dusts to any soil. I know one researcher-grower who added forty tons of rock dust per acre to farmed-out ground. He chiseled into the top 30" of soil. The results are amazing, and will continue to be amazing, he predicts, for at least twenty years. Finely ground rocks usually contain what we know of as major minerals and trace minerals. Other than calcium, phosphorus, and potassium, fertile soil utilizes iron, manganese, zinc, copper, boron, molybdenum, sulphur, magnesium, and possibly other trace minerals in plant production. Rock dusts are good mineral sources of these trace minerals.

Your soil test will chart available potassium. Potassium is a key cation used in energy metabolism and required for protein synthesis. Potassium salts can be added to soils and are present in many fertilizer formulations. Sol-po-mag, or lagbinite rock, contains a good amount of potassium. However, potassium is usually balanced in organic systems through additions of decomposed animal wastes. Which leads to our next soil test category, organic matter.

Organic matter (OM) is an indicator of the living energy in the soil. It is not really a count of the

Broccoli resisting pest damage

billions of micoherd members. Soil testing that gives some of those numbers is very expensive and not readily available. Instead, OM is a calculation of humus in soil structure. Humus is where carbon, hydrogen, and oxygen action occurs. Humus comes from the accumulated cycles of bodies of living organisms, including microbes, plants, fungi, and animals. Humus is where biological polymers, particularly proteins, are made and buffer soils, maintaining near neutral pH.

Good gardens can be grown on soils with low OM ratings if mineralization is sufficient. However, in a garden with an OM rating of 5.0, plant cells will be ex-

tremely healthy. Enzyme and hormone interactions, cation exchanges between minerals, and all the life of soil will remain heightened through all kinds of environmental stress. Harsh rains, cold winds, drought, and baking Sun all make plants weak and vulnerable to pests unless organic matter is sufficient to act as a buffer to promote stability of moisture, oxygen, and hydrogen (water) relationships. Organic matter is the key to having less "pest" damage in the garden.

How do you get organic matter into your garden? The best and fastest method is to use compost. Composted plant and animal wastes are loaded with living and dead microorganisms. Think of composting as inoculating your field with life, as you would inoculate bread flour with yeasts to bake living bread dough. Composts can be put on in relatively small amounts and still have an effect. Quantities of 1–5 tons per acre are sufficient to start a soil going in a super-fertile direction.

Another method of getting more organic matter into soils is to grow it. All plants eventually decompose. If you plant legumes such as clovers, vetches, peas, or beans for nitrogen fixation and biomass, with grains such as rye, barley, or oats for lignin and biomass, then till them into the top 3" of soil while they are green, you create an incredible food base for a microbe population explosion. Depending upon weather, this explosion generally lasts about 3–5 weeks. During this period, all that green material will be digested. It is amazing to watch. What is left will be digested more slowly. Humus is the result. Continual green manuring sweetens and gives dimension to soil in a way no other fertilization method can.

It is generally estimated that between 70 and 75 percent of "pest" problems in agriculture are directly related to imbalanced soil. Re-balancing through proper mineralization and additions of organic breakdown products like composts and green manures takes care of many pests.

Weeds: What They Tell and What They Do

In *Weeds, Control Without Poison*, Charles Walters, Jr. shows that all pests occur for a reason. Two of his myriad examples will illustrate his teachings. I urge you to read his book, available from Acres U.S.A.

Bindweed, field bindweed, and morning glory (*Convolvulus sepium*) are major garden pests and field pests. They reproduce from both seed and roots. They can be spread by birds and wind, but are often spread by tillage. Morning glory functions best where there is a lot of humus, but a disfunctional decay system. The biological energies in the decay system are foul, and support dominating hormone and enzyme systems that are just right for vine weeds but not right for other plant inhabitants. Dry-dead organic matter in dry soils, soils without enough moisture, or high enough temperature to properly decay, are often the first culprits. An imbalance of hydrogen (a function of water) and calcium, the major factors in pH, can also stimulate bindweed growth. Soil compaction can exacerbate this problem, as can sudden heavy levels of moisture that aid in putrification rather than decomposition of mounds of organic matter. Im-

proper spring tillage can make matters worse, leaving compacted soil or soil that might be friable one day but compacts under heavy rains the next.

Bindweed can be dealt a blow by reestablishing a decay system through introductions of composts and green manures. We have noticed that bindweed becomes part of a green manuring system, remains under control during the early part of a gardening season, and makes a vigorous return just as we till it under and plant winter cover crops for next spring's green manuring. In the places where it is most active, poor drainage is an aggravating factor. We manage this persistent pest with cultivation and attempts at better drainage so that microorganisms can perform proper breakdown activities.

The plant lamb's-quarters, (*Chenopodium album*) is a sign of high organic matter soil with good decay. It is a good indicator for phosphate being available on a dai-

ly meal basis, according to Charles Walters. We love our lamb's-quarters. We even sell it at farmer's markets as a substitute for spinach. But alas, it is invasive and competitive, so it must be cultivated. We leave patches of lamb's-quarter in our winter cover-crops. Small birds love the seeds of this welcome garden weed, and also that of pigweed. Both are signs for us that our biological systems are functioning well.

Not all "weeds" are weeded on our farm. Selective patches of various plants are left to attract pests. Wild lettuce is often home to hoards of black aphids. Ladybugs need these patches. If our horticultural plants are strong, not inviting attack, we encourage St.-John's-wort in hedgerows and certain other places. It is used as a medicinal herb, but along with many other species of unplanted plants it also harbors wasps, flies, bees, and a host of other good insects that need nectar. Many organic growers have begun planting nectaries for beneficial insects.

Insect Balancing

Organic growers tell many stories of insect populations suddenly surging to out of control proportions, and predator insects showing up or not showing up, or of birds and bats presenting themselves just at the peak of the infestation. These stories always have something in common. If fertility is relatively balanced, some other stress factor is present. Sometimes it is drought. Sometimes it is neighbors spraying fields or neighborhoods, and insects are escaping to the organic refuge. Sometimes it is temperature fluctuating in a manner that stimulates insect birth. Whatever the condition, the hard thing to do in organic growing is to wait for predators to do their work. Several years ago we had a sudden outbreak of black aphids on our parsley. They were doing some leaf damage, and were visibly weakening some plants. There were ladybugs in great numbers working the crop, but it took two weeks for them to clean out the infestation. Meanwhile, we wanted to harvest for market, and we worried that plants would be damaged and we'd have to replant for fall production instead of relying on cut-and come-again production from the plants we had already grown. What caused this infestation? My guess is that these plants had grown to maturity in waterlogged soils. We had a very late spring/early summer deluge that lasted over three weeks. Soils stayed damp and cool. Water hung in between the beds. Even though we foliar fed the plants with fish, they were under constant stress.

Waterlogged soil is incapable of proper nutrient cycling. The microherd functions within rather narrow windows of temperature and moisture. Bacteria, in particular, probably couldn't do its work in those 1993 soil conditions. We noticed fungi and algae both overpopulating the soil. Because of our high humus levels, good mineralization, and careful rotation of plant families, as soon as the floods ended and the water subsided, the gardens normalized. "Pests" were abundant in no more than normal numbers. "Beneficials" thrived and helped with balance.

We tried some human intervention during this crisis. After all, we needed to sell crops to make a living. How dare climate and pests threaten that? One of our interventions, one I've used often, was sprays of liquid seaweed and side dressing with seaweed meal. No one really knows why liquid seaweed works to control insects, but observations by Dr. T. L. Senn, formerly of Clemson University, and by others, (including me), indicate that insects such as flea bee-

tles stop chewing a plant sprayed with seaweed. The insects are not killed. They eventually leave or are eaten by predators. After the spray the plants show a glow and a vigor they didn't previously have. The plant's energy changes. According to Dr. Philip Callahan in *Tuning Into Nature* and other works (also available from Acres U.S.A.), weak plant energy waves attract predator insects. Perhaps the seaweed temporarily strengthens the plant, warding off the insects.

The crystalline elements in many bio-dynamic sprays appear to have a similar effect. Maybe plant/mineral energy fields interact, change sufficiently so that insects don't recognize the plant they are on as the one they thought they were on.

Fertility, diversity, and heightened wave energies are the virtues of proper organic management. Building highly fertile soils that will be passed to future generations is one of the major tasks we are here to do. In doing this process, pests are not so much problems as teachers, showing us how the process is working or where a system is heading despite our "management" skills.

HARRY MACCORMACK has been an organic farmer for twenty-four years. He serves as director of research and education at Oregon Tilth, as well as being the Oregon principal investigator for the Northwest Area Foundation Sustainable Agriculture Initiative. In addition, Harry holds a MFA in creative writing and teaches playwriting at Oregon State University.

Beneficial Nematodes

By Monica Wallace

Beneficial nematodes are nematodes that parasitize and kill insect pests of lawns, gardens, homes, and agricultural crops. Nematodes are unsegmented roundworms that can be found almost everywhere on Earth. Some parasitize animals and plants; others are free-living in the soil and feed on bacteria or graze on fungi, mosses, and algae. Some free-living nematodes are predatory and attack other nematodes. All are essentially aquatic animals and require moisture for survival. Moisture does not have to be in the form of free water; it can be found in the bodily fluids of an animal, in plant sap, or in high humidity in the air. Many nematodes, including beneficial ones, are very tiny and can only be seen with the aid of a microscope.

Biology

Insect-pathogenic nematodes are found in most soils worldwide (except Antarctica's) and have a very wide host range that includes the majority of insect families. Because almost all insects have at least one stage in their life cycle that occurs in the soil, they are ready targets for these nematodes. Two kinds of nematodes (*Steinernema* and *Heterorhabditis*) have been found to kill insects rapidly. They carry certain insect-pathogenic bacteria internally and introduce them into the insect host. The bacteria multiply in the insect's blood, and the nematodes feed on the bacteria and insect tissues. Eventually the insect dies from the combined attack (often within 24–48 hours), and its corpse is filled with a new generation of nematodes, which can infect other insects.

As with other nematodes, insect-pathogenic nematodes begin life as eggs, pass through four immature stages called *juveniles*, and become adults. In *Heterorhabditis*, the adults of the first generation are hermaphrodites, and no mating is required for egg fertilization (fertilization occurs internally). In

Steinernema, males and females are formed, and mating is required for egg fertilization. Although a few eggs may be laid in the insect, most hatch within the mother worm, and she is killed as the young worms develop.

Only juveniles which have molted twice (called *third stage juveniles*, or *dauers*) are able to infect another insect. When conditions inside the host insect become crowded and food scarce, the dauers move a short distance from the insect's corpse into the soil. They generally don't move far before becoming inactive. This inactive state reduces both their energy consumption and attractiveness to predators, and allows them to survive long periods in the absence of a host; it also makes them very useful as biological control agents, because they can be stored for long periods of time before application. When actively seeking a host or a penetration site, these juveniles lift their heads and wave them back and forth. They may lift their entire bodies until they are standing on their tails. From this position they can lean over and "bridge" gaps between soil particles to move from one to another. They can also leap into the air by bending over until their head touches their tail and uncoiling like a spring.

When the juveniles come in contact with an insect host, they generally enter its body through natural openings. *Heterorhabditis* possess a tooth which allows them to penetrate the insect's body.

Commercial Production

A number of commercial enterprises worldwide mass produce beneficial nematodes for use in agriculture. The nematodes can be cheaply grown on artificial media at the large scale necessary for commercial production. Much of the production technology is patented and not available to the public. Beneficial nematodes have some environmental impact, but are not thought to be an environmental risk. The United States Environmental Protection Agency has waived registration requirements for nematodes used in the biological control of insects. They are classed as macroparasites and are regulated by the United States Department of Agriculture.

Product Formulation and Application

Appropriate formulation and application are keys to success in the use of nematodes as biologicals. Formulation of nematode products involves the use of some sort of carrier to bring the nematodes to the target insects and to protect them from dehydration, temperature extremes, and the Sun's ultraviolet radiation. The carriers are inert and rapidly biodegradable. They include materials such as clay, vermiculite, peat, activated charcoal, and gels. Some of these materials are in the developmental stage and not yet available to the public. The finished product (carrier plus nematode) generally needs to be refrigerated until used. If left unrefrigerated, the shelf-life declines drastically, and effectiveness is lost.

Timing of application is critical. The nematodes must be applied when conditions are moist (soil is damp and high humidity prevails), and light is not intense. The best time is in the evening, but early morning may also be effective.

Nematode biologicals may be applied in various ways. Sprays are effective because a large area can be covered, and nematodes suspended in water are automatically protected from drying out. Most common agricultural spray equipment, ranging from hand-held sprayers to irrigation systems, is suitable. The nematodes can withstand application pressures of 300 pounds per square inch or more. Sprays have been effective against soil insects (white grubs, Japanese beetles, root weevils; foliar insects (gypsy moth larvae, leaf miners); and borers. Water containing beneficial nematodes can also be drenched into soil for more specific control.

Other specific application methods include mulches, gel capsules, and baits. Mulches containing nematodes in vermiculite or peat formulations protect plant roots from root-feeding insects. Nematodes in gel capsules may be incorporated with seeds. The gels are water soluble and degrade rapidly. This places the nematodes in close proximity to germinating seeds and protects young root systems from insects such as corn rootworms, onion maggots, and cabbage root maggots. Nematode-containing capsules may also be placed on the soil surface for control of insects such as grasshoppers and cutworms. Baits in either solid or liquid form may prove to be useful in managing insects such as grasshoppers, caterpillars, cutworms, and yellowjackets. The bait contains a carrier (corncob grits, peanut hulls, or water) and an insect feeding stimulant (sugar, molasses, malt extracts) as well as the nematodes. Insects ingest the bait and are infected.

Nematodes as biologicals also show some promise in the control of home-infesting insects such as cockroaches

Nematodes as biologicals also show some promise in the control of home-infesting insects such as cockroaches. For termites, results in trial studies have been conflicting. These insects have strategies for protecting themselves from nematodes (for example, termites often wall off infected individuals) and very high infection densities are necessary for achieving measurable control.

As is evident from the preceding discussion, beneficial nematodes represent an amazing potential for the management of many insect pests. They have potential for use in home gardens, lawns, golf courses, greenhouses, and crops. Once introduced into the soil, they are persistent, and re-application may not be necessary. Since organic gardening precludes the use of chemical pesticides, beneficial nematodes represent a natural and effective way to lessen insect damage and improve the quality of organically grown produce. They are safe for both people and the environment. The future for their use looks very promising.

Reference

Gaugler, Randy, and Harry Kaya. *Entomopathogenic Nematodes in Biological Control.* CRC Press, Inc., 1990.

MONICA WALLACE holds a Ph.D. in plant pathology and her area of specialization is plant nematology. She has had work published in several scientific journals, and is interested in becoming a technical writer.

Mistletoe Endangers Valuable Trees

By Deborah Duchon

Look up into the bare branches of wintertime trees and you may see bushy balls of green, as if small shrubs had taken up residence 30' into the air. It's not your imagination—it's mistletoe.

Steeped in myth, mistletoe is a plant that most of us think of affectionately. We hang little plastic replicas (after all, it's poisonous—but who cares?) from our doorways during the Christmas season for stealing kisses. Even though it is associated with Druid and Celtic practices, the Christian Church was unable to stamp out its ritualistic usage. Even though we know it is poisonous, the mere thought of it evokes positive emotions in most of us.

There is more to mistletoe than magic, however. It is, after all, a plant like any other. It plays a role in the ecosystem that is worthy of our attention, a role of sustenance to wild birds and danger to trees.

Botanists classify mistletoe as a semi-parasite. Although it makes its own chlorophyll, it sinks a root-like, fibrous organ, known techni-cally as a *haustorium*, into the host tree's vascular system to obtain water and minerals. An evergreen shrub, it remains green all winter, when its host is dormant.

Mistletoe grows slowly. A young, healthy tree tends to "outgrow" young mistletoe starts, according to University of Georgia forestry expert Kim Coder, Ph.D., but older, slower-growing trees often become hosts, especially if stressed by other factors, such as air pollution or root disturbance.

A large tree can tolerate one or two balls of mistletoe, although the branch beyond the plant may be stunted or killed. The more mistletoe growing on a tree, however, the more stressed the tree will become.

branches, to germinate. So high are these seeds sown that accurate observation is difficult. In the Dark Ages, mistletoe was thought to spring from bird dung rather than seeds.

In the eastern United States, mistletoe affects most hardwoods, but has a special affinity for large, slow-growing oaks, hickories, and pecans, causing problems on orchards. It also grows on sassafras, black walnut, and red maple.

The tree's resistance level to infection and disease will be affected. In cases of severe infestation, mistletoe leaves can even shade the tree's leaves, depriving them of much-needed sunlight. Although mistletoe itself rarely kills its host, its presence often contributes to a tree's demise.

According to Dr. Coder, the mistletoe family is unique in its growth habits. The root-like haustorium insinuates itself into the very structure of the tree. In fact, it secretes a chemical that makes the tree think the mistletoe is a branch. "From a biological engineering standpoint," states Dr. Coder, "it's an ingenious way to make a living."

Female mistletoe balls (there are male and female plants) produce sticky white berries, poisonous to humans but much-loved by wild birds. Birds eat the berries, but not the seeds. They unwittingly sow the seeds, in fact, by wiping them, sticky coating and all, off their beaks and feet onto tree

In the west, evergreen trees and desert shrubs are bedeviled by what is known as dwarf mistletoe. A much nastier breed, dwarf mistletoe lacks the ability to make chlorophyll and is entirely reliant upon its host. These plants live mainly within the tissues of their hosts, and emerge from the tree only to expose their sexual organs, a series of scaly spikes. Once fertilized, the female spikes swell up, retaining water as the seeds develop. When ripe, the water pressure builds up so much that the seed capsules explode, propelling the seeds at speeds up to sixty miles per hour. Enough land on unfortunate neighbors to grow and spread. These mistletoes don't even provide bird seed, much less offer pretty greenery for holiday parties.

The dwarf mistletoes are more host-specific than their leafy eastern cousins. There is a particular species that affects Douglas fir, another that aims for pinon pine. It is estimated that 40 percent of the commercial timberlands in Oregon and Washington are infected by the genus. In all, sixty-two tree species in North America are parasitized by some form of mistletoe.

Recommended treatment is removal of the diseased branch below the mistletoe ball. Dr. Coder cautions that if one simply removes the ball, the haustorium remains and can resprout. In the case of a full-grown ball, which can weigh as much as thirty pounds, it is important to remove the branch at least 14"–16" below the site to avoid reinfestation. Dr. Coder emphasizes that it is a mistake to wait until a tree is covered with mistletoe before removal. By that time, the tree may be so weakened that it is too late to save it. Mistletoe should be removed while it is still small and manageable if you are serious about keeping your trees healthy.

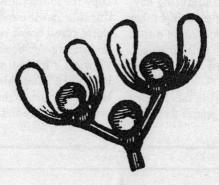

DEBORAH DUCHON is an ethnobotanist studying in Atlanta, Georgia. She has published articles in several magazines and newsletters, and is the founder of the Wild Foods Forum.

Cutworm Collars: The Natural Deterrent

By Harriet Amar

There is nothing as aggravating in vegetable gardening as spending hours and days planting your seedlings, only to come out one morning and find many of the plants chopped off at the stems. When you are sure that it cannot be small animals like rabbits or groundhogs, you can suspect small, quiet creatures called cutworms. You will not see them around during the day, as they stay beneath the ground during daylight hours. However, at night they become active and come out to find food. They will approach plants and chew them off at ground level.

To avoid having this happen to your young vegetable seedlings, you can construct a simple deterrent that will keep the cutworms away. It is called a cutworm collar, and is easily made from a sturdy, (yet flexible) piece of cardboard. The object of this collar is to act as a wall against cutworm intrusion since, as they cannot get through the barrier, the cutworms retreat and go elsewhere.

To make your protective cutworm collars, just measure and copy the illustration below onto durable cardboard from new shirts, cereal boxes, or other similar, strong-yet-bendable items. Plan on a height of 1½" and a length of 6". One third of the collar will go beneath the soil to prevent an underground approach by

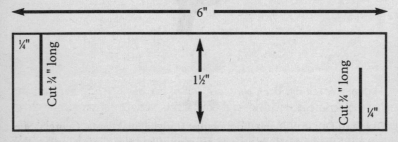

Cutworm Collar (not to scale)

the cutworm. The other two-thirds will be above the ground and successfully thwart the caterpillar from circling around the plant. Cutting a ¾" slit on each end from opposite directions, one from the top and one from the bottom, will serve as a clasp for the collar. This closure method is quick and economical if doing many collars. Though some suggest using paper clips for closure, there is the danger of losing the clips in the ground after the cardboard has disintegrated, and this could pose a hazard for unsuspecting wildlife, or even for your rototilling equipment. This also holds true for using nails around the plant stems; thus, that is not advisable, either.

Collars serve as very successful barriers to unwanted cutworm pests. However, you might also be interested in knowing that there are some other helpers nearby, as well. Birds, such as the red-winged blackbirds, love cutworms and will be happy to come around and eat them for you if you make them welcome. In addition, sprinkling finely-crushed egg shells around the plant stems and covering them lightly with soil seems to keep cutworms away, as the shells really hurt their bodies when they attempt to cross the area. Also, it has been shown that if the soil in the section to hold future seedlings is very well cultivated and remains free of any plant material for a fairly long period of time, the cutworms will starve to death of acute malnutrition.

To avoid visits from cutworms in the future, your best bet is making sure all grassy areas are well-mowed, and keeping after weeds as they emerge. In this way, you will eliminate the tempting, well-hidden places where the moth stage of the cutworm lays her eggs. In this case, the old adage is so true—an ounce of prevention is worth a pound of cure.

Good luck with your cutworm collars. Your plants will appreciate the protection and so will you.

HARRIET AMAR has been gardening all of her life. She and her husband have experimented with several small farms, and they are currently growing and researching the uses of the Jerusalem artichoke. Harriet also works as a desktop publisher, and in addition to the Jerusalem artichoke (and cutworms), one of her major areas of interest is the culinary and healing uses of so-called weeds, which she terms "misplaced plants."

Dealing with Damping-Off

By Eileen Powell

Excerpted from From Seed to Bloom © 1995 by Eileen Powell with permission from Storey Communications, Inc. Pownal, Vermont 05261.

If you find your seedlings lying prone on the soil with the leaves green but the base of the stems blackened and shriveled, they have probably fallen victim to damping-off. Damping-off is a fungal disease that can wipe out every seedling in a flat in less than a day. Damping-off can strike at any stage in a young plant's development and is usually due to excess moisture combined with a lack of ventilation. You need experience damping-off only once to be instilled with a life-long dread of this disease, and extreme caution is a small price to pay to avoid a visit from this grim reaper.

How To Avoid It

- Sterilize all seed containers and any instruments used in the process of sowing.
- Use only sterile growing media, such as vermiculite or sterilized soil.
- Sow seeds thinly to allow healthy air circulation between seedlings. Promptly thin over-crowded containers.
- Water seed trays from below. When growing plants that are particularly susceptible to damping-off, keep soil on the dry side.
- Damping-off can be stimulated by the presence of nitrogen. Always allow seedlings to develop three true leaves before using any fertilizer.

What To Do If You Detect It

- If even one of your seedlings exhibits signs of damping-off, remove it and, for caution's sake, its immediate neighbors, from the container at once.
- If the soil appears to be too moist, take immediate action by moving the containers away from other plants in order to increase air circulation and placing an absorbent material on the soil surface. Crushed charcoal is most successful, but in desperation, I've even used blotting paper.
- Resume cautious watering once the soil has dried.

Practical Application

Water in Agriculture

The Best Times to Pick Produce

Winterizing Your Garden

Raised Bed and Square Foot Gardens

Water in Agriculture

BY HARRY MACCORMACK

Many cultures celebrate four elements: Earth, water, air, and fire. Life on Earth is a mix of these four elements. Without any one of them life does not exist.

Most cultures tell stories of life coming from water. Each human comes from the waters of the womb. Many evolutionary theorists postulate life coming from the sea. Those of us who are growers know that seeds require water to stimulate germination. Water is indeed one of the four primary essences.

All life is sacred, but in ceremonies water, along with fire, is celebrated more frequently than are the elements air and earth. The qualities of pure water are those we wish for ourselves.

After all, our bodies are more than 90 percent water. We can exist without solid foods for a period of time, but without taking in water we wither and die quickly.

The atmosphere of Earth is such that water is continually recy-

❖∘∽∘❖

*Water spirit
dancing round
my head
Makes me
glad that
I'm not dead*

—NATIVE CHANT

❖∘∽∘❖

cled. Oceans, rivers, streams, rivulets, forests, and grasslands take in and release moisture. It is a fantastic process which humans in non-arid climates take for granted. Humans in arid climates tend to be more conscious of the limits related to water. The Hopi and Bedouin peoples, as desert dwellers, focus a lot of prayer, dance, and ceremony on rain. Serpentine icons in all the cultures of the Americas, Middle East, and Far East are reminders that water is what allows Earth and air to become life.

H (hydrogen) and O (oxygen) are free, colorless, odorless atmospheric gases which combined make H_2O—water. Both hydrogen and oxygen readily unite with other elements, especially with carbon compounds in cells, tissues, and bodies, generating growth. Water can feel magical when we stand by a waterfall and sense the abundance of negative ion energy as water reunites with air. We lift a handful of moist organic soil and realize that without water there would be no soil, or in a ceremony we participate in the energy held in charged water, water that has been blessed, water that holds the forces of lightning. I bring all this up because we do not think of water enough when we garden or farm. We should give continual thanks for water's presence. We should not misuse it. Ultimately, whatever the present economic condition worldwide, water cannot be owned or sold.

Basic Water Needs

To do agriculture we rely on fertile soil. Soil is not simply minerals. In soil with 5 percent organic matter, water should amount to 15–20 percent of the soil's total weight. Any amount less than about 7 percent is too dry to support life. What is life in the soil? Billions of microorganisms. Bacteria, fungus, algae. We don't see these creatures with the naked eye, but other creatures of the soil do. Worms, be they flat, annelid, earth, or nematode; mollusc-like slugs or snails; spiders, centipedes, or millipedes; are like rodents above ground. Living soil is loaded with all these critters, and they are very moisture sensitive. At above 59°F, bacteria will proliferate, but only if there is enough moisture—more than the minimum of 7 percent. Low mois-

ture levels stimulate growth of Actinomycete, a fungus-like bacteria that can constitute 10–50 percent of some soil populations. These creatures are particular to alkaline conditions. Balances between actinomycete, other bacteria, and fungus are directly related to soil moisture content. If there is too much moisture and many bacteria are consumed by rapidly proliferating fungus or algae. Temperature is always a factor in these population outbursts. In agriculture, moisture is the key. We want to stimulate balanced fertility, which means a balanced microherd condition.

To do agriculture we also rely on seeds. Seeds are repositories of germ plasm. This is where the chromosomes and genes that determine species, tribe, and variety are held. Collection and maintenance of seed stocks for agriculture is an almost-lost art, which fortunately is being regained in our time, out of desperation. Some people have become aware that we are losing thousands of species of plant organisms each year, and that the only way to save a few of them is to collect their seed.

Seeds will not sprout without adequate moisture. Some seeds need more than water to germinate new life. Gibberellic acids appear to be involved. Even so, water is needed for their work.

Germination of seeds is a primary life process. Germination in all its complexity is more important for children to understand than the three Rs. Seed germination can take place in any moist environment. Seeds of beans, sunflowers, and grasses like alfalfa can be placed in a jar with water in a warm place, and in several hours will begin softening. In one or two days the seed will break, and green life will begin to appear. In several more days, sprouting will have occurred. In even a simple germination demonstration such as the one just described, moisture is crucial. A lot of moisture is needed to soften the seed. Once germination and sprouting have begun, water is poured off and the seeds are rinsed daily, but they are not covered with water. Otherwise conditions are not life giving. Seeds can drown.

Also, too much moisture in a sprouting jar left too long will attract fungi and algae, and decomposition will begin. We should know all this as second nature from the time we are very small. Our lives depend upon this process, but most of us were never taught. Nor do we rehearse this process with our families, growing and eating our own sprouted seeds. We should.

Water and moisture levels are again key when the germination process is shifted to the greenhouse, where we are growing starts for transplant. The biggest problems in greenhouse production are fungus, algae, and mold. Too much moisture and fluctuating temperatures are the culprits. Moisture and temperature: these two elements are primary keys to good growth.

Greenhouse or potting soils are generally near neutral pH and are not usually nutrient heavy. During germination and early sprouting, plant nutrients are stored within the seed. Once rooting begins, we often supplement these nutrients through foliar feeding, placing soluble nutrients in water as a spray. Again, water is the key. We will speak more of foliar feeding later.

Field germination of seeds is more difficult than greenhouse or sprouting jar germination. Why?

Because both moisture and temperature variables are wider, more random, and outside our control. I can't tell you how often we and other growers here in Oregon have planted warm weather seeds such as corn during a warm spell, only to have a sudden change in weather: cool, rain-filled nights and days, just enough to waterlog the soil and rot the seed. Soil moisture can go from 15–30 percent rapidly during cool, sunless days. Meanwhile, corn seedlings, rooted inside a greenhouse and hardened off, can be transplanted into such cool conditions and will often thrive. Moisture and temperature are the keys.

In the garden or field, moisture levels need to be maintained at a steady level during plant growth and fruiting or flowering stages. Generally speaking, the root zone of the plant must be optimally moist. There is a wide range of requirements for garden plants in this regard, which can make adequate watering a nightmare if you plant for diversity. Lettuces have very shallow root systems, for instance, and carrots need at least 8" of damp soil. Corn can send down deep roots. Winter squash are known to probe sandy soils up to 12', seeking moisture and nutrients.

Essentially, you, the grower, want to establish a moisture conserve, a water holding bank. As everything in gardening and farming is related to everything else, we are now suddenly into the realms of tillage and fertility management. Improper tillage can release moisture into the air. It can also retain too much moisture, causing the soil to fall back into itself and close off the 20–25 percent (by volume) of oxygen needed for living soil to be healthy. Knowing your soil and your soil type and its essential characteristics is the key to water-holding capacity. Wilt points (dry soil that no longer supports life) occur rapidly in very sandy soils of low organic matter. Similarly, clay soils often remain too wet for long periods, then suddenly sear over, like meat in a hot pan, crusting and choking off the top several inches of moist life. Good amounts of organic matter in the top 3"–6" of soil are crucial for good water retention. Such an organic matter "sponge" also readily absorbs too much rain or too much irrigation, the holding capacity being significantly greater than soils of low organic matter.

Water is essential for fruiting of trees, vines, and shrubs. Although mature plants may have roots that go many feet into the soil, fruits are larger and there are more of them when ground moisture levels are adequate. Water can be a problem in these same crops. Apple scab, peach leaf curl, brown rot, and mold on raspberries and grapes can all happen as the result of too much water at the wrong time: wrong for humans bent on consuming the fruit, but right for bacteria, fungi, and other microorganisms also bent on consuming the fruit. A damp, warm, late spring in a fruit growing region brings out all our human "cides"—fungicides, insecticides, etc.—to fight the competition. Water and temperature. What a dynamic duo.

Water Delivery Systems

Rain is the basic agricultural water delivery system. There are signs over the 80,000 or so human generations back into the Upper Palae-olithic that people collected water. During at least 5,000 years of agriculture, people from the Dravidians in India, the Mayans in Guatemala, and the Chinese, to the Mandans of the Great Lakes in the U.S., all created ingenious ways to capture, control, and use water. Cisterns, canals, field irrigation ditches, buckets carried on yokes, whole fields flooded for rice production; the gathering and transport of water has been the basis for some of humankind's greatest engineering feats. Always it has been known that Earth herself holds water in reserve under her mantle. Wells dug by hand, pounded wells, and augured wells, were and are

centers for human development. Water in these wells was carefully guarded.

The industrial age changed all that. Water became a commodity as people were moved from the land for cheap city labor. Wells were dug deep with high-powered machines, allowing agricultural interests to pull 800–1,000 gallons per minute. Water was required both for production and as the medium for discharge as modern industrial agricultural systems were established. Cheap water has allowed a "cheap food" policy over the last decades. The sprawl of this style of water usage into underdeveloped countries places water as potentially the most volatile political issue during the first decades of the next century.

Of late, water problems have encouraged the assigning of dollar values to areas of abundant water. The Columbia basin, one of the largest water systems in the world, struggles with declining salmon runs. Yet the river has been dammed to create the electric power that fuels our modern lifestyle. That damming also supplies the high desert with water to grow abundant crops where in earlier times only sagebrush grew. The salmon and power interests say their water is worth $130.00 per cubic foot, while agricultural use water is estimated to be worth only $30.00 per per cubic foot. How much is the water used on your garden worth? Can we even think and talk this way when dealing with life? Interest groups and policy makers believe they can.

Once "free" water comes from the ground, a stream, or a canal or from the city water pipeline, how should we best use it on our gardens or in our fields?

With water so precious, old-style flood irrigation still fuels much of irrigated agriculture, particularly in the southwestern U.S. It is also prevalent in China, India, South America, and other zones. Much of this water evaporates into the atmosphere and is not absorbed by the soil. It does, however, pick up agricultural nutrients and pesticides, carrying them as pollutants downstream wherever the water goes: the ocean, reservoirs which are game preserves, or into municipal water systems.

Sprinklers are said to be more efficient in their delivery. Center pivot systems utilize misting sprinklers, as do roll wheel systems on large fields. Rain birds or other forms of sprinkler systems are in most urban areas. Much of the water delivered from these systems also evaporates, depending upon time of day used, wind velocity, and soil holding capacity.

Forms of drip or trickle irrigation are thought to conserve the most water and be the most efficient delivery mechanisms. In our use of these systems it appears that some plants do very well under drip and others do not do quite as well. Generally speaking, a well maintained, well engineered drip system can allow for gardens and farms to produce huge quantities of vegetables, fruits, and nuts with very little water. Capital investment and maintenance are the tradeoffs.

Foliar feeding is another form of water delivery, albeit water that is mixed with nutrients or poisons. Foliar feeding utilizes a spray nozzle to mist plants. This misting coats the plant with moisture. Foliar fed nutrients are carried directly into plant cells by a complex

mechanism of enzymatic reactions involved in the uptake of an amino acid or peptide into the plant cell. This process is used to offset poor soil fertility or to overcome slowness of plant growth during too cool, too hot, or drought periods. Plants can take water in through their leaf structures. Dew is carried into plants at dawn, helping their cells to grow when perhaps the day will be too hot and cell growth would all but shut down. Likewise, soluble nutrients can be piggybacked into plant cells at dawn or dusk. We use both soluble fish and seaweed fertilizers to feed plants when other soil mechanisms are under stress. Biodynamic growers use a host of plant and animal-based sprays. Foliar feeding is very efficient form of water management and is likely to find even more use in the future.

Water and Our Future

The Earth is a blue and white dot when viewed from the outer planets. Our atmosphere of oxygen and hydrogen mixes into water, all that blue viewed by satellites. However, most of the water is saline, too salty for agriculture. Our water resource is rather limited. It comes from rain, and then from all the chan-

nels and storage places where rain resides.

Rain is intimately linked to plant life, specifically to large forested regions of this earth. As these are cut down for human use, water itself becomes less abundant. The water that does come from the sky is not so well stored as it was by old trees and forested soil. For this reason, the future could require that we grow plants in much more efficient ways. Human diet is the cause for agriculture. Human dietary demands can be very complex, involving growth of foods which require massive amounts of water in order to get a small amount of useable nutrients. As a species, we could decide to utilize our intelligence to generate diets that can be grown simply in gardens that use no more than rain. Ultimately, a doubling of human populations during the next century will pose this water-diet issue. It behooves us as that small minority who are actually in touch with water-food relationships to learn how to grow food most efficiently and to promote simple diet as a way for humans to survive within the fabric of water, Earth, air, and fire.

HARRY MACCORMACK has been an organic farmer for twenty-four years. He serves as the director of research and education at Oregon Tilth.

The Best Times to Pick Produce

By Harry MacCormack

Gardens are productive spaces. As human managers of our gardens, we have to be keenly aware of time. Intimate involvement in the space-time continuum which is planting, transplanting, fertilization, weeding, and harvest requires of us a sense of real life. We work with nature's clocks while in the garden. Sun cycles, Moon cycles, and each plant's genetic time-clock replace our obsession with watches. The garden may be our last refuge from time, calculated by microseconds, that ticks away on the computer screen, payroll office, basketball court, or race tracks. In the garden, space and time are not fit into human constraints.

Why Are You Picking?

What are the best times to pick produce? This seemingly innocent and simple question is actually very complex and raises lots of issues. First of all, what are you picking for? Are you walking out into the garden just before a meal to pick fresh for that meal? Are you picking for a meal that will happen later in the day, or even the next day? Are you picking for market? If

so, what kind of market? Farmers' market or farm stand? Wholesale warehouse? Local store or restaurant? CSA (Community Supported Agriculture)? Canning, freezing, or a processor?

Picking for each of these uses requires a different sense of when best to pick. As conscientious growers, we want our garden product to be the best nutritionally. We want fullness of flavor. We want expected color and texture. Helping plants to fulfill our expectations is a lot of work. We want the fruits of our labors to be the best.

Nutritionally, there are specific times of day when cell chemistry appears to be superior, according to our needs. Some researchers have shown that lettuces, for example, reach a mineral and vitamin peak before dawn. Herbs have more of their potent oils before noon and are often less potent on cloudy days. Sugars in berries and capsicum heat levels in certain peppers change slightly depending upon the time and condition of the day. Some fruits are best picked while slightly immature to allow a maturing and nutritional change in storage.

Picking to Eat Immediately

Pick the ripe, (not overripe) berries, tomatoes, cucumbers, melons, greens, and medium-sized carrots, potatoes, beets, and kohlrabi. Apples, pears, plums, peaches, and other fruits should break easily from the tree.

Basically, we always want to pick when the mineral and vitamin content of these potential foods is best. With most vegetables and many fruits, picking early in the day, while great for post harvest storage under refrigeration, may not be the time of day when plant cells are most potent. We are picking for minerals, vitamins, amino acids, proteins, plant oils, and other nutritional reasons. We want to share cells. We cannot state as a rule what time of day nutritional content is superior, because there are myriads of variables—sunlight and temperature being the most important—that influence nutritional condition. In a world where individual humans were able to sense individual plant energies, harvest would happen like love-making happens, when the energy of the human-plant relationship was intense enough to allow for interaction, picking, and sustenance to happen. In the best garden experiences, the plants tell their gardeners when they are ready.

Picking to Eat Later in the Day

Most vegetables and fruits should be picked before the heat of the day. Greens should be picked early, washed, and refrigerated immediately. Post-harvest conditions for other fruits and vegetables are not so critical during the first twelve hours, if shade and moving air are provided.

Picking for a Farm Stand

Pick for daily sales, if possible. Otherwise pick early, provide immediate cooling with water, ice, or refrigeration on greens, berries, peas and beans, fresh herbs, carrots, and corn. Tomatoes, cucumbers, melons, squash, onions, and potatoes can be picked ahead and stored in a dark, cool room with good air circulation. Fruits can also be stored and brought to the stand as needed. Fruits, berries, and tomatoes should be picked after sugars are set but before totally mature.

Picking for the Farmer's Market

If possible, pick no more than twenty-four hours ahead of the market for greens, herbs, cucumbers, summer squashes, melons, berries, and tree ripened fruits. Use proper post-harvest storage practices. Pick for improper handling by customers. Pack as for shipping. Trucking stresses all produce. If marketing in the heat of the day, provide shade, ice, and water to avoid wilting and spoilage.

Picking for Wholesale

Generally, pick less than ripe but ripe enough that maturing will happen before use. Pick with storage in mind. Pick early, while produce is cool, to aid in refrigeration. Pick only what appears perfect. Often you must sort for size.

Picking for a CSA

Ideally, pick as farm stand or "later that day" use. Depending on clientele, you may have to pick for storage and shipping. Do not send very ripe produce to locations that will not use it immediately.

Plant Maturity

Like all relationships, picking items involves compromise. Not many people are going to wait for the nutritionally proper moment to pick. The sign most often used in harvesting is plant maturity.

Plant maturity is a function of what we expect from garden production. Do we pick baby carrots and greens? Do we pick squash blossoms? Do we wait for carrots and greens to mature? Do we eat small, medium, or large summer squashes? Many of the answers to these questions are cultural, having to do with diet as it has been passed down through generations.

Maturity is also a function of fertility. Generally speaking, greens, including all the lettuces, chard, spinach, mustard, kales, collards, some cabbages, kohlrabi, and especially oriental cabbages and mustard, should all be grown on very fertile soil. Rather than time of day or Moon position, harvest of these plants is usually judged by flavor and tenderness. The best flavors (which indicate heightened nutritional characteristics) are a result of very rapid growth and of being harvested before maturity. Slow growth on poorly fertilized ground makes the plants listed above inferior. They are often bitter, bug infested, and tough. To lend to the complexity, greens hit growth spurts somewhat unpredictably, usually as a function of light and temperature. The window for harvest is, because of all of the above, very narrow. Therefore I always suggest that gardeners plant, successively in small plots, only what can be picked and used over a two-

week period. Planting every 10–15 days usually allows picking over a one to two-week period.

Questions of quickness in production are raised in other ways by different plants. Cucurbits, for instance, from which we get cucumber, summer squashes, and melons, may take one to three months to grow a plant big enough for flowering and fruiting to take place. But once that flowering begins, look out. You must go to the garden at least daily to get cucumbers or zucchini if you are particular about the size you want or your customers want. Unlike lettuce or spinach, which are generally harvested as whole plants, cucumbers, melons, and summer squashes keep producing for a long time if the climate is right, they are adequately watered and fertilized, and they are kept picked. Usually plants of the cucurbit family are picked before the heat of the day because the fruit needs to remain cool. Night air is a natural form of cooling that is then followed by some form of refrigeration or shading. When do you pick a cucumber? It depends upon variety. You don't allow cucumbers or zucchini to develop tough skin. Melons, on the other hand, are judged by size and slippage (how easily they come from the plant). Flavor is the real determining characteristic. Eat what you grow at various stages and see what tastes best to you. It will likely be what others like also.

Some crops take a long time to mature but can be harvested at various stages for extended use. Onion, potatoes, carrots, and beets fit this category.

Planted very tightly, onions can be harvested for their greens. As with other salad greens, green onions should grow quickly, and be harvested while tender.

Storage onions or onions that are to be cured after picking will mature their skins as their tops fall down. We often aid this maturing process by removing irrigation and physically pushing the tops over. When the tops have turned toward brown, cut the tips and leave the pulled bulb on the ground, or in bad weather in a greenhouse. When the neck is no longer juicy, they are ready for storage or sale. In recent years we have picked green storage onions, onions that have full-sized bulbs but are not cured, for early sales in farmers' markets. We leave the roots on these onions and provide shallow buckets of water for them so that their tops remain fresh and green without the bulb becoming soggy.

Potatoes can be picked after the plants have flowered. Simply reach under the plant and feel around. We usually pick medium to large potatoes, keep feeding and watering the plants, let them remain in the field until their tops brown and fall, then dig cured potatoes from the same plants. Fresh, uncured potatoes do not store well. They should be used within a week or two. Cured potatoes should last for months in proper dark, cool conditions.

Carrots and beets are sweetest, crunchiest, and most vibrant looking if they are eaten within one day of harvest. We pick for flavor and color. We have found that carrots taste best if picked just prior to maturity. Some varieties hold in the soil and retain flavor and snappy tenderness better than other varieties. We try to plant only what will be sold over a several-week period. Home gardeners should use successive plantings. Plant what you actually eat. Late in the season we harvest carrots for keeping and long term sales. This harvest is done just prior to maturity, in the last quarter of the Moon, and before too much wet and cold weaken the roots. Beets, turnips, rutabagas, and celery are picked and treated in a manner similar to carrots.

Finally, some crops take a whole season to mature and are picked only once. Garlic and shallots are examples of this. Garlic is fall planted but doesn't mature until July. At maturity garlic tops brown and fall. We must wait for maturity of cloves, but if we wait too long we can get splitting of the bulbs or inclement moisture can ruin much of the crop. Because we sell garlic over a period of months, we also try to pick close to the dead of the Moon to minimize moisture content.

Ripeness

Many people judge picking time by ripeness. What is ripeness? Vine ripened tomatoes are usually not picked when they are dead ripe. They are too soft at that stage. Vine ripe usually means that some color and flavor have set. For tomatoes, in order to stand the rigors of the picking and sort bins, an orange flush is the sign. After picking, ripening continues. Depending upon variety, we have 3–5 days to sell what has been picked. After that the tomato may taste fine, but is too ripe and juicy for most uses.

Vine-ripened melons are picked at slip, although some varieties don't slip. We do a lot of melon tasting to figure out when a variety is ripe. If melons get too ripe they get mushy. If they are under-ripe they are crunchy and do not ooze sugar. Vine-ripened is a judgement call which you learn by experience within your peculiar growing conditions. One thing consumers can be almost certain of: vine-ripened usually never makes it to the supermarket. For shipping, most vegetables and fruits must be picked in a prior-to-ripened state. That is one of the big reasons why locally grown and marketed foods taste so much better than supermarket foods.

Some varieties keep better than others, and are therefore grown specifically for fresh market shipping. Strawberries are a good example. Supermarket berries cannot contain the sugars that are in some homegrown varieties. Shelf-life is a function of sugar and water content. Many June berry and everbearing varieties will lose marketability overnight, but they are the sweetest berries.

What is ripeness in a pepper? We grow many varieties of red, orange, golden, and purple peppers. We sell each of these at its green stage. Picking green peppers from the plant forces the plant into further flowering. To maximize production for a pepper plant, ripeness has a wide ranging defini-

tion. All peppers eventually turn color. Nutritionally, a red pepper is different from a green pepper, but there are many uses for green peppers. When the pepper's size is right, pick it.

Whole books have been written on the benefits of eating baby greens and sprouts. How do we know when to pick a lettuce, spinach, or sprout? There is a stage in plant growth in which it is easy to see or sense plant vigor and vitality. Many nutritional practitioners indicate that it is in that vital stage when humans should ingest greens. Usually plants are not very large at that stage. We've gotten use to purchasing mature plants of lettuce, artichoke, or spinach. We home gardeners have the advantage in that we can eat youthful plant energy. Nutritionally, the vitamin, mineral, enzyme, and hormone contents of these young plants are quite different from the larger versions of the same plant that have been off the soil, even for a day. Store versions, shipped several thousand miles, are nutritionally deficient when compared to youthful plants.

Varieties of plants and levels of maturity determine keeping or shipping quality. So do growing practices. Greens that are pumped up with nitrogen generally keep poorly. Greens grown with organic methods that include mineralization often keep well for weeks. Growing practices often determine ripeness, flavor, and picking time. Mineral-balanced soils allow us to pick many different kinds of crops over longer periods of time than is possible where mineral and nutrient deficiencies exist in the soil.

Picking Astrologically

Astrological time is a human projection that describes apparent cycles of energy. Gardens are spaces where Sun and Moon energies are very apparent. In *The Rulership Book,* Rex Bills assigns specific astrological signs to specific crops. Louise Riotte assigns planting and harvesting times in her book *Astrological Gardening.* Marua Thun, one of the researchers within the Biodynamic movement founded by Rudolf Steiner, assigns specific astrological qualities to plants and times of day. It is possible to construct an astrological mathematic that narrows picking times for various varieties to specific hour windows on a given day. Is this practical? Does this very human practice have anything to do with how plants live and grow?

We have found that there are astrological harvest rules that do make a difference to quality of fruits, vegetables, grains, and nuts. Position of Sun and Moon do make a difference, and should enter picking calculations.

The position of the Sun relative to your garden spot on Earth is crucial for growing. It is also very important for picking. Several examples will help. Cayenne pepper being picked for a processor who is using it to make medicinal tinctures requires that the peppers be picked at full, red maturity. Okay, the peppers begin turning in late August. They are picked in batches and dried. Our climate does not allow for Sun drying the whole crop, so a drier is used. A second picking is done several weeks later. Then the nights become longer. The mornings are cooler. The Sun has moved south on the horizon. Its heat is no longer like that of August, but like late September and early October. We harvest the last crops of peppers and dry them. All these peppers look the same. But the ones from the later pickings have less capsicum, (or less heat),

are therefore not useable for medicinal quality products. They are fine for culinary use. Sun was the variable.

Another example is early, everbearing strawberries. They bring a great market price, but their sugars do not peak until several weeks into marketing. In the fall they continue producing after the Sun has lost intensity. They are strawberries, but their flavor is less intense.

Watch the Moon phases. If you grow Moon-sensitive fruits and vegetables, such as tomatoes, you can plan events such as canning or selling canner boxes by the Moon. If tomatoes are green and starting to show signs of turning toward yellow at the new Moon, and if the Sun provides long days that are warm, you will have a large flush of ripe tomatoes in and around the full Moon.

When we think of "keeper crops," or crops that will be stored, we calculate harvest for the fourth quarter of the Moon. Grain, dry corn, storage onions, potatoes, carrots, garlic, apples, and pears are all slated for harvest in the dark of the Moon. Winter squashes, turnips, and rutabagas all have less water and therefore keep better if picked during the last of the fourth quarter Moon.

Fresh greens and Moon-ruled vegetables such as cucumbers and melons will have slightly longer shelf lives when picked in the fourth quarter. This piece of information is good for marketers. Over-abundant crops sold at this time to warehouses for distribution usually have better shelf lives.

Picking times really come down to what you want from your garden. Good growing practices are of primary importance. Deciding when to pick can very simple. Pick when you feel the time is right. Or, picking times can be very complex, utilizing nutritional, astrological, and climatological information to make calculations that are no more than human projections of expectation.

✦c✦

Harry MacCormack has been an organic farmer for twenty-four years. He serves as the director of research and education at Oregon Tilth, as well as the Oregon principal investigator for the Northwest Area Foundation's Sustainable Agriculture Initiative. In addition, Harry holds a MFA in creative writing and teaches playwriting at Oregon State University.

Winterizing Your Garden

By Penny Kelly

There was a time not so long ago when growing my own food was a simple ritual of pleasure. Every spring I tilled my garden, drove to the local nursery, bought seeds and young plants, then went quickly home to put them all in the ground immediately. Over the summer I struggled with weeds, bugs, and slugs because running a business of my own meant that I was always too busy to really take care of a garden, but I loved fresh tomatoes and cucumbers in my dinner salad, or crispy green beans for lunch.

Feed your soil's population of microbial tenants as you would wish them to feed you

When the first frost arrived I would breathe a sigh of guilty relief and allow the whole patch to fall into brown ruins. Winterizing the garden meant little more than pulling up the wooden stakes that marked the end of each row and putting away the tomato cages. Winter was the time to sit by the fire, or paint the laundry room, then withdraw to rest in the evenings, oblivious of weather, lettuces, and potato beetles.

That was before I understood firsthand the reality of what happens to a body that has been fed on foods grown in dead soils, laced with heavy metals and pesticides, and seriously deficient in a number of essential nutritional elements that prevent cancer, heart disease, arthritis, and a host of other subtle degenerative effects. That was before I made the decision that it was time to get serious about growing my family's own food.

These days I not only try to grow a few things right through December, I have discovered the importance of winterizing my garden. This means, in short, taking the money, time, and effort to assess the condition of the soil in the garden and then replacing the nutrients that were used by vegetables over the summer.

Your garden plot is home to millions of microbes that live in the soil, and these bacteria, fungi, and microorganisms are the secret to productive soil and its results—

healthy, truly nutritious vegetables and fruits. Winterizing your garden comes down to one simple rule: Feed your soil's population of microbial tenants as you would wish them to feed you!

What to feed them, when to feed them, and how much to feed them varies with the individual plot that you are trying to grow things in, but there are some general guidelines that apply almost everywhere.

First, bacteria, fungi, actinomycetes, and protozoa need both food and water. Their favorite dish is a plentiful supply of carbonaceous materials. These materials include familiar items like grass and tree clippings, unless you've recently sprayed them with weed or insect killers which will, in turn, kill your microorganisms. It also includes old leaves, kitchen wastes, animal wastes and manures, sawdust, weeds, old straw or hay, ashes from your woodstove, and even old papers and rags made of cotton, wool, or natural fibers. Of course, throwing old socks on the garden will not quite do the task; if you dump old newspapers on it they will probably be distributed over the whole neighborhood by the wind. The best approach is to do some serious spring cleaning; shred, cut, or chop everything that you possibly can into a compost pile. Add kitchen and yard wastes

over the summer, turning the pile about every three weeks. By September it will be finished compost.

When to feed your microbes? Autumn is the most important feeding time of the year as far as maintaining healthy soil is concerned. If you have made your own compost over the summer, fall is the time to spread it wherever it is needed.

If you have not made compost, seriously consider purchasing some and getting it onto your soil before the snow falls. If your soil is dead or collapsed, autumn is an excellent time to purchase liquid concentrations of microorganisms and spray them over the soil, then sow a cover crop, creating plentiful supplies of carbon-based materials for these microbes to digest. If your soil just needs a little balancing, this is the time to buy and put down any calcium, phosphorus, or trace elements needed.

If you make compost tea or manure tea, fall is the time to empty your tea barrel of whatever precious dregs it has left and spray it liberally all over the garden before the hard cold sets in. Doing so gives a powerful lift to the numbers of microorganisms in the soil's population of unseen helpers. Once it gets cold, microbial reproduction slows down considerably, but in the dead of winter you will often be able to see the difference with your own eyes. Snow on your lawn will continue to pile up in mounds of crusty white, while snow cover on the garden melts much more quickly because of the quantities of heat given off by microbial activities.

Putting compost on in the fall leaves plenty of time for it to do its work and mellow its way through the top few inches of earth. In spring most of us want to get out there and start planting right away. Waiting for warm weather is frustrating enough, and there can be an irresistible urgency to plant something, anything, especially if you have already purchased a few seedlings at a local store. The danger is that if your compost is not fully decomposed, it will finish its decomposition process and tie up precious nitrogen just when it's needed to support the growth and development of infant plants. Worse, if it is uneven in its composition, it can burn your tender seedlings to a fizzle.

Compost, compost tea, or other soil amendments should be added to the soil when there are still a couple weeks of warm weather left in the season. Warm temperatures will allow for rapid growth of the microorganisms and bacteria that are so necessary for plant health and vigor, and in spring your soil will be ready to receive transplants and seeds earlier.

If you would really like to balance, as well as restore, your soil for next spring, but have no clear idea of how to accomplish this, your best move is to collect soil samples around Labor Day and have them analyzed by a laboratory that does a complete soil analysis for the type of crop you are trying to grow. Vegetables, fruits, and grains all have different needs.

For years we dug up samples of soil from our gardens and vineyards and sent them off to the county extension office to be tested. The test was cheap, only around $7.00 per sample, and the result that came back every single year was the same short, simple comment: "No fertilizer needed." And yet the grapes and the gardens produced far below their capabilities. Worse, they were plagued by mildews and insects and seemed inordinately affected by every twitch of the weather.

Finally we broke down and got a complete soil analysis at a commercial lab that did both a La-

> ❧c❀❧
> *Amendments should be added to the soil when there are still a couple weeks of warm weather left in the season*
> ❧c❀❧

Motte test, to determine what was left in the soil once the growing season was over, and a Cation Exchange Capacity (CEC) test to let us know whether the minerals, elements, and nutrients actually in the soil were going to be available to our plants or were caught in such tight electromagnetic bonds that nothing would be released for translocation into the plants next spring. It cost us about $45.00 per sample and we had to wait nearly a month to get the results back, but it was worth both the money and the time.

The people at the lab who did the tests not only took considerable time to explain the many aspects of the test results, they also recommended sources in our area of the state for the soil amendments they were recommending. Since we were growing everything without the use of chemical fertilizers, pesticides, herbicides, or fungicides, finding someone who understood the sustainability concepts of organic agriculture and would work with us was extremely important.

I had no idea until then that you could buy chicken compost or mushroom compost, get marl (a nutrient-rich material from the bottom of ponds and lakebeds) de-

The main concept to understand about your garden is that it is not dead in winter

livered, or even what hard or soft rock phosphate was. Not only did the sources deliver, they mixed what we needed exactly to our specifications and were willing to bag it in fifty-pound bags. Some of them even spread it for us!

In an interview with Doug Murray, an IPM (Integrated Pest Management) specialist and agricultural consultant in Paw Paw, Michigan, he stressed that the main concept to understand about your garden is that it is not dead in winter. It has simply switched from a warm, green, fast-producing mode to a cooler, quiet, I-need-to-replenish-myself mode. The plants may be dead and gone but the soil is there, alive and biologically active.

To keep it that way, he offered several valuable recommendations. One is to broadcast rye, clover, or alfalfa seed throughout the garden at the end of August. Let it sprout and come up around your vegetables. The vegetables will be done growing just about the time the rye, alfalfa, or clover begins to take over. When it gets to be about 9"–10" tall (and before the ground freezes), till everything under and let the feasting microorganisms decompose it over

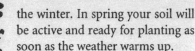

the winter. In spring your soil will be active and ready for planting as soon as the weather warms up.

Rye is a cheap and effective cover crop that can do wonders for the soil, as well as significantly improve the taste and sweetness of your vegetables. But rye has to be watched carefully and turned under before it gets too tall. Keep in mind that rye grows quickly and a week of rain can push your rye from 6" to over a foot in height. If you let it get more than 9" high, the root systems that it develops will be huge and tough and can leave your entire garden plot unworkable for nearly a year while the giant root systems decompose. Trying to rake them out of the garden removes most of the nutrients and carbonaceous materials you were trying to put back in.

Sweet clover is a great cover crop, but this is a more expensive way to get food for your microorganisms. If your soil has collapsed, is mostly clay, or is in really bad shape due to hardpan, clover is a miracle worker. It should be planted and left for at least three years so its magical roots can work their ways deeply into heavy clays or hardpans, breaking them up, greatly improving both soil structure and chemical composition.

Alfalfa is more expensive than rye, but cheaper than clover. When left in the ground it has much the same effect as sweet clover except the root systems are a bit slower, it does not have to be watched as carefully as rye, and it makes an excellent green manure and soil conditioner.

If you have struggled with serious weed problems, Murray recommends broadcasting a fairly heavy cover crop of oats throughout your garden at the end of August. Let the oats come up and grow without interference until the frost knocks them down. As the weather gets colder and winter arrives, the now-dry, brown oats will settle into a deep, matted cover over the entire garden, smothering the many perennial weeds that continue to grow well into winter and are the first to resume growing in the spring. Till the entire garden early in the spring at least one month before you intend to begin planting, and then till again just a few days before setting out plants.

His third recommendation is one that he uses in his own gardens. It does not involve cover cropping and assumes your garden soil is fairly healthy to begin with. Murray plants two gardens, each about 40' x 70', every year. In the autumn he buys a fifty-pound bag of lime and colloidal phosphate from the local hardware or mill and spreads about half on each garden. He then collects falling leaves, puts a layer up to 1' deep on each garden, and tills them in. Leaves have a fairly balanced composition of important elements brought up from deep in the ground by tree roots, and thus they provide a fairly balanced supply of nutrients for the soil. Over the fall and winter, the leaves decompose and worms crawl over and through the mixture of soil and leaves, depositing precious worm castings. In the spring the soil is in superb condition and ready to plant, leaving him free to concentrate on starting seeds and getting them into the ground.

Your rototiller, or tractor and tiller, also deserves to be winterized

Says Murray, "The goal to be reaching for is to be feeding only your soil, not your plants. Soil needs to be fed about three times a year, with autumn being the most important time on the feeding schedule. The other two times are in spring and again in early-to mid-July, with a side-dressing of good compost or balanced fertilizer. The July feeding is more important than the spring feeding because it is in midsummer that the plants are finishing their fruiting efforts and beginning the heavy work of nourishing fill to maturity whatever they are producing."

What about winterizing the more permanent sections of your garden? If you have a perennial patch with items like raspberries, herbs, grapes, rhubarb, sweet potatoes, strawberries, asparagus, or perennial onions and flowers, rototill around them or hoe thoroughly and weed. Then spread a layer of mulch around everything, banking it up to help protect stems. Compost can also be used as a mulch at this time, but it's a good idea to make sure the plants have been through two or three good frosts and are well on their way to dormancy. Compost can sometimes give a late boost to growth efforts. If the plant needs to be saving its energy for winter survival, a sudden splurge to produce new growth can weaken the whole system. If the winter turns out to be a severe one, you can lose the plant you intended to protect.

Prune raspberries back to about waist height, and consider mowing your asparagus and strawberries with your lawn mower. Set the blades fairly high so you do not injure the crowns. A soil test here will help determine whether you need nitrogen for healthy plants, or phosphorus for sweet berries and asparagus spears. A small amount of compost can be spread right over the rows to aid in crown development, especially for asparagus, which is a heavy feeder.

If you do not mow the strawberry patch, cut the runners connecting series of daughter plants or daughter-to-parent plants. This allows each plant to develop without drawing energy and nutrients from others. If the strawberry patch is getting overgrown, thin it out and reduce the row width to about 18" for easy care and picking. You can also sow oats in light to moderate quantities right in the strawberry patch. Let the oats grow until fall frosts knock them over, forming both a weed barrier and a nice, straw-like mulch the following year. If you plant the oat cover too heavy, the next spring it may be necessary to loosen the mulch it forms so that your strawberries can come up through it. You don't want to smother your berries!

Your rototiller, or tractor and tiller, also deserves to be winterized. Empty any gas-and-oil mixtures out of them. Clean and dry the spark plug, remove accumulations of soil or grasses that will hold moisture and cause rust to start earlier, and then put them away in your garden shed or garage with a dose of appreciation for the work this equipment saves your back and arm muscles.

Also collect and put away your shovels, rakes, hoes, hand tools, hoses, sprinklers, sprayers, and spreaders. Make sure they are clean and empty of soil, weeds, water, and leftover mixes. Clean and lubricate any moving parts, then put them to bed next to the rototiller until warm weather returns.

A common habit of hurried gardeners is to transplant glorious arrangements of flowers and vegetables, but never quite finish collecting the black, plastic cell-packs or trays they come out of. I have even found trays with a few cell-paks holding the forlorn remains of some specimens that never quite made it into the ground. As the flowers or vegetables grew taller, they completely hid the unfinished business, saving me from feeling any guilty pangs at such neglect. Now is the time to collect these leftovers and clear both yard and garden of anything that will be in the way of next season's start-up.

All baskets or pails should be emptied of leftover weeds or produce, then turned upside-down in a dry spot, or hung up in your shed or garage, especially if they are the old-fashioned bushel-basket type. One year I bought six new half-bushel baskets to make my harvesting easier. At the end of the season I didn't bother to collect and remove the discarded carrot tops and old cabbage leaves that had collected in two of them. A third one sat outside the shed all winter, collecting snow, ice, spring rains, and then mud. The following season I ended up with only three usable baskets. The bottoms of the two that held carrot tops and cabbage leaves had nearly decomposed with their contents. The other was so weakened and mushy from sitting in the snow and rain all winter that it was unable to carry anything of any weight. The plastic pails I had left out until temperatures dipped to near zero cracked crisply when I tried to pull them out of the snow and put them away halfway through the winter.

The end of the growing season may be the first time you've had all year to clean, sweep out, and reorganize the garden shed, or the garden corner of the garage or barn. As the growing season passes, most of us run in and out of the shed or the garage, grabbing tools, dropping off baskets, dumping bags or boxes of everything from nutrient sprays and new hose nozzles to watering wands and extra tiller teeth.

By the end of the summer you usually have at least a half-dozen ideas about how to make the shed work better, and now is the time to put those ideas into reality. Hooks, shelves, bins, racks, a table for assembling things—all these take only a half day to put in place and voila! The garden shed or corner seems twice its size.

When everything has been cleaned up and put away, it is time to winterize the gardener—yourself! Take advantage of the season to meander through your favorite bookstore and find out what's being written about gardening. Read about some aspect of gardening or agriculture that interests you. Research some problem that plagued you over the past season to find solutions. Look through your seed catalogs, keep abreast of the seeds offered on the market, and plan to experiment with growing at least one new flower, fruit, herb, or vegetable next year. Read something on nutrition. Explore cookbooks or magazines for recipes that might tempt you to try growing and actually eating something you've never considered before. When you head out to the garden the next spring, it will be a whole new world.

❖CƆ❖

PENNY KELLY is a writer, gardener, and small farmer raising Concord grapes for Welch Foods Corporation. She has been a tool and process engineer for Chrysler Corporation, and was an educational consultant specializing in brain-compatible and accelerative learning techniques for more than thirteen years. She was recently awarded a degree as doctor of naturopathy and is currently working on a Ph.D. in nutrition.

Raised Bed and Square Foot Gardens

By Leslie P. Nielsen

My own gardening experience goes back several years, and I have to admit that I learned by the "hit and miss" method.

Recently I started asking other people why they garden, and was surprised to get so many totally different answers. All of my neighbors are avid gardeners, so I started by asking them. Because we all live so close to each other, my thinking was that there would be some similar answers. There certainly were not. I also spoke to people in farm and garden stores and nurseries. I found that it takes no effort whatsoever to get an "expert" opinion.

One of my questions was, "What type of gardening do you do?" Most people grew both flowers and vegetables. What was of special interest to me, though, was that of the strangers I spoke to, just a few used raised bed gardens for their vegetables, and they seemed to use this method more for their flowers. Currently about 75 percent of my neighbors use raised beds. Five years ago I was the only raised bed gardener and, even as I write this article, I am the only square foot gardener. There are, however, a lot of questions over the back fence. I hope to share my enthusiasm for raised beds and square foot gardening with you. It will save you a lot of time and effort, which will make your garden that much more productive and rewarding.

Raised Beds

A raised bed is a roughly rectangular or square hill or mound of soil, usually about 8" high. These beds can be framed and made "permanment," or left without any supporting structure. For me, raised bed gardening makes a lot of sense, particularly since I am only 5'1" tall, and the way I have arranged the raised beds allows me to plant, weed, and maintain my garden all within my own arm's length. Because of this convenience, I refer to raised bed gardening as "no backbreaking gardening" or the "sitdown gardening method."

The three raised beds I work with are only 4' wide by 8' long, and are 16" high. They have been constructed out of 4" x 4" lumber, stacked four high. This gives me a nice bench from which to work, and makes the reach into the center of the garden only slightly under 2'. For me, one of the determinators of the size of my garden was *my* size. This method gives you a chance to get truly creative. There is no limit to the choice of structures that can be built using it.

When I asked my neighbors who do raised bed gardening why they use this particular method, their answers included ease of maintenance; a few said it was more aesthetically pleasing; others said it allowed them to plant on a slope; and others said they were able to plant earlier because the soil was warmer. The frost leaves raised bed gardens earlier than it does ground level gardens. There are also some additional reasons for raised bed gardening of my own that I would like to share.

First, the soil in a raised bed remains more easily workable. It doesn't need to be loosened up by roto-tilling. The initial turning of the soil can be done with a spade, to a depth of about 8"–10". This is very easy and a lot less noise polluting than a rototiller.

Another advantage to this type of gardening is that of time. Time spent in the maintenance of the raised beds is considerably less than that of row planting. It keeps

you seated in one spot longer to do your planting or weeding, rather than scooting both you and your knee pad along the rows (again compacting the soil). With the looser soil, our natural aerators the angleworms can do their work for us.

More consideration can be given to the irrigation of the garden. It's a very simple matter to run a network of soaker hoses through the garden, or to use any other method that you find effective. Depending on your skills with piping, you could develop a very sophisticated irrigation system. One of the blessings of raised beds is that drainage isn't a problem, as there are no pools of water left in the garden to promote fungus or otherwise rot your plants.

As you begin to design your raised bed garden, take some things into consideration beyond what you can, or can't, physically handle. Look at the location of your garden. How much Sun will it get? How much Sun do you need to grow what you want to grow? Usually you'll want a good six hours of sunlight, particularly for crops such as tomatoes. How much shade does your spot get, and at what time of day? If your area gets shade between 10:00 AM and 3:00 PM, you may wish to choose another spot. Think, also, about any tree roots that could in-

A garden with raised beds and square foot gardening.

terfere with your structure now or in future years. Yes, your raised beds should last you as many years as it takes that young maple tree to grow to its adulthood. You may also have a yard that includes an area for recreation, so you certainly don't want to place a raised bed where it interferes with a lively badminton game or the annual croquet tournament. In my case, three 4' x 8' beds still give me ample space in which to entertain.

After your structure has been built and you're looking into the hollow space, you should think about how and with what you are going to fill it. (In fact, it would be a very good idea to think about this well before you start your project.) You certainly don't want to fill it with anything that may damage the integrity of your topsoil application. As my structures were being built, I was fortunate enough to have had large quantities of sand, which had come out of the ground for the building of a garden pool. The sand found a nice new home in the bottom of the raised beds. I also cut some small tree limbs and put them into the beds. The initial hole requires a lot of "somethings" to fill it up. I know of one person who put some old chicken wire fencing in the hole. When the depth of your initial fill has come to about 10" from the top, you can start adding a mixture of topsoil, peat moss, sand, vermiculite, and an organic fertilizer.

Before putting in the topsoil, it is wise to have the soil tested to get a reading on the pH. Contacting your county extension service, a university in your area, or one of the better nurseries can tell you what you need for what you intend to grow. At the beginning of each growing season, I find that I need to "freshen up" the soil from the previous year and get some nicely composted material worked in for its spring tonic. There are no absolutes in giving formulas for soils, as each growing area and each intended crop will vary. The important thing to remember is that the soil needs to be soft and workable to give your plants' root systems a chance to develop.

Square Foot Gardening

When doing small-space gardening you'll find many advantages in utilizing the square foot gardening plan. In the early 1970s, a friend introduced me to her new gardening idea. This was her second year with this approach, and all was going well. Her garden was separated into sections by old boards placed on the ground. They formed smaller gardens, which seemed to be doing very well and looked nice and well-kept. The plants in each of the smaller gardens were organized into blocks, instead of the traditional rows. What she had was a simple gardening method that produced well in about 10' x 12'. This garden was feeding a family of four very nicely, with part of the harvest shared with friends. It was very intriguing to me but, I must admit, I was very slow to change from the row planting I had done for years (and which my mother had done before me).

When I constructed my raised beds, they seemed to cry out for a different type of planting. It was then that I started getting quite excited about the square foot method. The first year I measured out 1' squares, marking them with twine, much to the delight of the neighbors, who were asking, "What are you doing now?" (While they are still not square foot gardeners, there are no more smirks.)

The basic ideas of square foot gardening are very simple and, to my thinking, very sound:

- In a small space you can get big rewards.
- Seed conservation. There is no need to feel you're brutal when you have to thin and throw away a plant. Seeds are planted one at a time, usually about 1½' apart, and when one plant is harvested another can

be put in its place. The rule of thumb here is that the smaller the plant, the closer the seeds will be planted together. Pepper and tomato plants will each need 12" of room.

- When you have harvested your plant and are getting ready to place another seed in the ground, you may find this a good time to rotate your crop. Keep in mind, though, that you should be planting "friendly neighbors." (There are some very excellent writings on companion gardening, which make great wintertime reading.) Even plants like pole beans can be planted in this manner and are easily harvested. I have planted cantaloupe and watermelon using square gardening by placing the plants in tomato cages, and, when they start to vine, running the vine up the tomato cage. When they start to flower, I place a square piece of board under each flower to rest the soon-to-be-developing fruit. This also keeps the fruit from having a flat or undeveloped side.

- I don't need a lot of tools with which to produce my garden. The most important tool is my index finger, with which I make a hole to plant my seed.

A small trowel and a cup for water round out my tool kit.

🌿 Water conservation. This is where the cup is used. You merely pour small amounts of water around the seed, usually once a week. You'll be happier with your utility bill, too. Mulching around your plants as they start to grow will help conserve water. Grass clippings work very well around plants, provided you have a chemical-free lawn. If you have sprayed for broadleaf weeds, chances are you are putting toxins on your lawn; and you certainly do not want these next to your future food. Be cautious, too, about clippings that are offered to you, as they may not be a safe vegetable mulch.

As the ground warms earlier with the raised beds, you can plant earlier and have an earlier initial harvest. The growing season can be expanded by seeding again and again. Frost will touch these methods of gardening later, so, again, you have the advantage of producing more.

Using these two methods of gardening has given me a new enthusiasm for what I do. The ease of maintenance in both methods gives me additional time to read about my next project.

Further Reading

Bartholomew, Mel. *Square Foot Gardening.*

Riotte, Louise. *Carrots Love Tomatoes.*

LESLIE P. NIELSEN has been gardening for most of her life. She has also been a practicing astrologer since 1967 and, as an enthusiastic researcher, founded the Astrological Research Organization (ARO) in 1971. She began writing astrological articles in 1971, published and astrological newsletter for eleven years, and has authored five books.

The Lawn

Fermented Compost Tea

A Brief History of the Lawn

The Lay-on Lawn

Fermented Compost Tea

By Barbara Pleasant

Excerpted from The Gardener's Guide to Plant Diseases: Earth-Safe Remedies © 1995 by Barbara Pleasant, with permission from Storey Communications, Inc., Pownal, Vermont 05261. Tel.: 800-441-5700.

EDITOR'S NOTE: Compost tea is used as a liquid fertilizer, and is thought to boost plants' immunity to pests and diseases. It is generally considered safe for all plants, and should not "burn" them. See the article "Natural Fertilizers, Part Two: Liquids" on page 59 of this book for more information on compost tea.

❧c❍❧

1. Mix one part mature compost that includes some rotted manure (horse, cow, or chicken) with five parts water. A plastic milk jug works well.

2. Allow the mixture to sit and ferment in a shady place for ten days to two weeks. The effectiveness of the tea is highest when the tea ferments for a full two weeks.

3. Filter the mixture through cheesecloth to remove large particles. Do not attempt to remove all of the residue, for some residue gives the tea ex-

tra disease-fighting punch. Warning: this stuff can smell terrible—do your straining outdoors! The odor does vary from batch to batch.

4. If needed, (to prevent burning of delicate plants or to stretch the amount of tea) dilute the tea with more water, but keep the mixture at half strength, minimum.

5. Either spray on leaves with a pump or pressure sprayer, or dribble it on with a watering can. Coat both sides of leaves (so that more nutrient can be absorbed).

6. Reapply after 2–3 weeks.

7. The residue left after the tea is strained may be poured out on the ground below plants.

A Brief History of the Lawn

BY SHARON PARKER

In the beginning—if one can presume to know the beginning of anything natural in origin—the lawn was created to serve a useful function: to provide a pleasant, sometimes aromatic, surface on which to walk and play. Its role as a showpiece, a symbol of American suburban democracy and conformity, didn't become its primary function until advances of science and technology made these things possible in the mid-twentieth century.

The apex (or nadir) of the middle-class American lawn aesthetic may best be represented by the "Keep off the Grass" signs that dot our suburban and urban landscapes. The signs either warn us of the hazards of recently-applied chemicals or tell us that we must never walk on a particular lawn because it is only for show. Either way, in these instances the original function of the lawn has been usurped by its form.

As we near the end of the decade that saw the lawn become

> ❖c⊃❖
> *The original function of the lawn has been usurped by its form*
> ❖c⊃❖

what some have called an "obsession" for middle-class homeowners, we appear to be on the verge of moving away from the rigid lawn aesthetic, which has for so long dictated a strict monoculture that is inherently unnatural. We are beginning to appreciate that ecological diversity is both beautiful and necessary, and that the lawn's form must follow its function, not the other way around. Indeed, many are asking, "Do I need any lawn at all?"

The lawn was still a new invention around the first century AD, and was likely to consist of low-growing herbs and other ground covers that released their fragrance when trod upon. John Feltwell, in *The Naturalist's Garden* (Salem House Publishers, 1987), writes that Roman lawns were areas to "think, walk about and do exercises on." This continued to be the case right up through the Renaissance, when wealthy estates had lawns whose primary function was to provide a place for people to walk and play.

The English landscape movement that emerged in the seventeenth century began to see the lawn as an aesthetic device—to extend the views from park-like estates and contribute to a designed "natural" landscape. These lawns were patterned after meadows and kept short by grazing animals. They weren't necessarily places to walk or play—especially if they were, in fact, pastures where grazing animals left droppings behind as they obligingly kept the grass and flowers short.

The notion that the lawn should be a monoculture of only grasses—let alone only certain types of grasses—did not occur to anyone at that time, since it would have been impossible anyway. Warren Schultz, writing in *Harrowsmith Country Life* ("Greener Than Grass," October 1994), tells us that these early English lawns were "created from patches of sod, wildflowers, and weeds that were carved out of the meadows and transplanted around buildings. The meadows were kept short by browsing sheep, which grazed selectively; some flowers survived in the sod."

Wealthy landowners could maintain their lawns without the aid of sheep and their inconvenient (though fertile) by-products by hiring servants to trim them with scythes. The area near the manor house was maintained in this way—thus regaining its function as an area for walking and playing—while the more distant fields were still grazed by the sheep, which became part of the scenic vista. The sheep were kept off of the lawn by a wall sunk into a ditch, called a "ha-ha," which was invisible from the manor. Thus the view was uninterrupted.

When the English aristocracy crossed the Atlantic, they brought their landscape aesthetic along with them, and the Puritans brought something else: a deep distrust and fear of wilderness. This fear was based on a combination of the very real danger of wild animals and the perception that the wilderness represented nature unchecked by the orderly hand of God. The use of the word "wilderness" in the Bible emphasizes this idea. "If paradise was early man's greatest good, wilderness, as its antipode, was his greatest evil," writes Roderick Nash in *Wilderness and the American Mind* (Yale University Press, 1982). Rather than see the presence of God in nature, as was the case with both the "pagan" religions of pre-Christian Europe and the Native Americans (leading Christians to assume that these "nature worshipers" were somehow in league with the devil), the Puritans felt that they had to bring God into the wilderness.

Nash explains that the Puritans experienced the American wilderness—that is, nature—as something to be tamed and controlled in order to drive out its demonic influences. This idea of man versus the wilderness became a part of the American psyche, argues Nash. In *The Lawn: A History of an American Obsession* (Smithsonian Institution Press, 1994), cultural historian Virginia Scott Jenkins argues that by the twentieth century this idea was manifest in the drive to create lawns more like carpet than anything natural.

The artificiality of the lawn became an entrenched part of its very essence. Jenkins relates that as recently as 1976, the director of the Lawn Institute said, "A lawn, of course, is an artificial community of plants."

In fact, she cites advertisements from the late nineteenth century to the mid twentieth, describing lawns as carpets, such as this 1905 example: "What would we do without grass? For it really is the carpet of our outdoor living room." Because the lawn was supposed to have the even color and consistency of carpet, the constant effort of nature to reintroduce a diversity of species—both plant and insect—was the bane of the conscientious homeowner's existence. Nature was still considered the enemy.

This preoccupation with lawns as man-made environments at enmity with nature was a particularly male trait, argues Jenkins. While women were inclined to see their lawns as complimentary to their gardens, men were more likely to see them as representing their ability to impose their will upon nature.

The ideal and the reality were miles apart, however, largely due to the expense and sheer impossibility of lawns in an era when they had to be tilled and started anew each spring, when weeds were pulled by hand and grass cut either with a scythe or the heavy and cumbersome early lawn mowers. Lawns were a fashion of the upper classes, which could afford servants to help cut and maintain them.

But the aesthetic started to trickle down to the middle classes, aided both by the middle-class desire to be like the upper classes, and by the late nineteenth century introduction of the game of golf to America. The pristine golf green is still the ideal to which suburban American homeowners aspire for their lawns.

Schultz agrees that golf was one of two influences that popularized the American lawn and changed the aesthetic to favor a monoculture rather than the "flowery mede" of the English landscape. The other influence, Schultz asserts, was the invention of the lawn mower. The lawn mower, as it became more affordable and easier to operate, not only "democratized" the lawn, making it possible for all classes to maintain one, but also changed its nature. "The lawn mower wasn't selective like sheep. Every plant fell before its spinning blades. The lawn became nearly a monocrop," Schultz writes.

The ideal of a house surrounded by a green lawn gained prominence in the 20th century, especial-

ly among garden writers, who promoted it as a healthier alternative to the dirt "yards" prevalent in poor rural communities.

Now, there *is* something to be said for having a ground cover over dirt, to prevent erosion and minimize dust; in cities and suburbs today there is also the added concern of lead contamination in the soil. A "velvety carpet of green" is hardly the only way to accomplish this, however. Clearly, the health benefits of lawns were more image than substance.

Rather, it was conformity, and a belief that lawns somehow represented a democratic landscape, that really drove the proponents of lawns to become turf evangelists, pushing their ideas on the lower classes.

In an essay about mining communities of the upper Midwest, Arnold R. Alanen describes how company-built housing for immigrant laborers included lawns and gardens not so much because the residents desired them, but because the mining company executives believed it was an important way to Americanize the immigrants. The bosses believed that the immigrants "have been accustomed to ways of living which we must try to change." He quotes the U.S. Steel corporation in 1914:

Gardens and beautiful lawns help to make homes. A home means more than a mere shelter from the elements. The beauty of the gardens and lawns exerts a refining influence on the family, which shows inside of the house and in the behavior of the members of the family toward each other. (Francis, Mark, and Randolph T. Hester, eds. "Immigrant Gardens on a Mining Frontier." The Meaning of Gardens. MIT Press, 1993).

Peer pressure was considered by early lawn proponents an appropriate way to enforce their aesthetic. Jenkins relates that as early as 1875, a garden writer complained about those who "still" let the grass grow for "food for their critters," but added, "It is gratifying to know that such neighbors are not numerous, for the example of the majority will soon shame them into decency."

The wealthy made the naive assumption that the lower classes would follow their front lawn example without considering the considerable expense or the extent to which they themselves relied upon servants to help them do it. Lawns did not catch on among the working classes at this time.

By the post–World War II era, however, technology and science had made the lawn aesthetic an unavoidable requisite of suburban living. Homeowners felt the peer pressure to conform all too keenly. Michael Pollan describes in his book, *Second Nature* (Dell Publishing, 1991), how his own father chafed under the yoke of lawn conformity: "The summer [my father] stopped mowing altogether, I felt the hot breath of a tyrannical majority for the first time. Nobody would say anything, but you heard it anyway: 'Mow your lawn.'"

The neighbors finally pressured the one individual who got along best with Pollan's father to deliver the message that he should mow his lawn. His father responded by mowing his initials into the lawn and then putting the lawn mower away for the rest of the summer. They moved not long after that.

Technology alone did not lead to a "democratization" of the lawn aesthetic; but but the labor movement's success at shortening the work week and improving the financial means of the labor classes also helped to make this possible. Now the working man not only could afford to own a lawn mower, but had weekends off in which to attend to his lawn.

In the 1950s, public faith in science was at an all-time high, so it follows that the myriad of new chemicals available—some originally developed for chemical warfare during World War II—were seen as marvelous labor-saving devices that helped to make the "perfect lawn" a real possibility. Not until Rachel Carson published *Silent Spring* in 1962 did the public begin to question the environmental cost of such chemical warfare in suburban lawns.

As the means became available to create the perfect lawn, standards narrowed further regarding the lawn aesthetic. For example, whereas crab grass had hardly ever been mentioned before the post-World War II era, suddenly it was seen as a terrible menace.

Ironically, although chemical companies had helped to create the perception of the crab grass menace because they thought they had the means to eradicate it, their products were, in fact, no more effective than they were safe. In 1949, *Consumer's Research Bulletin* reviewed two popular crab grass killers that were on the market, made of arsenic or mercury. It concluded that the chemicals were not very effective and extremely poisonous.

Then followed a period in the sixties and seventies when chemical companies attempted to assure lawn enthusiasts that their products were safe. Certainly with the banning of DDT and the introduction of safety regulations there was some reduction of hazard—although anyone who watches a lawn chemical company employee don a Moon suit before spraying a yard may rightly wonder about this.

Chemical companies and lawn chemical enthusiasts had become quite defensive by the 1970s.

An article in *Horticulture* (April, 1972), contains not only a churlish defense of chemicals, but also reinforces the idea that lawns are not natural, turning the definition of "pollutant" on its head by using the word to describe weeds:

> The current rash of startling statements by alarmists on the danger of pollution from plant protection chemicals has frightened many into abandoning the use of modern labor saving weed controls. Actually, weeds are pollutants that need attention as much as some of the bogey men raised by extremists.

According to Jenkins, this same author regretted the banning of DDT. Another author of the time complained of the "anti-pollution bias" that made certain chemicals hard to find.

All this madness stemmed from the conviction that our front lawns should look like public parks or golf courses. So it is both interesting and heartening to note that the managers of both these institutions are themselves beginning to question the pristine lawn aesthetic as they weigh the environmental and economic costs, and respond to the concerns of a more enlightened public.

Rick Frederickson, superintendent of Woodhill Country Club in Wayzata, Minnesota, says that although there was a time back in the seventies when golf courses would spray liberally as a means to prevent possible insect, disease, and weed problems, things *have* changed. Rather than declaring that no weeds or insects are tolerable, landscapers set thresholds according to the amount of use a given area of the course receives: "So if we have an area that is more or less out of play, we'll leave that area go (by tolerating more weeds, for example). Our whole emphasis is to provide a real environmentally friendly atmosphere for our golfers to play in."

While golf course superintendents like Frederickson haven't abandoned the use of chemicals altogether, they have reduced their chemical use by incorporating integrated pest management (IPM), a system by which the most benign methods of control are tried before stronger measures are considered.

Frederickson has an added reason to keep chemical use at a minimum at his golf course: the twenty-five bluebird houses, and several wren, martin, and bat houses he has put up around the course. While some of these are for the aesthetic pleasure of encouraging bird populations, they also serve a practical function: to help control insect populations. He even installed some owl houses re-

cently, in the hope that the owls will help him control rodents.

Frederickson is not as unusual as he may seem. There is definitely a growing trend to manage golf courses using IPM techniques, says David Bishop, technical information services manager for the Golf Course Superintendents Association of America in Lawrence, Kansas. "We know that's happening, we know that superintendents are increasingly improving management strategies to reduce the need for pesticides," he says, further explaining that he can't really quantify reductions in pesticide use because pest pressures vary from year to year.

The organization calls IPM "integrated plant management" rather than integrated "pest" management because they want to put the emphasis on building healthy grass plants that resist pest and disease problems. "It's kind of a holistic approach," Bishop says.

While Bishop recognizes that many home lawn enthusiasts take their cues from golf courses, he warns that a golf course is still maintained at a stricter standard than a home lawn because of the nature of its use. "Lawns should not be maintained at putting green height," he says.

Many other golf course superintendents are also putting up bird and bat houses and augmenting their courses as wildlife habitat. In fact, the New York Audubon Society sponsors a cooperative wildlife program along with the United States Golf Association that is growing in popularity, according to Bishop.

In the public parks the beginnings of change in turf management and the lawn aesthetic are emerging. At the fall 1994 convention of the National Recreation and Parks Association, hosted by the Minneapolis Park and Recreation Board (MPRB), an indoor demonstration garden featured native plants rather than beds of annuals or exotic perennials.

The MPRB hopes to convert some of its existing turf to native prairie to reduce the expense and the environmental impact of mowing. Because funds are not yet available to start planting native grasses and flowers, the MPRB will start by simply discontinuing the mowing of certain areas.

"It's been something that has evolved from a concept of less manicured parks and that started with stream banks and lake banks and hillsides, and it got mixed up with economics and chemical use and prairies until they were all in the same pot," explains Tom Montgomery, an assistant superintendent in the Minneapolis park system.

Montgomery echoes earlier perceptions of the lawn as artificial when he adds, "It's tough to keep things alive and looking well in an artificial environment." He intends to plant a large portion of his own new home landscape with native plants.

While Montgomery admits that the major reason they introduced the "no-mow" areas this year is financial, concern about chemical use has played a part. Some years ago the Minneapolis parks banned the state's Metropolitan Mosquito Control District from spraying on park lands.

In parts of the country where water is scarce, front lawns have given way to xeriscaping—landscaping with plants native to the area that don't require the addition of water that turf grasses need. Some communities, such as Lakewood, Colorado, a suburb of Denver, have ordinances that require the use of xeriscaping over at least half the homeowner's lot.

Former natural lawn care executive for Ringer Corporation, Rob Ringer, believes that American consumers will have to change their expectations in order for a more natural lawn aesthetic to take root. "We live in a society of instant gratification; that's one of the problems with natural remedies ... sometimes they take longer to build up the defense systems (of the plants)."

While Ringer agrees that there is a growing interest in native landscaping, he's certain that the lawn aesthetic will take time to change. "I think it's going to hang in there a long time. I really believe it's one of these traditions that's ingrained in the American way of life: the obsession with lawns ... it's an obsession that has gone too far."

Currently researchers are looking into lawns that incorporate diversity of plant species, anticipating that consumers will develop a more environmentally sound aesthetic. Warren Schultz reports on research at the Oregon State University turf trial grounds that includes patches of test plots "speckled with small flowering plants. The plots bear a closer relationship to the flowery medes, or meadows, of medieval England than to a well-cared-for twentieth-century lawn."

Perhaps we will finally come full circle, as homeowners discover the joy and ease of lawns that mingle small flowers and fragrant herbs with grasses, a type that is not only environmentally sound, but also attractive, especially to the types of beneficial insects and microorganisms that keep at bay the very problems that plague the monoculture lawns of the suburban ideal. Perhaps lawn enthusiasts will discover that nature is not the enemy after all, and that a lawn is primarily something to be walked and played upon.

Sources

Feltwell, John. *The Naturalist's Garden.* Topsfield, MA: Salem House Publishers, 1987.

Francis, Mark, and Randolph T. Hester, Jr., eds. *The Meaning of Gardens.* Cambridge, MA: MIT Press, 1993.

Jenkins, Virginia Scott. *The Lawn: A History of An American Obsession.* Washington, D.C.: Smithsonian Institution Press, 1994.

Nash, Roderick. *Wilderness and the American Mind.* New Haven, CT. Yale University Press, 1982.

Pollan, Michael. *Second Nature: A Gardener's Education.* New York: Dell Publishing, 1991.

Schultz, Warren. "Greener Than Grass." *Harrowsmith Country Life.* October 1994; p 47-49+.

Interviews

David Bishop, technical information services manager, Golf Course Superintendents Association of America, Lawrence, Kansas; March 10, 1995.

Rick Frederickson, supervisor, Woodhill Country Club, Wayzata, Minnesota; March 6, 1995.

Tom Montgomery, assistant superintendent for operations, Minneapolis Park and Recreation Board, Minnesota; February 16, 1995.

Rob Ringer, formerly of Ringer Corporation, Minneapolis, Minnesota; February 17, 1995.

SHARON PARKER has been gardening for more than twenty years, and grew up in a family of organic gardeners. She writes for the gardening section of the *Southwest Journal*, a community newspaper of southwest Minneapolis, Minnesota. She is a member of the Men's Gardening Club of Minneapolis, and enjoys gardening at home with her husband and children.

The Lay-on Lawn

By Janet LaBarre

Every spring, my lawn is the first to green up, and I must admit to taking some small pride in that. What makes me feel *really* good about my lawn is knowing it's safe to walk barefoot on, lie on, and is not polluting anything around it. Best of all, it is extremely low-maintenance and virtually sustains itself. This allows me to sit back, sip lemonade, and enjoy the view.

My goal is to tell you how to get to this same place with your lawn. Organic lawn care covers a large spectrum of possibilities, from doing nothing more than mowing and leaving the clippings on the lawn, to doing extensive initial renovation, annual fertilization, and weeding.

As a master gardener, I teach classes and give talks. My favorite demonstration is a listening test. First, I spread newspaper on a table and ask the audience to close their eyes and listen carefully. I crumble a handful of soil onto the newspaper, and it makes a sharp, harsh, staccato noise. Then, the next handful gets dropped, with a decidedly softer, gentler sound. When I ask the audience if they can hear the difference, 90 percent of them raise their hands. The audience opens their eyes and looks at the soil. When I ball the first sample up in my hand, it just falls apart and sifts on out. The second, quieter sample forms a nice, moist ball in my hands and crumbles richly as I move my hands together. The difference is just one year's application of compost to the moist, rich sample. These are side-by-side samples of lawn soil, collected within moments of each other! Which soil do you think requires less watering? Which do you think holds onto its nutrients longer? Which requires less work? Yes! It's the compost-enriched soil!

First, we will discuss the easiest approach to organic lawn care: Learn to love your weeds. Many people simply mow their lawns and leave the clippings on. This actually is a form of organic lawn care, as the clippings do supply some of the nitrogen needs of lawn grasses. This is not enough for them to thrive, but about half their annual needs can be met this way. When you do this, you will find weeds creeping into your lawn, but what's wrong with a few weeds? Who decided a beautiful lawn had to be a vast expanse of monoculture grass? I personally think great clumps of clover in bloom are gorgeous, find dandelions cheerful and tough, and wouldn't be without plantain and chickweed for their wonderful medicinal uses. Your lawn, managed this way, will become a mix of many different plants, capable of sustaining itself through heat and drought.

A second approach involving minimal work is to simply start applying an organic lawn food like Ringer's Lawn Restore, or Gardens Alive! twice a summer. This program will do wonders for your turf, allowing it to thicken and grow healthier. As your grass becomes denser, it crowds out weeds, further reducing your work. Ringer's organic products are available almost anywhere lawn and garden items are sold, and the Gardens Alive! catalog is available free of charge at 5100 Schenley Place, Lawrenceburg, IN 47025, or by calling (812) 537-8650.

The next approach involves a little more time and expense up front. In the long run you will save money and time by purchasing ex-

actly what your lawn needs, after you have your *soil tested*. Yes, tested! This is relatively easy and inexpensive to do. In my area, it costs $7.00 for the basic test, and you need only call your local extension agent to obtain the test kit. The phone number is listed under your county government section in the phone book as "extension service." While you're on the phone with the extension agent, ask for the list of bulletins on gardening and lawn care. If they have a master gardening program in your county, you can also get free gardening advice from one of the master gardeners. Ask for someone familiar with organic techniques.

So you've done the soil test and know that your lawn needs, for example, lots of nitrogen and a little phosphorous. Armed with this information, you decide what product meets these specific needs. You might also find your soil is too alkaline or too acidic. This is known as its pH. Grass grows best in a fairly neutral pH (around 7), but will tolerate some variance. If you find you need to raise or lower pH, you can apply ground limestone or acidic peat product. Limestone will raise the pH, and acidic peat will lower it. Next, apply fertilizer. If your test shows you need nitrogen, you can use bone meal, blood meal, any composted manure, alfalfa meal, or a prepackaged organic fertilizer with high nitrogen levels. If your test shows you need phosphorous, some good sources are wood ash, marine animal waste, composted animal manures, blood meal, and cottonseed meal. The third nutrient necessary for good grass growth is potassium, usually referred to as potash. Potash rock, finely ground, not only adds potassium, but many other trace minerals as well. Greensand is also a good source of potassium, and is most effective in hard or clay soils, where its sandy nature can help with drainage. Potash is a better choice where soil is already sandy. Compost is always good for lawns, and can be applied no matter what your test shows.

Once you've decided what to apply to the lawn, you need to find a way to apply it. While you can always scatter fertilizer or seeds by hand, two more uniform methods are to use either a drop or broadcast spreader. You can use these items for many different materials: composted manures, limestone, meals, seeds, etc. Make sure you have everything spread as evenly and as deeply as you want. It may take several passes and a little raking to get it right, but it's worth it.

After you have all your lawn amendments in place, the next optional (but highly recommended) step is to overseed the grass. By this I mean throwing on additional grass seed over the top of everything else you've just put on. This step will greatly enhance a thin lawn, but you must keep the new seed watered well until it germinates. The best time for this is spring or fall, but if you can keep the seeds moist enough, almost any time can be successful. During warm weather, you might need to water the seeds several times per day. Don't let them dry out. If you're really ambitious, or are trying this during hotter weather than spring or fall, get some straw and shake a covering over the entire lawn after you've watered it generously, keep watering, and check daily for germination of the grass seedlings. When the seeds have sprouted (in anywhere from 3–10 days), remove the straw immediately. Take care not to disturb the new seedlings as you remove the straw, and continue with the daily watering until the new grass needs its first mowing. At this point, gradually harden the new grass off by going to every other day watering, then every third day, and so on until you're down to weekly watering, after about six weeks from the first mowing. If it rains, you can skip the supplemental watering, but make sure the grass gets at least 1" of water per week during its first summer. A rain gauge is helpful with this.

A continuing problem for people who don't want weeds in their lawn is getting get rid of them without harsh chemicals. Rumor has it there's an organic control for dandelions on the way, but until then, hand-pulling is your best bet. When the ground is soft (in the spring or after a rain), pick out a patch of ground to work on, and, using a weeding tool, go to it. Pop out those weeds, getting at least 1" of root, and work until you're tired or bored, returning as needed. The dandilions will eventually be gone, and you can get a lot of thinking and relaxing done while weeding. Another option is to hire the neighborhood kids. Pay them a penny or nickel per weed with at least an inch of root, and you'll not only get your weeding finished, you'll become acquainted with your neighborhood children and provide some employment.

Finally, when you need to mow your grass, consider using one of the old-fashioned push mowers that our grandparents used. You can find them at garage sales, auctions, or even new in some stores and mail-order catalogs. Just make sure the blades are sharpened on the old ones. These do a beautiful job of cutting the grass without noise or air pollution, and give you a nice workout, besides.

I hope these tips get you started on your "lay-on" lawn. When I see another lawn greening up as quickly as mine next spring, I'll know someone else has gone organic!

JANET LABARRE is a master gardener for Sherburne County, Minnesota. She has appeared several times on a call-in gardening radio show on the Minneapolis-based station WCCO. She has done promotional work, grant writing, and fund raising for the Minnesota Landscape Arboretum Plant Development Center, and is the gardener at Kelly's farm, an 1800s historical interpretive center.

Herbs

The Virtue of Tea

By Betty Wold

The invitation means the same thing whether you are in the Australian outback, a New York penthouse, or a rural southern cafe.

"Ow about a cuppa, mate?"

"We'll serve on the terrace."

You have just been offered the second of the world's three top-rated drinks. Water is first; coffee is third in popularity, but tops in economic value.

Strictly speaking, tea is an infusion of the flowers, berries, leaves, bark, roots, or seeds of an edible plant. By that definition, coffee is a tea. When you are offered "tea," the beverage is usually an infusion of the leaves of *Camellia sinensis*, which grows as a low shrub. Any other infusion is called "herb tea." Beyond this distinction, you have further choices: regular or decaf, hot or iced, and sweet or plain.

The History of Tea

Tea has had a long and colorful history. It has been the driving force behind tariffs, taxes, trade agreements, economic development, and wars. It was not until after the sixteenth century that it became a popular beverage in the Western world. In China and India, where it originated, only the wealthy or royal classes could afford it, and among them it was used for medicinal or ceremonial purposes. It was picked by hand and went through elaborate processing. Black and green tea come from the same plant; black tea is fermented, green tea is not.

By 1200 BC, tea was being offered as tribute to powerful leaders, although it was still most commonly used for its medicinal properties. Preparation included pounding the leaf to a pulp, which was then formed into cakes and used as currency.

In 793 AD, after its introduction in Japan, one of the first tea taxes was levied: It was a "donation" of the choicest leaves to the reigning emperor. Tea bricks, made by steaming green leaves, pulverizing them, and forming them into cakes, were easily transported and became essential trade items.

Venetian and Portuguese trading ships introduced tea to southern Europeans. Mongolian camel caravans carried it to Russia. Dutch mariners brought the first consignment of green tea from Java to England in 1610 and for many years monopolized the trade from China and Japan. Until the late 1600s, all the tea in England was imported from Holland. In 1664, a group of wealthy merchants, early lobbyists, formed the British East India Company. They presented a gift of two pounds of tea to King Charles II, consequently persuading the Crown to levy heavy duties and later to ban Dutch tea imports.

Charles' wife, Catherine of Braganza, brought the custom of tea drinking from her native Portugal, where it had become the fashion. By 1689 tea was the drink of the British upper classes, and it all was brought directly from China by the British East India Tea Company.

In 1717, Thomas Twining (whose tea is still available) opened the first tea house. By 1750, everyone was drinking tea, though one pound of the cheapest variety cost one third of the average clerk's weekly wage. Wealthy people passed used leaves down to their servants, the first "trickle-down" scheme.

Tea played an important part in maintaining British colonial rule in India. Britain resented the Chinese monopoly and wanted to establish plantations in India, which was then a British colony. It met with little success, for the Chinese guarded their plants and methods jealously. Finally, in the 1820s, some native plants were found growing near the Burmese border. Seeds from these plants eventually made their way to the province of Assam. Whole forests were cleared to make room for tea estates, which became the producers of some of today's finest black teas, Darjeeling and Assam.

Every American schoolchild knows the story of the Boston Tea Party. In 1773, a group of Boston citizens, protesting a tax on tea, boarded three tea ships in Boston harbor and threw 340 chests of tea overboard. This led to similar raids in other colonies and was a spark for the American Revolution.

On a darker note, the British fondness for tea led to the Opium Wars. Tea consumption in Britain had risen to nearly five billion cups

Her tea cargo paid for the cost of building the ship, and provided an equal sum as profit to the owners. A well-known grocery chain, the A & P, began as the American and Pacific Tea Stores, outlets for the importers, the Great Atlantic and Pacific Tea Companies.

Herbal Tea

Herb teas, for the most part, followed a kinder, gentler tradition. The dark exception was the persecution of thousands of women accused of witchcraft because of their herbal knowledge. Until the seventeenth century, herb teas were used mostly as medicines. The popular beverages of the time, even for breakfast, were wine, beer, cider, and ale. Herb teas were considered best for invalids.

a year by the 1800s, but no tea was yet being grown in India. The Chinese did not want to exchange tea for the British trade staple, heavy broadcloth, so the British turned to a surplus product of the Indian colony, the opium poppy. Opium was smuggled into China and traded for silver, which remained in China as payment for tea. It was a great deal for the British, but not for the Chinese. In 1839, the Chinese emperor ordered 20,000 casks of opium burned on the beaches of Canton. The British retaliated by declaring war, which they easily won. They then legalized the opium trade, causing the addiction of millions of Chinese. It remained a legal trade item until 1908.

In colonial America, herb tea replaced imported tea during the Revolution as a protest against the tea tax. The most popular native teas were Colonial tea, *Monarda didyma*, and Liberty or New Jersey tea, made from leaves of the shrub *Ceatiothus americana*. It was thought to taste most like green tea. Betony, *Stachys officinalis*, substituted for black tea.

The British East India Company monopoly was abolished in 1833, and American freelancers took over the tea trade with sleek, three-masted clipper ships. The first of these, the *Rainbow*, sailed for China from New York in February and returned in September.

The war ended, America gained control of the tea trade, and South American coffee became a staple. Herb teas became a bit of arcane folklore known only to old women back in the hills.

And so it might have remained had it not been for the so-called "hippie generation" and its desire for a simpler, self-sufficient way of life. Blending mountain-grown herbs collected in the wild proved so tasty and so popular that it led to the formation of the first herbal tea company to promote herbs as a social drink.

Today you can walk into any grocery store and find as much shelf space given to herb blends as to the traditional green and black teas. Health food stores stock flavorful mixtures, and boxes of single herbs for you to blend as you choose. Packages give directions for preparation, but by law cannot make claims for health benefits. However, you will find any number of books written by reputable herbalists who share information on traditional uses for those boxed herbs.

In addition, studies have verified many of the benefits attributed to herbs. Feverfew has been proven to reduce fevers, alleviate arthritic pain, and relieve migraine headaches, and old-time mothers knew what they were doing when they gave their colicky babies dill tea.

Growing Herbal Tea

You know they taste good, you know they're healthy, but they're pricy. How to deal with that? Grow your own! Ask yourself: What do I like? Where can I grow it? When should I start? Why should I do it? How shall I grow it?

What

Start with the culinary herbs and concentrate on the most aromatic and flavorful. Choose from peppermint, spearmint, chocolate mint, and their relatives; lemon and lime balm; lemon verbena; rose geranium; Mexican marigold; anise hyssop; lavender; catnip; and yes, even parsley, sage, rosemary, and thyme.

Where

All of these can be grown in pots on a balcony or patio, but if you have a plot of ground with good drainage, at least six hours of sunshine, and access to water, you have a perfect spot for a tea garden. Soil does not have to be ideal—in a small plot of ground such as you want, it's easy and inexpensive to add amendments. If you can only grow indoors, limit your choices, set up a good light source and don't over-water.

When

Start right now, while your interest is high. Pick at least three of your favorite flavors, go to an herb grower, and buy seedlings. Later you can grow from seeds, but you want to use these herbs immediately.

Why

These tea herbs satisfy all your senses. They look good, with their various shades of green, unique leaf shapes, and special growth habits (bushy, upright, or sprawling). They smell wonderful, even when you do nothing but gently brush the leaves. Just a leaf or two adds special flavor and aroma to beverages. Add them to green or black tea, light wines, or even to warm lemon juice. Best of all, they will be much fresher than dried store-bought blends. Some of those ingredients may be as much as a year old before they are packaged.

How

Learn all you can about the herbs you want to grow. What special needs might each have? What qualities does the tea have: is it invigorating, relaxing, or sedative? How have the herbs been used medicinally? They may make a delicious beverage, but have they also been used for salves or poultices? What other culinary uses have they? What interesting folklore is associated with each?

What makes a good cup of tea? Your own sense of taste and one simple rule are all you need: start with fresh, clean, cold water, even if you want hot tea. Cold water contains more oxygen, making for a better tasting brew. Bring it to a full rolling boil in a stainless steel or enamel tea kettle. Warm a china or silver teapot, if that's your style, with warm water.

Some teas are infusions, which are usually made with leaves or flowers. Start with cold, fresh water. Bring to a full rolling boil. Empty the teapot, add boiling water and herbs, steep for four or five minutes. Strain, sweeten with sugar or honey if desired; but first try to develop a taste for the natural flavor. Infusions are served hot or iced. Americans add milk to tea less frequently than the British do. That opens a whole new discussion: Should milk be added first or last? Some say first, to protect delicate china cups from hot liquids. Some say last, so you can judge the strength of the tea.

Some teas are decoctions. These are boiled or simmered for a prescribed time, then allowed to steep until cool before straining. Decoctions are usually made with seeds, barks, roots, or stems. These materials do not release their oils, minerals, or other benefits readily and are often for medicinal use. They should always be covered during preparation to prevent volatile substances from escaping. Decoctions are usually served at room temperature and in small amounts. Sometimes they are sipped, sometimes taken by the spoonful. It's important to re-

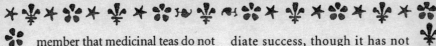

member that medicinal teas do not work as quickly as prescription drugs. Some may take two or three days before showing any effect, since they work on whole body balance. Certain others, like anti-nausea teas, usually work quickly.

A cold extract preserves volatile oils, but may require a larger amount of herb. Sun tea, in which herbs are added to cold water and allowed to stand in the sun for several hours, is an example.

Teas can also be made from herb juices, but these should be used quickly. If you do not have an extractor, chop the herbs, add water or juice, press and squeeze through cheesecloth or similar material and drink immediately. "Weed" juices, made from such beneficial wild herbs as dandelion, nettle, chickweed, or dock, are delicious combined with pineapple juice.

Tea Bags

Americans deserve the credit—or some say, the blame—for the inventions of iced tea and the tea bag. The first was introduced at the St. Louis World Fair in 1904. East Indian growers were trying to promote black tea to Midwesterners, but having no success with hot tea in the humid summer heat. In despair, Richard Blechynden, their representative, poured some tea over a glass of ice. It was an imme-

diate success, though it has not caught on in other countries.

The tea bag was invented fifty years ago by tea merchant John Sullivan, who sent out samples of his teas in little hand-sewn silk bags. Americans like the convenience of the bag, even though it is more expensive and often does not use the finer grades of tea. Half of the tea sold in America now comes in bags, and tea bags are rapidly gaining favor in other countries.

Black and Green Tea

All of the suggestions for preparing herb teas apply equally to green and black tea. And, just as we have always known the health benefits of many herb teas, and the Chinese have always used green tea for their well-being, modern science is giving us more good reason to drink them instead of coffee. A study in *The Journal of Nutrition* suggests that coffee raises cholesterol levels, while tea lowers them.

Both black and green tea contain polyphenols; they were once incorrectly called tannins, and they give tea its pleasantly "puckery" taste. Polyphenols have been shown to boost immunity to disease and inhibit absorption of cholesterol. Because they are anti-oxidants, they can help eliminate unstable oxygen molecules, called free radicals, from the blood stream. Free radicals damage DNA

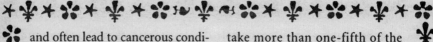

and often lead to cancerous conditions. Researchers in Shanghai demonstrated that people who drank green tea had significantly less esophageal cancer. Later studies showed that black tea had almost as much of the cancer-fighting substances: good news for Americans who prefer black tea.

Tea also contains three stimulants, theobromine, theophylline and caffeine, the best known. Caffeine gives tea its "lift." There is more in black tea than in green, but only about half as much as in coffee. Finer-cut leaf, such as is used in tea bags, and longer brewing time increases the amount of caffeine. The other two stimulants open the bronchial passages and relieve respiratory problems. Both black and green tea contain more fluoride than fluoridated water, and, along with the tannin, help to prevent tooth decay.

Collecting Herbs

Be sure you know what you are collecting. Take a class, or go with a knowledgeable wildcrafter. There are a number of look-alikes in the plant world, some of which are dangerous, even deadly. Do not collect plants along the side of the highway, where they may have been sprayed, and surely will have been subjected to hydrocarbons from passing cars. Never collect a plant on the endangered list. Don't take more than one-fifth of the plants in an area; leave plenty to propagate for future use. Collect at the proper time for your needs. As a general rule, pick flowers and leaves in the morning, dig roots in the late afternoon or evening. Take seeds only when you are sure they are ripe, and leave plenty for re-seeding.

It takes years to become an expert tea blender, but only a few tries to create a good herb tea blend. Begin by making herb tea with just one of your home-grown herbs, preferably the most fragrant. Taste and decide whether you want more or less flavor. Choose a leaf from another herb, crush it between your fingers, and hold it over your steaming herb brew. Do the flavors seem to blend? Make your next pot of herb tea with a combination of the two, not in equal portions. Allow one flavor to prevail, letting the second add an accent note. Use the same technique to add other combinations (usually not more than a total of four).

When you have enough herbs to dry some, strip the leaves from the stem, leave whole, and dry them until they are corn-flake dry. Use a dehydrator, an oven with pilot light, even your car or a camper parked in the sunshine. If the latter, cover the herbs so they are not in bright sunlight. When they are

completely dry, leave them whole and store them in glass jars away from direct light. Check the jars every day for the first week; it's easy to spot moisture condensing on the inside. If you see any, pour the herb out and dry more thoroughly.

Whole leaves retain flavor better as they dry, but crushing them just before using releases more flavor into the hot water.

You might blend one mixture for a relaxing tea, another to lift your spirits. Your herb book will suggest herbs for each purpose. Consider mint and rose geranium, rosemary and lavender flowers, lemon balm and thyme, marjoram and catnip. You may find herbs said to be energizing or relaxing do not have the same effect on you. Over-the-counter and prescription medicines often produce similar reactions.

Pay attention to what your body tells you. Pick the herbs, make the tea, and enjoy.

Bibliography

Buchman, Diane Dincin. *Herbal Medicine.* Gramercy Publishing, 1980.

Huxley, Gervase. *Talking of Tea.* John Waggner and Sons, 1956.

Lust, John. *The Herb Book.* Bantam Books, 1980.

Mabry, Richard, ed. *The New Age Herbalist.* Collier Books, 1988.

Rodale's Illustrated Encyclopedia of Herbs. Rodale Press, 1987.

The Book of Tea and Herbs, The Republic of Tea. The Cole Group, 1993.

BETTY WOLD, herb grower, author, teacher, and speaker, has been growing and using herbs for more years than she cares to admit. She has been a featured speaker at the International Herb Growers and Marketers Association Convention, Great Lakes Herb Symposium, New Zealand Herb Federation Conference, and many regional herb meetings. She is a member of the Herb Society of America and several local herb groups.

Herbs of the Zodiac

By Susan Wittig Albert

EDITOR'S NOTE: Before trying any new herbal remedy, be sure to consult a doctor, herbalist, or reference work to find the appropriate uses and dosage.

From the dawn of human understanding, the Earth and its creatures were all intimately and mysteriously connected with the cosmos as part of an ordered, organic whole. In fact, the word "cosmos" represented the idea of order, built on the harmonic energies that kept things from falling apart. Philosophers, scientists, and physicians could apply their observations and understanding of one aspect of the cosmos—the planets, for instance—to any other aspect, the human body, say, or the plants on which humans relied for food and medicine. But you didn't have to be learned to understand the cosmic connection. Even the ordinary person knew that humans, the Earth, and the stars all belonged to the same family.

Then along came the analytic science of the Enlightenment, destroying the earlier sense of organic, natural order. In its place was imposed a mechanistic view of the universe, built on parts instead of wholes. Traditional knowledge was discarded, and ideas that once commanded respect were jeered at. For three centuries, we have lived with that kind of science, but things are changing once again. With the advent of ecology (a word that derives from the Greek word for "household"), we are returning to the idea that all things on Earth and in the heavens are part of the same family of matter, energy, movements, and cycles. We all belong to the same universe. As above, so below. Our task now is to reclaim the ancient knowledge, infuse it with our modern energy of inquiry and observation, and see how we can use it in our own lives.

Astrology, Gardening, and Herbs

When people first began skywatching, they saw that the Sun, the Moon, and the planets moved in regular, predictable cycles: the cycles of the zodiac. They timed their activities, including agriculture, by these cycles. Over the centuries, a vast reservoir of wisdom was accumulated, identifying the ideal astrological conditions for planting, tending, harvesting, and storing crops. Today, as we return to the idea of the cosmic household, many people are turning to the ancient practices of gardening astrologically: planting, tending, and harvesting by the signs of the Moon.

But plant astrology went farther. For thousands of years, healers understood that there was a connection between the changing cycles of the zodiac, the energies of the human body, and the energies of plants. They systematized this understanding by assigning every plant to the rulership of one of the seven known planets: Sun, Moon, Mercury, Venus, Mars, Jupiter, and Saturn. Their assignments were based on simple physical observations. For instance, if a plant produced the sensation of heat, it belonged to fiery Mars. Plants associated with water belonged to the Moon, which ruled the tides. Physicians prescribed plant medicines according to the way the planets interacted in the birth charts. Physicians with a less specific knowledge of their patients' natal stars relied on the astrological relationship between parts of the human body and certain plant medicines. Venus governed the throat, for example, so a Venus-

ruled herb such as goldenrod would be used to treat a sore throat.

Much of what was known about plants and astrology was handed down orally, from one healer to another. But in the seventeenth century, a physician/astrologer named Nicholas Culpeper wrote down everything he had learned from a variety of sources, many now lost. It is largely thanks to Culpeper that we know as much as we do about the astrology of the healing plants.

While medical science has not confirmed the connection between the birth chart and certain diseases, it is now beginning to reaffirm the marvelous healing properties of herbal medicines, many of which have recently been discovered to be effective treatments for exactly the conditions for which ancient healers prescribed them. So, whether or not you believe that your ailments are related to your stars, the traditional zodiacal assignments of herbs remain as a folk-guide to their uses. At the least, they can help you remember which herb was used for which condition. At the most, they may suggest that the mysteries of our intimate, interwoven connections to the cosmos have not yet been entirely revealed.

Zodiac Healing Herbs

Aries Herbs
(The Ram, March 21–April 20)

The first sign of the zodiac, Aries, is ruled by the fiery planet Mars. People born under Mars have a fierce need to be independent and to initiate their own actions. Herbs governed by Mars may be prickly; some are red in color. They are stimulants, particularly acting on the circulatory system and/or the muscles. (Both the circulatory and muscular systems are ruled by Mars; Aries rules the head.) Garlic is a Mars herb, which is known to reduce blood pressure and lower blood cholesterol. To tone the system, eat three cloves (or the equivalent) every day.

Mustard is used to stimulate circulation and, as a poultice, to relieve muscular pain. To reduce fevers (which are under Mars' rule), try a tea made of mustard seed. Nettle (covered with stinging prickles) is rich in Mars-ruled iron. The plant has traditionally been used to reduce hemorrhages (including excessive menstrual flow), and as a general system tonic. Recent research suggests that it may also help stabilize blood sugar. Other Mars-ruled herbs include cayenne, red clover, sassafras, yellow dock, and ginger.

Taurus Herbs
(The Bull, April 21–May 21)

Taurus rules the throat; the planet Venus, which governs this sign, also rules the metabolic system. People born under Taurus tend to love comfort and beauty. Venus-ruled herbs are soothing and often have beautiful blossoms. They also help to regulate the body's metabolism by acting on the endocrine system. Violet is a lovely and powerful soother and emollient, helpful in easing sore throats. Violet-leaf poultices have been used for centuries to help heal skin infections and wounds. Daisy combines beauty and healing strength; the flower heads contain a mucilage that makes both tea and tincture helpful in cases of sore throat. A tea made of plantain soothes the inflamed mucous membranes of the throat, and is often used to treat bronchitis. For more Venus herbs, see Libra.

Gemini Herbs
(The Twins, May 22–June 21)

Mercury, with all its swift changes, rules the respiratory and nervous systems; it also rules Gemini, which governs the shoulders, arms, and hands. Mercury people are apt to think fast and speak quickly; they may be nervous and distracted, finding it hard to focus their attention on one thing for very long. Gemini herbs often have finely divided leaves that seem to "twin" on either side of the stem. They are usually nervines that calm and soothe the nervous system. Among these, lobelia is helpful for stressed-out, hyperactive people. It has powerful alkaloids that both stimulate and relax the respiratory system. Use the tea or tincture with caution. (EDITOR'S NOTE: Lobelia is a very powerful herb, and can be poisonous in large amounts. Do your research before attempting to use this herb medicinally.) Valerian is perhaps the best-known Mercury herb. It is a relaxing substitute for chemical sedatives. Combine it with skullcap, hops, and passion flower for a bedtime tea that will help you fall asleep. Licorice is used to treat bronchial problems and coughs; it also has a marked effect on the glandular system because it contains a natural precursor of the adrenal hormones (as such, it has an affinity with Venus). For Mercury's herbal applications to the intestinal system, see Virgo. For more nervous-system specifics, see Aquarius.

Cancer Herbs
(The Crab, June 22–July 23)

Nurturing, maternal Cancer, ruled by the Moon, governs the upper digestive system, the breasts, and women's reproductive organs. People strongly influenced by Cancer are very much in tune with others and with their environment; they want to help, nurture, and protect other people. Cancer herbs were traditionally used to treat indigestion, enhance mothers' milk, and heal women's reproductive ailments. Motherwort (related to the Sun and also to Venus) stimulates the menses and is a relaxing tonic during menopause. The herb stimulates the flow of blood to the pelvis. Try 10–15 drops once or twice a day to lessen the severity of hot flashes and reduce menopausal stress. Meadowsweet is one of the best digestive herbs available. A cup of meadowsweet tea reduces stomach acid and eases nausea. The herb also contains salicylic acid compounds that relieve headache and reduce fever. Kelp protects against some of the dangers of our century, particularly strontium-90, a by-product of nuclear power. Other Cancer herbs include agrimony (another valuable digestive remedy) and adder's tongue, the root of which was cooked in milk and the milk drunk to heal stomach ulcers. For additional lunar herbs, see Pisces.

Leo Herbs
(The Lion, July 24–August 23)

Ruled by the Sun, Leo is associated with the cardiac system. Leo people are warm-hearted and generous, often to a fault. Herbs related to Leo strengthen and tone the heart, regulate blood pressure, and relieve depression. Sparteine sulphate, the active principle in broom, makes it helpful in raising blood pressure. Mistletoe reduces blood pressure (its cardioactive principle is viscotoxin) and eases arteriosclerosis. (EDITOR'S NOTE: Mistletoe is poisonous. Please consult an expert before attempting to use it medi-

nally.) Juniper berries have recently been shown to reduce blood pressure and improve heart action; hawthorne berries are one of the best and safest tonic remedies for the heart and circulatory system. All cardioactive herbs should be used only in consultation with a qualified professional.

Virgo Herbs
(The Virgin, August 24– September 23)

People born under the sign of the Virgin display many of the characteristics of Mercury. They are thoughtful, discriminating, analytic, and sometimes very critical of themselves and others. In its rulership of Virgo, Mercury governs the abdomen and the lower intestinal tract. Virgo herbs assist in digestion, help to expel gas, and/or have a laxative effect; they also treat intestinal cramping and intestinal parasites. Licorice tea is an effective laxative, at the same time relieving gas and cramps. Senna is used in Europe as an ingredient in over-the-counter laxatives. Coriander stimulates the secretion of digestive juices. Fennel, another Mercury-ruled herb, promotes digestion and relieves gas. Try a tea (steep 1–2 teaspoons of crushed seeds in 1 cup freshly-boiled water for ten minutes). For other Mercury herbs, see Gemini and Aquarius.

Libra Herbs
(The Scales, September 24– October 23)

Venus-ruled Libra is traditionally associated with the kidneys and the bladder; under Libra, Venus also rules the endocrine system. Librans are usually gregarious people who enjoy the company of others and prefer balance and harmony, but may have trouble making up their minds. Herbs traditionally associated with Libra are specific to the urinary system and the kidneys, and have Venus' soothing capabilities. Thyme has traditionally been used as a mild astringent to prevent childhood bedwetting; its volatile oil, thymol, makes it helpful in the treatment of upset stomach, as well as the prevention of infection in cuts and scrapes. Goldenseal is an Native American herb, first used by the Cherokees. As well as being a general tonic for the mucous membranes, it is particularly useful in toning the glandular system. Other Libran herbs include yarrow (an excellent urinary anti-

septic) and cornsilk, both soothing diuretics that aid kidney function and help to heal cystitis. For more Venus herbs, see Taurus.

Scorpio Herbs
(The Scorpion, October 24– November 22)

Mars was the first ruler of Scorpio; astrologers now give this sign to Pluto, discovered in 1930. Whatever the emotion, Scorpio people feel it intensely, cling to it passionately, and find themselves transformed by their feelings. Pluto rules the processes of catabolism and anabolism, the continual death and regeneration of body cells. Scorpio traditionally rules the genitals. Herbs related to Scorpio are revitalizing, rebuilding, cleansing herbs associated with Mars. Horseradish is a folk remedy used as a stimulant and renewer. Ginseng is valued by the Chinese above all other plant medicines. It is used as a general tonic, restorative, and aphrodisiac (Mars rules sexual desire). Sassafras is a powerful revitalizer because it contains large amounts of iron salts. It has a general tonic effect, as well as cleansing the intestines. Wormwood, a Mars herb, is an effective renewing tonic, in addition to its uses in treating indigestion, intestinal parasites, and infections. (EDITOR'S NOTE: Wormwood was once used to make absinthe, which is highly addictive and considered to be an aphrodesiac. Wormwood is now considered poisonous, or at least dangerous for human consumption. Consult a professional before attempting to use wormwood medicinally.) For other Martian herbs, see Aries.

Sagittarius Herbs
(The Archer, November 23–December 21)

Jupiter, the largest planet, is responsible for growth and aging, as well as the body's largest glandular organ, the liver. Jupiter-ruled Sagittarius governs the hips, thighs, lower spine, and the autonomic nervous system. Jupiter's people are often expansive and optimistic, with a great deal of physical energy, and sometimes overdo it. Sagittarius herbs are used to treat lower back problems, arthritis, rheumatism, and the liver. Black willow is used to reduce joint and muscle pain and inflammation, as well as headaches. Its chief constituent, salacin, is the primary ingredient in aspirin. Dandelion is perhaps the best-known Jupiter herb; it stimu-

lates bile production in the liver, acts as a diuretic, and at the same time replaces lost potassium salts. It is also helpful in the treatment of chronic rheumatism. You may safely use this effective herb as a tincture, brew a tea from the root, or add the young leaves to your spring salads. Sage has been used for centuries as a powerful preservative. It contains antioxidants that slow spoilage in food and may, in the human body, resist the deteriorations of aging.

Capricorn Herbs
(The Goat, December 22–January 20)

Saturn rules this sign. Saturnine people seem to have a strong need for structure and organization, and may be highly disciplined. They get things done. Physiologically, Saturn rules the systems that give the body its structure and form: the skeletal system, the skin, teeth, joints, and knees. Plants associated with Capricorn are usually high in calcium, and Saturn herbs are useful in treating ailments of the skeleton and skin. The seed of mullein, Culpeper says, "bruised and boiled in wine and laid on any member that has been out of joint and newly set again, takes away all swelling and pain." Comfrey ("knitbone" or "boneset") leaves boiled in water make a sticky paste that dries plaster-hard; this was once used to set broken bones. It is also helpful in such skin diseases as psoriasis. Fumitory has a long history of use in the treatment of eczema and acne. Slippery elm is one of the most important remedies in herbal medicine; it was traditionally used to treat scurvy and leprosy. Bathing with it was thought to heal broken bones. And according to Culpeper, elm "mollifies hard tumours and the shrinking of the sinews."

Aquarius Herbs
(The Waterman, January 21– February 19)

Mercury ruled this sign until the surprising discovery of Uranus in 1781. Psychologically, Uranus represents change, often so powerful that it comes as a tremendous shock. It rules the electrical impulses of the body's nervous system. Exhaustion brought on by stress and environmental change is related to Uranus. Aquarius also rules the lower legs, the calves, and the ankles. Since Uranus was discovered after the plant/planet correspondences were established,

Aquarian herbs are those governed by its former ruler, Mercury. Lavender gently tones and strengthens the entire nervous system, making it a very valuable herb. The tea is an effective calming agent, easing headaches, promoting healthy sleep, and relieving depression. It is also widely used in aromatherapy, and research suggests that the scent alone has a calming effect on jangled nerves. Skullcap has a history of medicinal use in Chinese medicine as a treatment for convulsions and epilepsy. It was first introduced into the West to treat the convulsive symptoms of rabies. Now, it is widely used to relieve nervous tension, PMS, and the effects of drug/alcohol withdrawal. Valerian, one of the most useful relaxing nervines that nature has given us, is a powerful soother. A bedtime tea of valerian and skullcap virtually ensures a restful night's sleep.

Pisces Herbs
(The Fish, February 20– March 20)

Pisces rules all water plants, including the seaweeds and the mosses; in medical astrology, it rules the feet. It is also associated with infectious diseases such as tuberculosis, with psychotic disorders, and with all forms of substance addiction. After the discovery of Neptune in 1846, that planet was assigned to its rulership. Piscean herbs belong to the watery Moon, which formerly ruled this sign. Poppy represents the distortion of Pisces' wish to escape reality. Herbalists use the non-poisonous red poppy to treat coughs. Goldenseal has an antibiotic effect on most infections. Echinacea, the most important medicinal plant of the American Plains Indians, fights many bacteria and viruses, at the same time strengthening tissues. Hallucinogenic herbs, such as marijuana and peyote, also have Piscean overtones.

Uses for Zodiac Herbs

The medicine chest isn't the only place you can use your understanding of herbs and the zodiac! Here are some other ways to incorporate this ancient wisdom into your daily life.

Garden by the Moon

There isn't anything complicated about using the Moon's phases as a guide to planting, maintaining, and harvesting your garden. This almanac and other books on the reading list below offer excellent guidance and plenty of how-to. Just remember to use your common sense when you work with this or any other guide. For example, astrologically, the time may be right to harvest your basil. But if it's raining cats and dogs, you'll have to choose another day—less astrologically ideal, perhaps, but in tune with the meteorological conditions in your local environment.

Zodiacal Garden Journal

This project can be a great deal of fun and very instructive, too. Buy a blank book and mark it into twelve sections, corresponding to the twelve signs. You might also use one of the astrology texts cited in the reference section to fill in a bit of additional information about each of the signs. And of course, use the information in this almanac to incorporate the Moon's signs and phases. Use this format to note what you planted, where and when; the dates you cultivated and weeded; your observations about the growth of your plants; and information about your harvest yield. Of course, it's always a good idea to keep a garden journal. Organizing it astrologically will also help you to get acquainted with the signs and seasons.

Plant a Zodiacal Garden

The zodiac is drawn in the form of a circle divided into twelve sections or "houses," each ruled by a sign and planet. (The first house, ruled by Aries, is located in the lower left quadrant of the circle.) The circle is also a traditional herb garden form, easily divisible into twelve sections. You might create your own circular herb garden, planting Mars/Aries herbs in the first section or house, Venus/Taurus herbs in the second, Mercury/Gemini in the third, and so on. You could personalize your garden by placing a terra cotta Sun (available from garden catalogs) or other decorative object in your Sun-sign house. For instance, if you are a Capricorn, you would place your object in the tenth section (the tenth house). If you don't have the time or the space for a larger garden, why not create a container garden of herbs related to your sun sign? If you know your Moon sign and/or your rising sign, you could include herbs associated with those planetary rulerships, as well.

Pressed Herbs

You don't have to plant a garden to enjoy the symbolism of herbs. For instance, you might enjoy collecting a variety of herbs, pressing them in the pages of a telephone book, and mounting them, together with drawings of the signs to which they're related. A framed collection of these herbs would make a fascinating display on an empty wall. If you're not sure where to collect samples for pressing, ask the owner of your local herb store for suggestions. Herbalists are generous people who are delighted to share their passion—and their plants!

Create Herbal Rituals

Your birthday—astrologers call it your solar return day—is a special time. Honor it with a special herbal ritual, featuring your Sun-sign herbs. If you are born under Leo, for instance, treat yourself to a bouquet of sunflowers, marigolds, or calendula—Leo's flowers. Or craft a tussy mussie, featuring your solar flowers together with lamb's ears, a bit of artemisia, a sprig of rosemary (Sun-ruled), a spray of baby's breath, bound with a bit of orange ribbon. You might also drink a cup of chamomile tea (the Egyptians assigned chamomile to the Sun) and enjoy a bit of chopped fresh rosemary sprinkled over your baked potato during the last few minutes in the oven!

If Venus rules your chart, create a birthday potpourri of Venus' floral herbs—violets, perhaps, with rose petals, tangy mint leaves, and a bit of goldenrod to remind you of your planetary affinity for all things beautiful. Sip a glass of iced mint tea, dip into a bowl of spring-fresh sorrel soup, and nibble on your favorite minted chocolate.

But herbal delights need not be confined to birthdays. Mealtime can be more fun if you remember that the culinary herbs are all associated with the planets. Parsley belongs to Mercury, sage to Jupiter, rosemary to the Sun, thyme to Venus, basil to Saturn, cayenne, mustard, and all hot peppers to Mars. Bathtime can be an herbal joy if it's celebrated with Mercury-ruled lavender—a lavender soap, a few drops of lavender essential oil in your bathwater, a lavender-scented candle. Bedtime can be Venus' ritual hour if you slip off to sleep between rose-scented sheets, with a mugwort pillow under your head. Sweet dreams!

The pleasures of herbs and the fascinations of astrology have gone hand-in-hand for centuries, linking humans to the earth, the heavens, and to each other in a community of common knowledge. We can recreate this community, but only if we are mindful of the treasures nature has given us. All this is possible if we take time every day to listen to the voice of the green world and heed what it has to tell us about ourselves, our bodies, and our cosmic spirits.

Further Reading

Culpeper, Nicholas. *Culpeper's Complete Herbal & English Physician*, enlarged. Facsimile edition, 1990. Meyerbooks, P.O. Box 427, Glenwood, IL 60425.

Daath, Heinrich. *Medical Astrology.* Sun Publishing Co., P.O. Box 5588, Santa Fe, NM 87502.

Landis, Knight. *The Astrologer's Manual: Modern Insights into an Ancient Art.* CRCS Publications, P.O. Box 1460, Sebastopol, CA 95472.

Muir, Ada. *Healing Herbs & Health Foods of the Zodiac.* Llewellyn Publications, 1993.

Riotte, Louise. *Astrological Gardening: The Ancient Wisdom of Successful Planting & Harvesting by the Stars.* Storey Communications, Pownal, VT, 1989.

Weed, Susun. *The Wise Woman Herbal: Healing Wise.* Ash Tree Publishing, Woodstock, NY, 1989.

SUSAN WITTIG ALBERT is the author of the China Bayles mystery series, including *Thyme of Death, Witches' Bane, Hangman's Root,* and the new *Rosemary Remembered,* released in November 1995. Susan is an herbalist and astrologer, and is currently working with her husband, Bill, on a new historical mystery series under the name of Robin Paige. The first book in this series is called *Death at Bishop's Keep.* If you would like to order any of Susan's books, write to China's Garden, Drawer M, Bertram, TX 78605.

Preserving Herbs the Natural Way

By Harriet Amar

Drying your freshly-grown herbs is a healthful, nutrient-saving way to preserve your harvest, as well as a very satisfying experience. Another great advantage to this method of preserving herbs is that they will retain the same delightful, pleasing scents as were in the original growing plants. They will also stay quite close to the lovely original hues, which you want, since the herb's strength is judged by its retained depth of color (which seems to vanish with many of the commercially-dried ones). Also, and very importantly, they will have almost no loss of their unique healing abilities.

The very best time to pick your herbs for drying is on a warm, dry, clear morning after all the dew is gone from the plants, yet before the warm Sun starts to disperse the flavor-bearing volatile oils. Take the time to pick them slowly. Lay them gently on a tray or wire screen or in a clean cardboard box next to each other, rather than piling them heavily on top of one another. Plan on several harvests during the summer, rather than one massive one. In fact, if you just clip the leafy tops of some of them, the plants will be encouraged to become bushy and provide a second cutting.

Before beginning any drying process, you will want to check the herbs for clinging soil, insects, and weeds. Gently and carefully remove them so as not to disturb or damage the plants, which will already be shocked after being pulled or cut. Before moving the herbs, it has been suggested by professional herbalists that all the leaves, stems, stalks, roots, and flowers to be dried first be laid out in the sun for a short time to avoid any chance of fungus attack. After taking care of this, the herbs are ready for drying. This procedure is best done away from the Sun, in a cool, shady area. Wherever you decide to dry the herbs, do plan on as short a time as will do the best job, so that the healing qualities and unique flavors and essences are not destroyed. In other words, the faster the drying method, the better for preserving the herbs' value.

This leads us to the three most popular ways to dry your fresh herbs, and which of these will work best depends on which herbs, and how much of them, you are drying.

It is always a good idea to start small. If this is, indeed, your first venture into drying your freshly picked herbs, you can pick up valuable pointers, as well as correct possible errors, with a small amount of the plants. Your later, larger attempts will be more successful based on the experience gained during your early experiences.

A very small amount of herbs can be dried on trays in a cool room indoors. Be sure to leave a window open for the necessary circulation of air.

Another handy, quick method is to put your herbs on cheesecloth-covered racks in the oven, at the lowest setting, with the door held ajar several inches by a small block of wood. Your herbs will be dry in a matter of hours—the small, delicate ones first, and the heavier ones a few hours later. Checking them every two hours will tell you when each type is thoroughly dried. To

do this, you can take a sampling of each kind and set them on a nearby clean tray. After they have cooled off for a few minutes, check each one. If not dry enough, return to drying rack or tray for another few hours.

A second method is good for larger amounts or fuller herbs. This is the hanging-upside-down-in-bunches-treatment, and can be done in just a few days if the area you hang them in is warm and dry. Whether they are hung in an attic or an outside shed, make sure that a window is open for thorough circulation of air throughout the bunched plants. Also, the place you dry in should be dark, because light takes the color away from herbs as they dry. Thus, it is advisable to put shades on any windows in the drying area. If this cannot be done, cover the herbs themselves with large paper bags, leaving just the bottoms open for air. If some of your drying herbs have seeds you wish to save, place a large, open paper bag under each of those to catch the seeds as they gently fall from time to time. If some seeds still remain after the herbs have thoroughly dried, you can carefully lower the herb into a bag, close it around the inverted stems, and, shaking gently, release the balance of the seeds. Always make sure, of course, if you are saving seeds, that they are fully ripe when picked so that they will be viable for replanting. This can be determined by tapping a few of them gently. If they fall, they are ripe and ready to be removed.

The third way to dry really large quantities of herbs is to construct a number of reusable, multi-tiered drying racks to be set up in a small, separate area of any outbuilding, such as a garage or shed. This works well for all kinds of herbs, and the racks are easily constructed from wooden-tiered frames covered with taut cheesecloth. Air and heat can be provided by an open window and a small electric heater. In a very large room, you would probably do better with a propane or natural gas forced heater, instead.

Once your herbs are completely dry, you can remove them for storage. The most effective storage containers have proven to be clean gallon glass jars. They keep out moisture and discourage insect and rodent infestations, which cardboard boxes, paper

bags, and plastic jars do not. For smaller amounts of herbs that you plan to use sooner, you will want to use quart and pint glass jars instead. The reason for the smaller jars is so that smaller amounts of herbs will be exposed to air and moisture when the jar is opened. Make sure when you put the herbs in each jar that no moisture appears on the inside of the jar. If this should happen, those herbs need further drying before storage. The larger jars will stay closed (which helps them keep better and longer) until ready to transfer to the faster-used quart or pint glass jars. Be sure to store the glass jars of herbs in a closed, dark cabinet so that they will keep well.

Drying your own home-grown or wild herbs can be a very rewarding experience. Start with a few favorites, and take your time doing the drying, experimenting as you go. Your resulting combination of flavorful, nutritious, delightfully colored, aromatic, health enhancing herbal specimens will give you great pleasure. Plan to start preserving all sorts of wonderful herbs soon.

HARRIET AMAR has been gardening all of her life. She and her husband have experimented with several small farms, and are currently growing and researching the uses of the Jerusalem artichoke. Harriet also works as a desktop publisher.

The Stinging Nettle: Nature's Doctor

By Mary Brown

As gardeners, ramblers, and short-trousered children know only too well, the nettle is found almost everywhere. Its name originally meant "to twist" (as in fibers), for the crushed stems make excellent rope and coarse cloth. Nettles were cultivated in wort beds or herb gardens by Anglo-Saxon monks, who had many uses for them.

Nettles can be found on verges by the roadside, on wasteland and woodland, and in gardens both large and small. The nettle has a creeping root system and is very invasive, soon colonizing any patch of land left uncultivated. The plants will grow as high as 4'–5' if left undisturbed, and disappear only briefly in the winter months. With the first hints of spring, up they come again. ·

As children we all knew that close contact with the nettle proved very painful, and we quickly learned to look for large dock leaves to cool the itchy rash on arms and legs. It is strange that the age-old remedy usually grows nearby. We knew that it would work better if we sang, "Nettle out and dock in, dock removes the nettle's sting."

Our ancestors knew all about nettles and their many uses. The stems could be used for cloth, rope, and even paper-making. The leaves could be dried and powdered to use as snuff, which would stop nosebleed. Ailments of the chest could be cured by a syrup made by boiling the juice of the leaves and roots with honey, while the leaves in a decoction were an excellent diuretic and could also cure worms in children. An old herbal tells us that the decoction of the root was excellent for washing "fistulas, gangrenes, corroding scabs, and the itch."

Nettle seeds were said to cure dog bites, and claims were even made that they were effective against such deadly poisons as hemlock, nightshade, henbane, and mandrake. The Romans swore by nettles as a cure for rheumatism. The method they used was to thrash the affected joints with the whole plant—a most painful remedy, by the sound of it.

There were many superstitious beliefs about the nettle. It was said to be under the dominion of Mercury in the age when all plants were assigned to a particular planet according to the doctrine of astrological botany. The nettle's folkname was "devil's needle," no doubt because of its sting. This link with the devil led to many myths about its supernatural powers, for it was believed to ward off all kinds of danger and misfortune. The plant was said to give courage in time of danger, and people were advised to carry a small piece of it, which would protect against lightning, evil spirits, and sorcery. Part of this "magic" was due to the belief that the nettle usually grew around the hidden entrances of fairy dwellings. The saying "grasp the nettle" refers to the belief that a person ill with fever could be cured if a relative took hold of a nettle firmly and pulled it up by the roots, at the same time repeating the name of the patient and the patient's parents.

Nettle juice combed through the hair was believed to cure baldness (this claim is also made for rosemary), and the juice was supposed to be able to seal cracks in barrels. The nettle was said to increase laying in chickens and to deter flies if hung in the kitchen. If fruit was packed in nettles it would keep longer. The juice of nettles could also be used in place of rennet to curdle the milk for making cheese. The plant was so useful and so highly thought of that there was a saying about it: "If they would eat nettles in March and eat mugwort in May, so many fine maidens wouldn't go to clay" (meaning the grave).

We know now that the old wives' tales weren't far off. Nettles do indeed have many uses, even today. The plant is very rich in vitamin C and minerals. The leaves should be collected before flowering if the plant is to be dried and stored, though the fresh plant can be used. An infusion (nettle tea) made with 1 ounce of the dried leaves, or 2 ounces of fresh leaves to 1 pint of boiling water, taken in doses of 2 fluid ounces at a time, relieves high blood pressure and cystitis, and also makes a good

Nettle

blood tonic for anemia. For diarrhea, a decoction of the root is used. Boil 1 ounce of the cleaned, chopped root for twenty minutes in 1 pint of water. Leave to cool and then strain.

Homeopaths use a fresh plant tincture to treat asthma. To relieve nettle sting more effectively than the dock leaf method, take a handful each of the flowers of chamomile, comfrey, and marshmallow. Crush them and make into a paste with boiling water. When cool, apply to the rash.

The crumbly, greenish flowers of the nettle are a favorite food of several species of butterfly, which in itself will provide you with much pleasure. Apart from this and the possibility of a soothing nettle tea, the leaves can also be used to make a fine wine, or nettle beer. The young leaves can also be cooked and eaten like spinach. Boil for at least six minutes to destroy the formic acid, which is what

makes the sting so painful. Strip the leaves off first, as the stems are tough. Eat with a little butter and feel it doing you good.

Another way in which the nettle can benefit your garden is as a compost activator, for its special properties make it a fast rotter, and it will help to break down other ingredients in the heap. Allow a bucketful of leaves to rot down in water, and you have an excellent liquid fertilizer that is also a pesticide. Strain and use directly.

Nettles share a strong affinity with soft fruit bushes and should be allowed to grow between rows. The fruit bushes will bear more fruit and suffer less from their usual pests. In fact, nettles tend to help stimulate the growth of all the other garden plants, flowers, fruit and vegetables alike, so don't be too hasty with the machete. It's still a good idea to keep your gloves on, however!

MARY BROWN is a freelance writer from England specializing in folklore and British seasonal customs, gardening, and history. A regular contributor to *Prediction* magazine, she also writes book reviews for *Organic Gardening*. At present she is writing her third novel. She lives on a farm in Somerset.

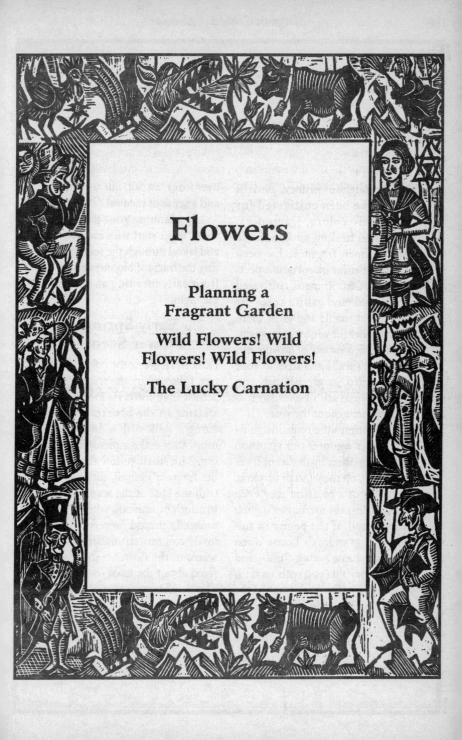

Flowers

Planning a
Fragrant Garden

Wild Flowers! Wild
Flowers! Wild Flowers!

The Lucky Carnation

Planning a Fragrant Garden

By Kristine M. Distel-Bennett

Throughout history, gardens have been cultivated for their colors, fragrances, tastes, and healing powers. Since ancient times, fragrance has been one of the most important aspects of the garden. Romans cultivated the damask and gallica roses for their sweet smells and grew them in hothouses for winter enjoyment. By planting a variety of flowers and blooming shrubs and trees in your garden, yard, or greenhouse, you can enjoy nature's beautiful fragrances throughout the year.

Sometimes the most insignificant flower captures our attention and imagination by the scent it reveals to us, on the wind or up close. The odor of a blossom may even invoke pleasant memories—such as the smell of the peony in full bloom at grandma's house when you visited as a young child—and the memory fills you with warmth and security. The fresh smell of the moist Earth heralds the onset of spring, and the lush smell of new vegetative growth, intermingled with the scents of molds, fungi, and decaying vegetable matter left over from last fall, fills us with joy and a sense of renewal.

In planning your garden for scent, let us start with early spring and travel through the seasons, letting the fragrant blooms delight us from early morning and on into the night.

Early Spring Flower Scents

Early April greets the colorful crocus, followed by the fragrant hyacinth that sends its sweet scent wafting in the breeze. Planted along a walk with a dwarf early tulip, they make a pleasant greeting. The small yellow flowers of the fragrant jonquil, interplanted with the blue of the scented grape hyacinth or muscari, with its blue, umbrella-shaped flowers, create a lovely contrast, naturalizing themselves in the flower beds or scattered about the lawn or meadow. The delicately scented Dutch iris, or *Iris reticulata*, is a treasure among the early irises, and is best enjoyed planted in small groups.

Scattered among the spring bulbs are a few scented species of tulips. These tulips are smaller than the hybrids, and they have only one or two flowers per bulb. For example, the 12" Saxatilis tulip blooms in mid-spring. Its cup-like pale lilac flowers, with their yellow bases, are from Crete. Later in spring comes the 6" Australis tulip from France and Algeria. Its petals are yellow inside and reddish outside. The Sylvestris tulip is 8"–12" tall and yellow. Clusia tulip, or candlestick tulip, is the tallest of the tulips at 15". Candlestick tulips are white or yellowish. The outsides are striped with a pinkish red. They hail from Iran and Afghanistan, and have naturalized throughout Southern Europe.

Spring Woodland Scents

Fragrance is not lost in the partially shaded woodland area. In the planted woodland we may find the early-blooming *Magnolia x loebneri,* "Merrill." Its large, white, sweetly-scented blooms can be detected a block away on a warm spring afternoon. Underneath the magnolia branches, and in the partial shade, the wildflower *Phlox divaricata,* with its scented blue flowers, can be found with the woodland and odorata violets, the latter being the more fragrant. Also growing in the woods is the white-flowered sweet woodruff, which is highly prized for its scented, dried leaves. In large patches of shade, lily of the valley can be found, with its familiar odor and white flowers. Near at hand we may find the large, flowered, white *Chionantha* primrose planted along the border for its soft fragrance.

Scented Spring Trees and Shrubs

Above the shade flowers, flowering crabs bloom in colors ranging from white to pink to red, sending out their famous fresh, sweet, apple blossom scent. They are followed by the lovely but short-bloomed hawthorn tree.

In the month of May, the northern garden can be a riot of scents and odors. The purple wisteria vine, called "Aunt Dee" in the North, coupled with the other va-

Tulips

Azalea

rieties of the South, adds a delicate beauty to the landscape with its hanging flowers.

Springtime flowering shrubs seem to conspire to drown us in their multitudes of scent. The shrub daphne, with its tiny trumpet flower, has a fragrance worth noting. The white flowers and blue fruit of the tall serviceberry or juneberry can be intoxicating next to an open window, and spicy azaleas, with their large flowers, attract hummingbirds. The Nanking cherry, *Prunus tomentosa,* is covered with scented blooms, and later with luscious red fruit.

The many varieties of lilac begin to bloom in May, starting with the common lilac and the French hybrids. Next to bloom is the Chinese or Persian lilac, with its foliage more delicate than the common varieties. The shorter Korean lilac,

at 5' tall, has the most heavenly scent of all. When planted beneath the bedroom window, it fills the morning with its perfume. The Canadian hybrids and preston lilacs, with their pink to lavender blooms, are followed by the Japanese tree lilac, with its large, white flowers.

Scented Summer Trees and Shrubs

In June, the profuse bloom of the mock orange adds to the perfumed fragrance of the later lilacs with its scent of citrus and orange blossom. A few of the viburnums emit a spicy odor from their clusters of white flowers. The bayberry is prized for its scented foliage, used in the making of candles.

Two fragrant shrubs are also attractive to butterflies, making them doubly useful in the landscape garden. The buddleia begins to bloom in July, and continues until hard frost. Its elongated, honey-scented flowers are very distinctive. Hummingbirds are attracted to the white spikes of the clethera. The "pink spire" clethera blooms a little later and adds its fragrance to the garden for a few weeks in the heat of summer.

Creating another level of the fragrant landscape are the ornamental and shade trees. The shortest, at 15', is the fringe tree. Its open form and long panicles of white flowers are a delight to the eye. The 40' robinia, with its golden yellow foliage and white blooms, makes a lovely accent tree in the landscape. The basswood, or American linden, is taller yet, giving us its soothing and fragrant white blossom and its refreshing summer shade. The most dramatic of the summer flowering trees is the catalpa. The large, white flowers remind one of the tropics. The long, pendulous, bean-like fruits hanging from under the large leaves add to its exotic appearance. A dense, cooling shade can be found underneath.

Shady Summer Scents

Lorvcera x heckrotti, the honeysuckle vine, will bloom in partial shade with a soft, sweet fragrance that lifts the spirit. Plant this rosy red and yellow vine along a wall or near a walkway to enjoy the summer scent that lingers into the fall.

In the shade of the trees grows the hosta in all its splendor. This plant comes in sizes from 6"–4', and leaf colors from green to blue to yellow, and variegated mixes. There are three commonly known hostas with outstanding scent. This is not to say you won't find others at your local nursery, for they are one of the easier plants to breed, and new varieties arrive on the market every year. The most pop-

ular, the *Hosta plantaginea* and the *Hosta royal standard,* have fragrant white blooms appearing in August. Their scents can be enjoyed on into the night. The hosta honeybell is the first variety to bloom in the summer. Its fragrant lavender blooms appear in July. It has lighter green foliage than the others, and can withstand some sun without burning.

Scented Summer Perennials

The perennials of summer include the familiar tall, bearded iris, with its vast array of colors and elusive scent, which has made it an outstanding flower for the garden for centuries. The spicy garden phlox is also an old standby, with large flower heads and extended blooming period. The evening primrose opens after sunset, casting its fragrance into the night.

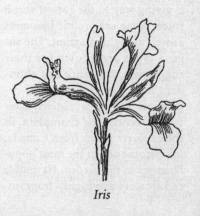

Iris

Rose

Roses have always been held in high esteem because of their fragrance and beauty. For some people, roses rank number one above all other flowers of the garden. The heavenly sweet smells begin in June in great abundance, and recur throughout the summer until frost. The most highly-prized roses for their outstanding beauty are the hybrid teas. In the northern climes, the tender beauty of the hybrid teas is giving way to the robust shrub roses. Some are prolific bloomers as well as highly fragrant. The rugosa types are known for their ruggedness, fragrance and abundant hips. The clove-scented rugosa rose "hansa" is relatively carefree. Recently, the champlain, in the explorer series from Canada, has become one of the most popular roses in the garden. Its double red flowers are highly fragrant, bloom continuously, and make excellent dried flowers.

Summer Herb Scents

Many perennials have scented leaves as well as flowers. Some herbs are best known for their foliage only. The bergamots, or bee balms, have oregano-scented flowers as well as leaves. The English lavender casts its refreshing volatile oil into the air from both its leaves and flowers on a hot summery day. The purple flowers of the licorice mint, or anise hyssop, are loved by bees. Both the flowers and leaves are edible, and delicious in teas and salads. The mints are favored for their flowers as well as scented leaves. Lemon catnip leaves make a refreshing tea. Spearmint, peppermint, pineapple mint, and chocolate mint are just a few of the many mints available for their fragrant leaves. Pearly everlasting is a white prairie flower whose leaves are more pungent when dried, making it useful for flower arrangements.

Many culinary herbs have a place in the fragrant garden. They add color and texture to the garden as well as adding flavor to our food. The most common are the blue-green rosemary, the silver sage, the rapidly spreading oregano, with its small purple flowers, the French herb tarragon, and the versatile thyme, with its many flavors.

Summer Scented Border Plants

The lilium create drama in the fragrant garden. The exotic Oriental lily "stargazer" is not only beautiful, but it is highly scented. It is one of the most sought-after flowers for arrangements. The trumpet lily, *Lilium aurelians,* is also highly fragrant—so fragrant, in fact, that some people place it well back in the flower border to lessen its impact on the olfactory organ. *Lilium regale* is a tall beauty, with burgundy buds opening to purest white.

Some of our most fragrant flowers can be found in the annual border. The sweet peas start off the spring with their sweet scent. Low to the ground, in pots, or climbing on a fence or trellis, they are a welcome addition to spring. In low ground borders, the sweet allysum sends its fragrance into the wind from spring to late fall. Its colors range from white, to pink, to purple. Sweet William, a biannual dianthus, is one of the showiest in a multitude of colors, scented in spice. The other dianthus, carnations, garden pinks, and phlox, join in for spring and summer color and spicy scent.

Stocks and sweet sultan "dairy maid" make excellent cut flowers for floral arrangements and bedding plants. Stocks have a magifi-cent sweet and spicy clove scent, and "night-scented" stock has a deliciously powerful scent. Sweet sultan "dairy maid" has a chocolate fragrance. *Berlandiera lyrata* also has the aroma of chocolate, which can fill the patio. Its leaves are silver and its flower yellow-bronze, making it a colorful asset in the garden.

The strongly-scented heliotrope is wonderful in a basket at nose level. Its purple flowers are surrounded by soft leaves. The old-fashioned mignonette may be leggy, but its pink flowers send a romantic fragrance into the air.

Scented Summer Nights

In the evening hours, a stroll into the garden can be all the more romantic by moonlight, with the scent of flowers in the air. The evening primrose and the *Hosta plantaginea* are two that were mentioned earlier. The tall, old-fashioned evening-blooming nicotiana, or flowering tobacco, sends its soft scent into the air. Four-o'clocks have already had a head start on the evening fragrances by opening their blooms in late afternoon. Datura sends its deeply rich perfume into the air from its large downward-facing trumpets, which catch the moonlight, creating a haunting atmosphere. Climbing

Hyacinth

upon the garden fence, the large white flowers of the moon-flower vine emit their pleasant fragrance for the night visitor from evening until noon the next day.

Autumn and Winter Scents

Clematis sweet autumn is the last to bloom in the northern climate. It is an outstanding perennial vine covered in a multitude of small fra-grant white flowers. In warmer climates it may retain its leaves and act as an evergreen.

Throughout the winter we can enjoy the fragrance of the jasmines, such as the gardenia, or jasmine sambac, or the vigorous night-blooming jasmine. The tuberose sends a heady scent into the air. The tall gingers give the appear-ance of cornplants, but give off the most beautiful tropical smell. The famous Hawaiian white ginger grows in the tropics. Since not all of us do, we can grow these in pots indoors in a sunny window with humidity and still enjoy their fra-grance. Another way to bring scent into the indoor winter landscape is to force spring bulbs in containers. Hyacinths, jonquils, and freesia make for a relief of winter and an anticipation of spring.

KRISTINE M. DISTEL-BENNETT has been an organic gardener all her life. Her main gardening focus is to help people create harmony within them-selves and their environments through landscaping and gardening.

Wild Flowers! Wild Flowers! Wild Flowers!

By Carly Wall

Is there something missing from your fall flower bed? Are you searching for that special touch to make your fall a glorious blaze of color? If you are, then you might want to consider a fall-blooming wildflower bed. A corner of the yard that contains a bed of wildflowers can speak a gentle poetry to our senses. The delightful discovery of these forgotten flowers will kindle many special moments and make for fascinating research. There are many varieties of wild blooms, and you are sure to find favorites among them, as well as varied colors. They're beautiful, fun, and, best of all, almost effortless. And now's the time to plan for next year's show!

Delving into wild beds alters some gardeners' whole view on flower gardening. Karen Young, mother of two and a tentative gardener from the Columbus, Ohio area, was coaxed into trying her hand at a small wild bed. "I couldn't believe it. When I was planting the seeds, I thought, well, this is going to be another disaster. Last year, I spent all spring planting

some roses, which promptly died. I have the worst black thumb ever. My family laughs at my projects. But then something happened. I ignored this wild bed, and one morning, it was like a grand explosion of color. From then on, wildflowers were my passion. Now, the cultivated beds just don't have the charms of their wilder cousins."

Creating Your Own Wild Beds

Marilyn Zwayer, gardener at Companion Plants, an Ohio mail-order firm specializing in the more unusual herbs and flowers, states, "The best and easiest time to start creating such a garden is in the fall of the year. This is the time the wild flowers generally set their seed. And they need the cold weather for proper germination in the spring."

The easiest way is to prepare the bed several weeks in advance of planting. Work up your soil well. Turn over several times and let the sun bake it to kill any top layers of weed seeds. Rake out any grass clods and smooth out the soil,

Yarrow

adding compost. You may also want to add an edging to outline your bed—for beauty, as well as to keep out grass or wandering feet! When the weather is cool and your bed is ready, just toss in some seeds in an even manner and lightly cover over with a rake.

The bed is entirely up to you. Do you want a particular color? Then plant a mixture of all white flowers, or pink, or yellow. Perhaps you just enjoy one particular type of plant. Or you may want surprises of color. It's according to your own tastes.

"Wildflowers are the easiest things to grow," adds Zwayer, "if you follow a few tips. One, try to recreate the natural habitat of a particular flower. It won't grow in the sun if it likes the shade. And two, don't be too particular about weeding. Many times a gardener will weed out their bed only to learn later in the season that they have pulled up their flowers!" Her wildflower picks are the native ironweed and Queen Anne's lace, which she says are naturally beautiful and are surprisingly lovely when added to indoor bouquets.

There are thousands of varieties of flowering plants to suit your area, but sadly, they are fast becoming rare because of our changing landscape—there aren't very many wild places left, which makes it all the more reason to map out a wild area of your own backyard. With this in mind, remember that if you see a wildflower out somewhere growing strong and healthy, help it out by just enjoying its natural beauty, not by picking or digging up the plant.

You can plant wildflowers that bloom throughout the season, but here are some which bloom specifically in the fall, if you want to create a colorful end-of-season bed.

White Blooms

INDIAN PIPE (*Monotropa uniflora*) It has waxy, white, ghostly blossoms, but wilts immediately when exposed to the sun. It is a weird, leafless plant which Native Americans used to cure eye irritations. In the deep south it blooms in November and December. It likes pine trees and shade.

RATTLESNAKE PLANTAIN (*Epipactis tesselata*) With green-white flowers and patterned leaves, it loves the acid soil and shady spots of the Indian Pipe. It blooms from July through September and grows 5"–8" tall. Many Native American women believed if they rubbed their bodies with this plant, it would make their husbands love them more.

SWEET SCENTED BEDSTRAW (*Galium triflorium*) It blooms in the summer, and grows across the northern and midwestern states. Country folk used the dried foliage to stuff mattresses because of its sweet vanilla scent, which appears only on drying.

YARROW (*Achillea millefolium*) From the daisy family, it was imported from Europe and blooms early in the summer to September.

Blue Flowers

CHICORY (*Cichorium intybus*) It has shaggy blue flowers the color of the sky, which close with rain and open with the sun. It is most often seen along roadways. The blooms can be used in salads, the roots ground and roasted to add to coffee or used as coffee substitute. It blooms summer and fall.

FORGET-ME-NOT (*Myosotis scorpioides*) This is the state flower of Alaska, but it has been naturalized in many parts of the country. It is

Forget-me-not

fragrant, with enchanting tiny blue blooms which make lovely small bouquets. It is the symbol of loving remembrance and friendship, and it blooms spring through fall. It especially likes wet, marshy soil.

PICKERELWEED (*Pontederia*) It has a stiff blossom spike which appears August through September. Deer love it. It grows near pond edges or shallow streams from Nova Scotia to Florida and Texas.

PURPLE CONEFLOWER (*Echinacea pupurea*) This is a late summer to autumn flower with deep violet-toothed petals. As summer ends, it gives a colorful tribute. It likes the Sun.

Yellow Blooms

SEASIDE GOLDENROD (*Solidago sempervirens*) It grows along shores and beaches of Cape Cod and the Eastern seaboard. It blooms Sep-

Pink

tember through October with rich gold tones, and attracts the migrating monarch butterflies.

GERMAN CHAMOMILE (*Matricaria chamomila*) This is where the famous chamomile tea comes from. The tiny, daisy-like flowers bloom in late summer and the plants like full sun to partial shade.

SUNFLOWER (*Helianthus annus*) Revered by Incans in Peru as the image of their Sun god, the seeds are a source of oil and food for both humans and birds. The leaves can be dried and smoked in place of tobacco. It likes the sun and blooms late summer and fall.

Pink Blooms

DEPTFORD PINK (*Dianthus armeria*) With clusters of tight crimson flowers, the petals are jagged-edged, resembling sweet William, and naturalized here from Europe. It is named after a town in England, where it grows in abundance. It grows in sunny fields, dry meadows, and along roadsides. It blooms in summer and fall.

MEADOWSWEET (*Spirea latifolia*) The flowers resemble tiny apple blossoms, and they are fragrant! In old times the plumes were used in garlands and wreaths. It's a sun-lover that grows 2'–4' tall.

Conclusion

This article lists only a few of the many wildflowers you can grow yourself. Please see the list of sources for further ideas and information. Tempt butterflies, hummingbirds, and bees with your wonderful wildflowers!

Sources

Since there are so many varieties to choose from, here are some catalogs that specialize in wildflower seed:

COMPANION PLANTS
    7247 N. Coolville Ridge Road
    Athens, Ohio 45701
    (614) 592-4643

CLYDE ROBIN SEED COMPANY
    P.O. Box 2366
    Castro Valley, CA 94546
    (415) 581-3468

Organizations

Here are two organizations to contact for more information on wildflowers:

NEW ENGLAND WILDFLOWER SOCIETY

180 Hemenway Road
Framingham, MA 01701-2699
(508) 877-7630

The New England Wildflower Society was founded in 1922. It features the botanical garden (Garden in the Woods), and promotes conservation, research, and education, as well as acting as a clearinghouse for plant projects. They have an international seed exchange, garden tours, classes for adults and children, and a newsletter.

NATIONAL WILDLIFE FEDERATION

Backyard Wildlife Habitat Program
8925 Leesburg Pike
Vienna, VA 22184
(202) 797-6800

Anyone who gardens for wildlife may apply here for certification as having an official Backyard Wildlife Habitat. Ask for your booklet, which explains the program and offers suggestions for getting started as well as how to apply. No matter how large or small your project, you are welcome.

❖⊂⊃❖

CARLY WALL is a midwestern gardener and aromatherapist. She has written a book called *Flower Secrets Revealed: Using Flowers to Heal, Beautify and Energize Your Life,* A.R.E. Press. It's available at your local bookstore for $14.95, or you can order direct by calling: 1-800-723-1112.

The Lucky Carnation

By Carly Wall

Ever wondered why the scarlet carnation (*Dianthus caryophyllus*) is considered a lucky flower? In 1904, the red carnation was adopted officially as Ohio's state flower in memory of William McFinley. He considered it a lucky flower because during an early campaign for a seat in the U.S. House of Representatives, his opponent gave him a red carnation for his buttonhole. Since he won that election, he continued wearing this flower throughout his career.

A Literary Flower

The carnation is actually a member of a large group called *Dianthus*, containing many family members. There are three main groups; sweet Williams, pinks, and carnations. All of these require full sun and a well-drained, slightly alkaline soil. All are delightful in their own way. For now, we'll explore the carnations: the perpetual-flowering and the hardy border types. This ancient flower was known and loved centuries before the Christian era, and many have referred to it as the "Divine" or Dianthus. The Greeks and Romans often used it in garlands for their best athletes. In fact, it is a part of literary history, being mentioned in Chaucer's *Canterbury Tales*, where he called it "clove gilofre," derived from the Greek *caryophyllus*. Later, Shakespeare took the liberty of calling them "gillyflowers" in *A Winter's Tale*. Before that, the monks of the Middle Ages grew them in their monastery gardens as ingredients for their wine-making.

The perpetual-flowering carnations are an all-year-round plant that can be grown in greenhouses in changeable climates, while the border carnations are the more easy-going characters, requiring only good sun and moist conditions for them to fill your summer with bright color. It's not hard to grow these beautiful, varied flowers, and it's a shame that the carnation has for the most part been turned into a "florist" flower, for the joys of growing this beautiful plant in your own garden or greenhouse are unmatched.

Cooking With Flowers

Please remember that some flowers are not safe to eat: know what you are eating. Also, florist shop flowers are for the most part treated with chemicals, so don't eat these. Eat only flowers which are pesticide and chemical-free.

Whenever I tell someone that I'm cooking with flowers, they look at me in that wondering way—as if they aren't sure whether I'm joking or not. Many haven't even heard of such a thing, and the ones who have think it's mainly a decorative endeavor (garnish for a salad or drink). Actually, flowers (the edible kind), have exciting and varied tastes and textures which add zest and even health benefits. For years I've candied violets, made lavender bud cookies, and added chopped chrysanthemum petals to soups. I've also made dandelion jelly and wine, which is quite a welcome treat on cold winter nights. There are actually about five flavor variations which flowers fall into; very flavorful, mildly flavorful, sweet, slightly bitter, and very mild. The carnation falls into the very flavorful category. It has a spicy bite. What do you do with it? Add the petals to salads, soups, or sandwiches. I like to add the red to herbal vinegars because it adds a pretty pink sparkle to the finished product. The clove-scented varieties add something special to sweets. Here, I share a few of my favorite recipes using carnations:

Carnation Butter

½ pound sweet butter, room temperature

1¼ cups carnation petals, chopped

2–3 tablespoons milk

Whip or blend petals into butter until well mixed. Press butter into a pretty container or server. Cover tightly and store in refrigerator about a week before serving to let the petals impart their flavor to the butter. Good served on banana bread or shortbread.

Carnation and Lavender Sugar

This floral sugar can be used in cakes, puddings, or sugar cookies. Take a 1-quart, sterilized mason jar, half-full of white granulated sugar. Fill the rest with 2 parts carnation petals and 1 part lavender buds. Pour this into a bowl and mix well, then return to the mason jar and close tightly. Leave the jar sealed 1–2 weeks, shaking every three days. Spread out the con-

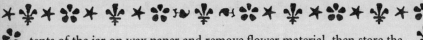

tents of the jar on wax paper and remove flower material, then store the sugar in the jar in a cool, dry place. Sprinkle on cookies or desserts.

Carnation Jam

¾ cup boiling water
1 cup carnation petals, chopped
5¾ cups granulated sugar
1½ cups water
1 (¾-ounce) package of powdered pectin

Have 6–8 sterilized jelly jars on hand. Pour boiling water over carnation petals. Mix remaining water with powdered pectin (such as Sure-Jell). Bring water-pectin to boil over high heat. Add carnation petals and sugar. Stir constantly. Bring to a full rolling boil and boil for one minute. Fill jars to within 2" of the top. Wipe edges, cover with lids. Screw bands tightly. Invert jars for five minutes, then stand upright. Check seals after one hour. If jars haven't sealed, place in a boiling water bath fifteen minutes.

And That's Not All

The Victorians had an obsession with flowers, and created many ways to add them to daily life. They even adopted the use of the nosegay to add hidden messages of sentiment, and fragrance. The nosegay is simply a small scented bouquet (usually no taller than 6") which can easily be hand-carried or pinned onto a blouse or lapel.

Create a tiny nosegay of carnations by gathering a bunch of the smaller blooms. Cut the stem ends short and even. Tie together, wrap ends with a piece of wet paper towel. Cover the paper towel tightly and completely with tin foil. Take a paper doily and wrap around the stem and tie with a pretty ribbon.

CARLY WALL is a midwestern gardener and aromatherapist. She has written a book called *Flower Secrets Revealed: Using Flowers to Heal, Beautify and Energize Your Life*, A.R.E. Press.

Specialty Gardens

Growing Organic Garlic for Home and Market

Tips for Growing Hot Peppers

Asian Vegetables

Storing Seeds

Growing Organic Garlic for Home and Market

By Tim King

Garlic is a high-value crop that is well-suited to home gardens and small market gardening enterprises. It, like every crop, has a few cultural idiosyncrasies that make it interesting to grow. Once you learn those, and have a workable marketing strategy in place, garlic can become a respectable addition to your market basket of produce.

The most important thing for prospective northern growers to know is to plant in the fall, not in the spring! There have been reports of successful spring-planted garlic as far north as Jamestown, North Dakota. In general, though, if your soil is frozen into March, you will have a better chance of harvesting dry garlic if you fall plant.

If you live in a section of the country with very hot summers, fall planting is also advisable. Recomended planting dates in California range from September through November for the desert valleys to November through February for the Santa Carla Valley.

For the best results, plant garlic 4–6 weeks before freeze-up. This gives it plenty of time to develop a healthy root system before frozen ground halts growth.

Why does garlic have a different rhythm than almost everything else in your garden, you ask? Garlic, like June-bearing strawberries, has an internal sundial. That sundial is set to the seasonal cadences that dance around the long days of summer solstice. When garlic leaves pierce the cold soil surface in early spring, they immediately begin to collect nutrients from the soil and energy from the Sun. They can get busy photosynthesizing more quickly if they've got a set of fall grown roots. They photosynthesize as long as the daylight hours increase. When the summer solstice arrives, followed by slightly shortening days, garlic leaves shut down their light and nutrient gathering functions. Then the bulb takes over and nutrients and energy are transferred underground. Within six weeks of the solstice, the leaves are largely brown and useless and, if you've treated your garlic right, your garden will bless you with a harvest of fat bulbs.

There are a cantankerous few who insist on experimenting with spring planting in cold climates. If you must be one of those, be prepared to have nice looking, vigorous leaves, but poorly developed, wet, and unmarketable bulbs.

Seed Bed Preparation

Garlic needs a weed-free environment to thrive. The flat, low leaf of garlic is a poor sunlight receptor. Weeds easily out-compete it. The best way to accomplish a weed-free seed bed is to fallow or green manure it the summer prior to planting. A clean bed can also be established by growing a well-weeded row crop, such as carrots, where you plan to plant garlic next year. Most people I know plant garlic in beds, rather than rows. If you're going to cultivate with a tractor, however, you may want to consider row plantings of garlic.

To prepare a bed, plant buckwheat about 3' wide by the length you desire. You may consider planting the buckwheat early and letting it start to go to seed. Then, till it under with a rototiller. If the soil is moist, you can get a second crop of green manure before frost. David Stern of the Garlic Seed Foundation (GSF), recommends a seeding rate of 70 percent per acre for buckwheat.

You may create a weed problem by letting the buckwheat go to seed. However, the annual buckwheat weed, which is easy to pull, is preferable to annual and perennial grasses, or many of the other weeds that are fond of your garden. The buckwheat will even choke some of those weeds out.

In addition to suppressing other weeds, the buckwheat adds much-needed organic matter to the soil. Garlic loves a high organic content. Build the humus up in your garlic beds with buckwheat or other organic matter.

The GSF suggests rotating garlic ground with legumes to replace the nitrogen used by the garlic. A leguminous green manure could add organic matter as well as nitrogen. Winter rye, an excellent weed suppressant, might also be used, although when it is well established, it is hard to till under with a rototiller.

Sheet composting of leaves or other material may be a good alternative to living green manures.

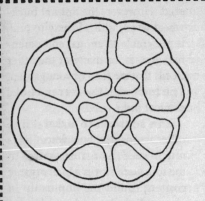

Cross section of ripe softneck garlic

Simply spread the organic matter evenly over the soil and till it in well in advance of planting to achieve proper decomposition and nutrient development.

Selecting a Variety

There is about one more garlic variety then there are hairs on your dog. The chorus of varieties come in two general groups—topsetting or softneck. You may find softnecks referred to as "artichoke types" and hardnecks may be called "ophios," after their Latin subspecies name, *ophioscorodon*. Hardnecks may also be referred to as "bolting" garlics.

Topsetting garlic grows little bulbuls on a stiff stem, or scape, during the early portion of the summer. Bulbuls are great finger food and may actually have commercial potential. Softnecks don't have bulbuls.

A number of seed catalogues carry garlic bulbs, but only a few tell you if the variety is topsetting or softneck. Locating a variety that grows well in your area is an experimental process. California Early and California Late, which are offered in many catalogues, probably won't grow well if you have to fall plant. Since garlic responds to the length of day, these varieties will think they are still in southern California and will be confused by endless June days.

Find a variety that has been grown successfully in your area, or at least in your general latitude. Then experiment with it for a few years to see if it works for you. If the variety does well, it will actually change slightly in color and taste as it makes itself at home in your garden's microclimate. GSF claims that hardnecks do better than softnecks in the north country. That seems to be only partly true, as some northern growers have had some success with softnecks.

In areas where there is little or no garlic grown, obtaining large quantities of seed stock at moderate prices is difficult. Although that is a problem, it is also an entrepreneurial opportunity. If you are one of the savvy first garlic producers in your area, you can sell garlic seed stock to the growing numbers of garlic enthusiasts who want to plant their own.

Planting

Garlic bulbs and cloves come in different sizes and shapes, so estimating how much garlic you can plant in a specific garden spot is educated guessing. An acre of garlic requires between 700 and 1,000 pounds of cloves. Plan using between three and four pounds of cloves for every 100' of row.

Individual cloves of garlic are planted, not the entire bulb. Some growers don't break the bulbs up until they put them in the ground. Others break them up before planting. Both groups claim their system is more labor-efficient. Most people plant garlic, even in large quantities, by hand, although some enterprising growers in northeastern states have developed semi-automated planting systems.

Timing your planting is critical. "The clove of garlic sends its roots down when the tip hits moist soil. The clove is a modified storage leaf and has only has so much energy. Green above ground in the fall is wasted energy," Stern will tell you.

To avoid green above ground, plant no more than six weeks before freeze up. Use only medium and large cloves that are healthy, have their parchment intact, and are worm-free for planting. Place individual cloves 4"–6" apart, with the root side down. One method is to plant them in a trench twice the depth of the length of the clove. Push the cloves gently into the soil so they will stay topside up as you back fill the trench. You can dig your trench with the corner of a hoe in lose soil.

Stern's experience is that it is hard to plant garlic too deep. He plants 3" deep, and then throws soil alongside the plants during summer cultivation, adding another 3".

Fall mulching prevents spring frost heaving. Some growers suggest removing hay mulch in spring so the soil warms quickly and emergence is hastened. That approach adds labor. Some garden sites not prone to frost heaving may be able to get away without any fall mulching. If you choose not to mulch, proceed with caution.

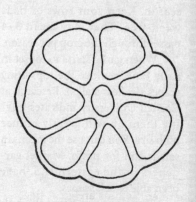

Cross section of ripe topsetting garlic

Mulch prevents frost heaving by evening out soil temperatures during spring thaws. Heaving soil tears roots and can destroy your crop.

Garlic has modestly high water requirements. If you need to water any crops, you'll need to water garlic. Both overhead and drip irrigation work well.

Culture

Water and weed are the by-words for successful garlic growing. Although root systems vary with the variety, garlic roots are fairly shallow. Keep your beds moist, but not water-logged. Keeping the mulch on or replacing it after emergence will help retain moisture. Stop watering garlic in early July, about 2–3 weeks before harvest.

Since the leaves are small and narrow, the plants can't take any weed competition, even late in the season. Keep your rows or beds weed-free. That may mean 3–4 passes through the crop per season.

When garlic starts to topset in early June, remove the topsetting scapes (leafless stalks). Research at Cornell University indicates leaving them on will greatly reduce bulb size. You can use the greens in salads and for pesto. Market gardeners in the eastern U.S. have been able to sell scapes.

Some growers plant the bulbuls from topsetting plants as a safeguard against losing a variety.

These are planted away from the main bed to avoid disease problems, according to Stern.

Most growers report few or no insect problems with garlic. California, where most of the commercial garlic in the U.S. is grown, reports garlic as having many of the same insect problems as onions. Don't plant garlic where onions were planted the year before.

Garlic does appear to have some virus problems. Occasionally there can be some crop loss due to it. There is no clear way to prevent this.

You may also have to deal with varmints. Some Minnesota deer have developed a taste for young garlic shoots. New York deer don't have such civilized tastes, according to Stern, and have yet to bother a garlic crop.

New York gardeners, however, have developed a market for tender garlic greens. Harvesting the greens by deer or humans precludes harvesting market-sized bulbs.

Harvest

As the bulb expands and absorbs the nutrients from the leaves, the leaves yellow and then turn brown. When they are around two-thirds brown, or when the neck of the plant is nearly dry, it's time to dig. Don't wait too long, or the cloves will start to separate or shatter. Stern suggests digging a few bulbs as the ripening process proceeds. "Always trial dig. To dig your crop you want to see full tight skins, and when you cut the bulb you want a very slight pulling away from the center," he says.

You can dig garlic with a spading fork. Some growers use an old one-row potato digger pulled behind a tractor. Be careful not to injure the bulbs. If you do, they won't store well. There are a blessed few who can actually hand pull garlic. It all depends on the condition of your soil.

Ron Engeland, from Washington State, the author of the excellent book *Growing Great Garlic*, doesn't trial dig or count the number of brown leaves. He counts the number of green leaves left on a plant.

However you do it, proceed with caution. Garlic harvested too late will begin to break through the "wrappers" around the cloves and start to fall apart in the ground.

Stern says New York growers are washing the garlic right after pulling, rather then waiting till the dirt is dry and brushing it off. Ron Engeland opposes washing, and hand-cleans each bulb after it dries. He says washing reduces quality. Engeland gets assured quality. Stern gets reduced labor and insists he loses little or no quality. There is never one absolutely right answer in farming. You must experiment and determine what works on your farm.

Cure the garlic in a shaded, moderately-humid area for a few weeks. Then you can brush the dirt off, clip the roots and tops, and clean it up for market.

One of the advantages of garlic is that it is not particularly perishable. If you have a good harvest, it can be stored for months before you eat or sell it.

Long term storage is best at 65 percent relative humidity, and temperatures just above freezing. Garlic does lose up to 15 percent of its fieldweight during curing. If you sell uncured garlic, let your customers know it will continue to dry down and that it should be stored in a ventilated area.

Marketing

Most of the garlic sold in the U.S. is grown in California. Some very cheap garlic is being imported from China. You can easily compete with the low quality of this imported product by emphasizing the freshness, color, or size of your locally grown, unique variety. Don't be willing to easily accept the low wholesale prices that Californian and Chinese garlic brings. Your garlic will be better.

You can also focus on specialty markets. Chefs in urban areas want fresh garlic and they use lots of it. If you can find a variety that peels easily, chefs are buying large quantities of pre-peeled cloves. You can also look at the health food store market. If you are an organic grower, you can obtain a premium price. Some growers sell braids with a fair amount of success. Other people are developing catalogues to service the mail-order market with seeds, braids, and other garlic gift items.

Resources

The Garlic Seed Foundation newsletter *The Garlic Press* is an excellent source of useful, humorous, and arcane information for new and experienced growers. It's a bargain at $10 per year and can be obtained by sending a check to GSF, Rose Valley Farm, Rose, NY 14542-0149.

Ron Engelund's book *Growing Great Garlic* covers everything from philosophy to marketing and can be obtained by writing to Filaree Farm at Rt. 2, Box 162 Okanogan, WA 98840.

Louis Van Deven's book, *Onions and Garlic Forever*, is a no-nonsense gardeners' approach to growing garlic and all of its allium relatives, including onions, leeks, and and a mysterious chive-like, cousin called a kurrat.

Incomplete List of Seed Sources

FILAREE FARM
Route 2, Box 162
Okanogan, WA 98840

GARDEN CITY SEEDS
13254 Red Crow Road
Victor, MT 59875

GREG ANTHONY'S
P.O. Box 407
South Prairie, WA 98385

JOHNNY'S SELECTED SEEDS
Fosshill Road
Albion, ME 04910

MERRIFIELD GARLIC MERCHANTS
Rd. 1, Box 184
Auburn, NY 13021

NICHOLS NURSERY
1190 N. Pacific Highway
Albany, OR 97321

❖∞❖

TIM KING is an organic market gardener, growing garlic with the help of his wife, Janice, and son, Colin. He is also an agricultural and community journalist. If you would like more information about organic garlic, Tim can be contacted by mail at RR #2, Maple Hill, Long Prairie, MN 56347.

Tips for Growing Hot Peppers

By Michael VeSeart

Five years ago, I started growing hot peppers for no other reason than to see if I could grow anything all. You see, I grew up in Los Angeles, and I've always felt that I knew more about the beach and surf scene than the gardening scene. I have always had a passion for hot peppers, and like a growing number of collectors, I have assembled a rather extensive collection of pepper sauces from around the world. So one fine day I found myself thinking seriously that I could and would make my own pepper sauce. I began experimenting with recipes, and then cajoling my friends and family to try all my latest concoctions. Finally, I felt that I had come up with a recipe that satisfied both my friends and me. Well, there you have it. Bang! Here I am in the "peppa sauce biz."

First, I learned that in order to make pepper sauce, I needed the peppers in abundance. Okay, I have the space for a garden; I guess I'll grow some peppers. Not a problem. The very next thing I learned is that everybody has a better way to grow anything you are growing. I also learned to listen only to those gardeners who have nice-looking gardens themselves. You know, just like you wouldn't want a haircut from someone with "bad" hair.

I won't elaborate on my—let's call it "first"—growing year, except to say it was fun, it was a true learning experience, and it *was* productive. My first year was a small adventure into the wide world of gardening. "Peppers and pumpkins, that's all I grow," I would boast to the neighbors. (Remember, they all have a better way, but still want to know how you do it.) By the way, I grew pumpkins because their leaves are a wonderful, rich green and I figured that if the peppers were a failure, at least my daughter and I could carve jack-o-lanterns at the end of the growing season.

Needless to say, I also learned about many things, including: water, weather, weeds, wilt, work, and worms. Actually, I learned a whole host of words that I hadn't thought about until I began my exploration of gardening and hot peppers in particular. What I learned then now seems simple. You usually can find answers to questions in two re-

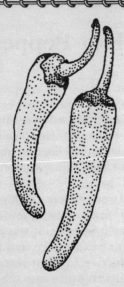

As my garden gets bigger each year, I discover new "tricks" to make it easier and even more productive than the previous year. Perhaps that's what "growing" is all about. Anyway, here are some of my tried and true tricks:

Journals

Writing down even the simplest information helps in many ways. It can help make astute comparisons of plants, soil conditions, and start-up times, or it can be an easy jog to the memory, for things that you thought you would never forget. For example: "When did I start the seedlings? When did I actually put the plants in the ground? When was that late April freeze that killed everything?" All of this information becomes incredibly important as you continue your gardening year after year.

liable ways. One is to read books from your local library. Stay away from complicated dissertations about gardens; I always look for the photographs, pictures, and graphs that are clear and readable—the more straightforward the better. The other way is to go to a local, well-established nursery and ask questions there. I have found this strategy to be an especially enlightening way to find the answers to a great number of my simple and not-so-simple questions. An informed nursery staff can not only answer your questions, but they also can give you options. *Lots* of options, with humor and insight and many years of experience. Options to deal with all those "w" words—and words that begin with every other letter too!

Weeds

It's back-breaking, tiresome work. I am blessed to live in a neighborhood with lots of families with children, and I have always believed that kids need some good, old-fashioned, regular work to do, especially during the summer months when things get just too dull for them to bear. I "hire" these neighborhood kids to do the weeding. Some important things to keep in mind before hiring children to work are: make certain their parents know you are hiring them; make certain you are very precise with your instructions to them; and always keep an eye on them and the work that they are doing. Make certain that they know the difference between a weed and one of your plants. You need to make some simple agreements, like how much they will be paid, and whether their work will be paid by the hour or whether they will just work until the job is finished for a set fee. Then, of course, I make sure I hire the most reliable kids over and over again. Word spreads fast in our neighborhood, and I usually have abundance of workers for my garden.

Water

This is one of those "I have the better way" issues. All I can say is this: I *always* water from above. It just seems to be the natural thing to do. It makes the plants look fresh, clean, and happy. A happy plant is a productive plant. In New Mexico and throughout the Southwest, water is the great elixir, the cure-all, the remedy for all ailments, the healer, a panacea. I can honestly say that I've tried a variety of ways to water: in the furrows, between rows of plants, drip systems two or three times a day, one big watering once a day, etc. The method that seems to work best for my garden is a gentle spray from a 5' mounted sprinkler twice a day (morning and evening). That's it.

Bugs

Yazow! This is the big question, that I'm not sure will ever be really answered. The way I see it: Live with them, kill them, or make them go live in your neighbor's garden. Here is where nursery people are at their best. They know countless schemes to achieve all three options. These days I mostly live with the bugs—although will someone please write to me and tell me how to keep those pesky aphids off my seedlings? In my modest garden, bugs and other pests haven't taken more than their share—yet. I have found that a little netting keeps the birds from pecking at the tender plants and the netting also helps keep the damaging rays of our hot, New Mexican Sun off the plants, at least in their formative stages.

Compost

Composting has turned into a real joy for me. I feel that I've gotten a handle on it. I've built an original composting mechanism in the corner of the garden and even in the dead darkness of winter, there is a sublime feeling of Earth-care that comes over me as I trek out to the compost heap to put more "stuff" on the pile.

Cross Pollination

A curious thing I've noticed as this gardening fascination has taken hold is cross pollination. I must grow at least forty or so varieties of peppers. I can also guess that least thirty or so of these so-called varieties are beginning to look and taste exactly alike.

Picking the Peppers

Picking hot peppers is an art all unto itself. My daughter Josephine helps me. "Only pick the totally red ones," I say to her. She says in return, "But Papa, they burn my fingers." I try to remind her never to rub her eyes, and of course tell her that there is no cure for the burn. In fact, the searing burn is the rea-

son that I've gotten myself into this business. Let's face it—I'm joyously, happily addicted. Like all bona fide pepperheads.

I've had fun growing hot peppers, and along with the enjoyment has come a marked improvement in all my gardening skills. In fact, my neighbors often come by and ask me how I do it. I can proudly say that I grow all the peppers for the sauce that I make. Each year that I've made my pepper sauce my production has expanded and I have never had a bottle of sauce left at the beginning of the next season. All my friends like it and I have a good time while learning about gardening.

How can you go wrong? Try it! But don't rub your eyes …

MICHAEL VESEART is a theater technician and artist living in New Mexico. In addition to pepper growing, his hobbies include fishing with his daughter. Michael produces limited batches of his hot sauce for sale annually. If you are interested in trying VeSeart's New Mexican Pepper Sauce, Michael can be contacted at (505) 345-6973.

Place
First Class
Stamp Here

Llewellyn Publications
P.O. Box 64383-K915RC
St. Paul, MN 55164-0383

Asian Vegetables

By Deborah Duchon

The plants that grow in America's gardens reflect the diversity of our culture. A typical gardener cultivates plants native to several continents. A few examples are corn, native to North America; potatoes, native to South America; cabbage, native to Europe; and okra, native to Africa.

Until recently, however, the vegetables of Asia were not available to American gardeners, probably because immigration from that area of the world was historically low. But things are changing. In the past twenty years, immigrants and refugees from nearly every nation on that far-off continent have moved to many different areas of the United States, and they have brought wonderful things with them to add to our cultural mix. Among those things are vegetables rich in flavor, texture, and nutrition. Some are variations on familiar plants, such as garlic chives and eggplant, while others, such as bitter melon, seem brand new to us.

These plants are not always available in mainstream garden centers or seed catalogs. The best source for starts may be by cultivating friendships with Asian immigrants in your area. Another source is your closest Oriental market, which offers fresh and exotic produce as well as information and possible seeds or starts.

Although these plants may look new and unfamiliar, as gardeners we can see them as part of the larger scheme of things. They are, after all, simply "new" varieties of plants we are already familiar with and know how to grow. For instance, if you examine the leaves of bitter melon, one of the strangest-looking plants I've seen, you see that it really *is* a melon. It requires the same growing conditions as any old cantaloupe or watermelon. Because the fruit is small (about the size of a cucumber), it can be grown on a trellis to save space. Culturing these plants should not be any more difficult than any other vegetables.

If you are good at growing peas, you should be good at growing Chinese long beans (also called yard-long beans) which can grow to 30" in length! They're better eating at a modest 12"–18", however. Prepare them by cutting into 1" lengths and boiling or adding to stir fry.

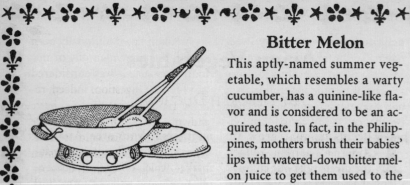

This article will introduce you to only a few of these new vegetables, in the hope that you will experiment with one or more next gardening season.

Japanese Eggplant

Eggplant is an important staple in Asian cuisine, which tends to be lower in meat than Western diets. It adds bulk and a meaty texture to vegetarian dishes. Long, skinny Japanese eggplants have a reputation for being creamier, finer-grained, and less bitter than our bulky familiar counterpart. Thai eggplant, rounder and light green or lavender, is naturally spicy. All Oriental eggplants have a thin, delicate skin that doesn't need to be peeled.

Oriental eggplants are grown easily, needing the same conditions as any other eggplant, such as full Sun. Seeds are available from a wide variety of seed catalogs and other sources. They are good deep-fried, grilled, or braised.

Bitter Melon

This aptly-named summer vegetable, which resembles a warty cucumber, has a quinine-like flavor and is considered to be an acquired taste. In fact, in the Philippines, mothers brush their babies' lips with watered-down bitter melon juice to get them used to the flavor. The bitter flavor is thought to be cooling in hot weather.

A vine, the plant is generally grown on trellises, and is edible at all stages of growth. Even the tendrils are eaten. Bitter melon is eaten while green. Once it turns yellow, it is overripe. The darker the fruit, the more bitter the taste. It is eaten cooked, cut in half with seeds and interior membranes removed. Blanch or salt the flesh to remove some of the bitterness, and add to soup or stir fry. Even if you never develop a taste for bitter melon, its unusual appearance will make it a real conversation piece in your garden!

Bok Choy and Napa

This is closely related to our familiar head cabbage, but with a mustardy flavor. Other Asian versions of cabbage are: *choi sum* (Chinese flowering cabbage), which has slender stalks and delicate yellow flowers, which are cooked as part of the vegetable; and napa, or Chinese cabbage, known for its thin, delicate leaves and slightly sweet flavor. To stir fry, cut stems into ½" pieces. Stir fry stems for one minute, leaves for 30 seconds, then add 1 tablespoon of liquid (such as broth), cover and cook for an additional 2–3 minutes.

Asian cabbages form the basis of most (but not all) pickles commonly found in Japan, Korea, and China. In fact, the national dish of Korea is *kim chee*, a pungent fermented cabbage dish which is served at nearly every meal. To make your own kim chee, see the recipe at the end of this article.

Daikon Radish

These huge Asian radishes are juicy, with a fresh, clean, even sweet, taste. There are two major varieties: Japanese radish, which is long and slender, and the Korean daikon, which is shorter and stouter. They look like large, white carrots, and should be eaten while young. They get tough, woody, and even musty-tasting as they age. In Korean cuisine, they are shredded and added to soups and sauces. They can be added to stir fry, too, and with a short cooking time will retain their flavor. The greens, too, can be braised or stir-fried. Even the flowers can be eaten, making this a highly productive, no-waste crop that yields a useful edible both above and below ground.

Daikon has traditionally been served to complement oily or raw foods, because it was considered good for the digestion. Indeed, recent laboratory studies have shown it to be a significant source of diastase, amylase, and esterase, all enzymes found in the human digestive tract. Grated daikon, then, is good for one's digestion when added to a meal, but it must be eaten raw and grated within thirty minutes of serving, as half of the enzymes are lost in that period of time. Research done at Tokyo's College of Pharmacy has shown that daikon juice inhibits the formation of carcinogenic chemicals that form in the stomach when one eats processed foods, so raw daikon may reduce the risk of some cancers.

Burdock, or Gobo

If your garden is bedeviled by this common weed, you'll be pleased to know that it is considered a delicacy in Japan, where it is known as *gobo* and has been cultivated for nearly 1000 years. A biennial, the edible root is best eaten the first year, before the plant sends up its flower stalk, prickly burrs and all. The root of the second year plant is tough, woody, and virtually inedible. The first year plant resembles rhubarb, with large, heart-shaped, dark green leaves and thick stems.

Wild burdock, although abundant and certainly edible, has a shorter root and stronger flavor than the domesticated varieties. Because of its growing reputation as a valuable medicinal plant, seeds of domesticated burdock are becoming widely available from such herb specialists as the Richter catalog (1-905-640-6677). Although it is becoming trendy among American herbalists, burdock has been used in the Orient as a blood-purifier and general tonic since ancient times. It is a good source of B vitamins, and is usually prescribed to clear up skin disease and gain strength after an illness.

Burdock root has a nice "rooty" flavor, and can be prepared much like potatoes. You may cube it, boil for 30–40 minutes (add a little baking soda to the water), drain, mash, add chopped onion, and fry in patties, for a tasty side dish. Another way to prepare burdock is to make *kinpira*, a popular side dish in Japan, usually eaten in fall and winter. To make kinpira, see the recipe at the end of this article.

Kim Chee

There are many recipes for kim chee, varying in spicy hotness and pungency. Here is one recipe, adapted from *Cooking with Japanese Foods*, by John Belleme and Jan Belleme, Avery Publishing Group, Inc. Garden City Park, NY, 1993.

    1   large head Chinese cabbage
         salt for rubbing cabbage
    1   small carrot, slivered
    1   teaspoon minced garlic
    ½   cup minced scallion
  1½–2   teaspoons cayenne pepper
    ½   apple, peeled, cored and coarsely grated
    1½   teaspoons sea salt
   1–2   teaspoons ginger, freshly grated
    ⅔   cup water

Cut the head of Chinese cabbage into quarters. Discard the tough core. Rub tablespoons of salt into the cabbage, concentrating on the thicker bottom portion, and using less on the upper leaves. Place the cabbage in a bowl, cover with a plate or other lid that will press down, and add about

5 pounds of weight on top. Press for 8–10 hours. If desired, you may then rinse the cabbage to remove excess salt. Gently squeeze out liquid. Cut the cabbage into 1" square chunks and set aside.

Combine carrot, garlic, scallion, cayenne pepper, apple, sea salt, ginger, and water. Add the mixture to the cabbage and toss well. Place all into a wide-mouthed jar or crock and let sit in a cool place for 3–5 days before eating. After this time, keep in the refrigerator. Will be good for about two weeks if refrigerated.

Kinpira

This recipe is adapted from *Cooking with Japanese Foods*.

    3 burdock roots
    1 large carrot
       sesame oil
    ½ teaspoon salt
    2 tablespoons Japanese sweet rice wine, divided
    1 tablespoon soy sauce
       pinch cayenne

Scrub burdock roots well, and cut into thin, 2"-long julienne strips. Immediately submerge in cold water. Cut carrot similarly, but a little thicker. Heat teaspoons of light or dark sesame oil in a skillet or heavy sauce pan. Drain burdock and sauté over medium heat for several minutes. Lower heat, add a little water if necessary to prevent scorching, cover and cook for 10–15 minutes, or until burdock is nearly tender. Add carrots, salt, and 1 tablespoon Japanese cooking wine (*mirin*) and sauté briefly. Cover and let cook, checking often to be sure that vegetables are not sticking. When burdock and carrots are cooked dry, add the remaining tablespoon of mirin, soy sauce (*shoyu*), and cayenne, if desired. Toss, cover, and cook briefly until tender, adding 2 tablespoons of water, if necessary.

DEBORAH DUCHON is an ethnobotanist studying in Atlanta, Georgia. She has published articles in several magazines and newsletters, and is the founder of the Wild Foods Forum.

Storing Seeds

By Rhonda Massingham Hart

Excerpted from Dirt-Cheap Gardening © *1995 by Rhonda Massingham Hart with permission from Storey Communications, Inc., Tel.: 800-441-5700.*

Y ou can find good, cheap containers for storing seeds around your house, including old prescription bottles, glass jars with screw-on lids, and plastic film canisters. These containers all protect from outside moisture and pests. If you have some very small packets of seeds, label and store them within a larger container.

Seeds must be kept dry and cool, otherwise they rot or sprout. Humidity of less than 60 percent, and temperatures between 32°F and 41°F are ideal. Add a packet of desiccant powder (such as silica gel) or powdered milk, to combat high humidity. The gel absorbs best.

Vegetable Seeds: Storage Life and Viability

SEED	YEARS	SEED	YEARS
Asparagus	3	Muskmelons	5
Beans	3	Okra	2
Beets	4	Onions	1
Broccoli	5	Parsley	1
Brussels Sprouts	5	Parsnips	1
Cabbage	5	Peas	3
Carrots	3	Peppers	2
Cauliflower	5	Pumpkins	4
Celery	5	Radishes	5
Corn	2	Spinach	5
Cucumbers	5	Squash	4
Eggplant	5	Tomatoes	4
Lettuce	3		

Hi-Tech Gardening and Building

What Is Hydro-organic Gardening?

Artificial Lighting

Harvesting Organic Data from the Internet

Indoor Air Pollution: Problems and Solutions

What Is Hydro-organic Gardening?

By Gilbert Schoenstein

A substantial portion of our precious gardening hours are often dedicated to preparing the soil and reacting to the variety of problems that can arise from it. Unfortunately, the soil acts as host to guests we gardeners find irreverent to our wishes to grow plants for our pleasure. From the tiny nematode and the ubiquitous weed seed to the gopher, in addition to other accompanying soil-toil and trouble, there is no shortage to the tests of a gardener's patience.

Hydro-organics, growing plants using a soil-less medium with a liquid organic solution, is a means to overcome these problems. Here are some reasons to consider adding hydro-organics to your gardening regimen.

Reasons to Go Hydro-organic

- If your soil has been chemically gardened, leading to a build-up of toxic salts and pesticide residues.
- Solvents, oil, etc. have been dumped on a potential garden plot, or it was subjected to severe compaction.
- You don't have soil to begin with. This is true for people who have rocky, hardpan clay, and sandy ground. Also for those who live in apartments without a yard. Hydro-organics can grow more plants using minimal space. It is ideal for indoors, balconies, and rooftops.
- Less time and labor needed. Hydro-organics acts with a sterile medium, so you will never, ever have to pull a single weed. There are no soil-dwelling pests such as snails, slugs, moles, etc.
- Soil has varying traits. The pH in soil can vary from one plot of ground to the next, resulting in inconsistent plant performance. Hydro-organic mediums are uniform throughout, simplifying pH control. Adjustment of pH is difficult once plants are in the ground. With hydro-organics, addition of a concentrated pH adjuster will instantly correct

an unacceptable pH reading. Soil porosity varies, therefore root systems receive inconsistent amounts of air and water.

❧ Greater and quicker yields. Hydro-organic mediums can support far more fine feeder roots per area than the most well-nurtured soil. There is little competition between plant root systems for available air and nutrients, thus tighter plant spacing is possible, increasing yields. With this physiologically different root structure and an air-rich medium, a complete organic nutrient diet is recirculated to the roots. More of the plants' energy is spent on leaf, fruit, and flower production than on root growth and pulling nutrients into the plant.

❧ Greater nutrient control. In soil, once you have added your nutrients, you are stuck with the results. In the flowering stage, for example, the amount of fruit and flowers can be significantly reduced with too much nitrogen, usually from animal manures. Hydro-organics allows the gardener to simply drain the nutrients out of the reservoir and adjust the recipe to make a quick recovery. Nutrient intensity can be measured by a ppm (parts per million) meter. Readings can be taken to record a desired plant response, and used as the standard for on-going recharging of the nutrient solution.

❧ It's easy to work with plants in hydro-organic systems because they are often set up at waist level. This also makes hydro-organics more popular with the elderly and disabled.

Benefits for Commercial Growers

❧ There is no need for capital for weed control.

❧ There is no need to wait for certification. Many organic certifying groups stipulate that you can not be considered organic for a three-year period from the date chemicals were last used. This discourages growers from going organic. Hydro-organics starts with perlite, vermiculite, and peat moss, all recognized organic mediums.

❧ Hydro-organics outproduces per acre what can be grown in soil. Hydro-organic tomatoes, for example, can produce 12–30 times more fruit per acre.

❧ Hydro-organics, in conjunction with greenhouse use of HID lighting, opens up an untapped area of the produce market—off-season organics.

Ecological Reasons to Try Hydro-organics

❖ Hydro-organics is more efficient in use of nutrients and water. It utilizes recirculating watering systems (in which nutrient is pumped to the medium, caught, and returned to reservoir). In soil, nutrients and water are lost as they seep below the root zone.

❖ Hydro-organic food can be grown in the region in which it is to be consumed. After all, a head of broccoli travels an average of 1,300 miles before it is eaten. This great waste of fuels, etc. can be significantly reduced. This harvest to consumption proximity also translates to an increase in freshness and nutrition.

❖ Less space is required. A hydro-organic farm with far greater yields could ultimately decrease the need to farm in sensitive areas, that could otherwise be used for native plants and animal habitat.

Hydro-organics Disadvantages

❖ Start-up costs are greater than conventional organic methods.

❖ Many systems require electricity, albeit a very minor draw from submersible pumps and/or air pumps.

❖ The pH can fluctuate on a daily to weekly basis and must be monitored, whereas in soil, pH remains much more stable, and once it is on target, it doesn't need to be fussed with.

❖ Due to pump failure, plants can be stranded without water.

❖ Working with soil is a very gratifying and wonderful process. There is something irresistably enjoyable about getting dirt under our gardening fingernails. Yet the same wonder and satisfaction that comes with growing plants as can be experienced with the simplicity of hydro-organics.

GILBERT SCHOENSTEIN is a freelance garden magazine writer who has devoted many hours to hydro-organic experimentation. He is the owner of Gilby's farm, America's first certified organic hydroponic farm.

Artificial Lighting

By Gilbert Schoenstein

I magine a garden giving you gardenias in full bloom, a ripe plucked mango, a fresh picked tomato, and pungent homegrown basil any time of the year at any latitude, no matter how much snow, wind, or rain is coming down outside. Any plant grown under the Sun can be grown in the "great indoors" with the use of HID (high intensity discharge) lighting.

HID lights can be hung anywhere in the house, garage, or as a supplement to the greenhouse. By choosing the right HID, a gardener can use a bulb with a particular band of light to induce greater flower and fruit yields than what can be produced under sunlight. Other HID bulbs encourage a more compact plant, promoting more green leafy growth. The Sun has obvious advantages, but when it's not available, or specialized plant performance is desired, previously unimagined gardening potentials can be realized with the use of HID lights.

There are two common myths associated with HID lights; one is that they are too expensive, and the other is that they are the same as fluorescent grow lights. Fluores-cent grow lights should be labeled full spectrum. These lights are great for seedlings, but high light-requiring plants (any plant other than house plants) require much more light than they provide. Seedlings left too long under fluorescents stay scrawny and grow very slowly.

HIDs utilize a glass tube within an outer glass envelope. The inner glass tube contains a mixture of up to five different gases, through which electricity is channeled. The three major types of HIDs each have a different blend of gases, each one producing its own range of light color. HIDs are sold with either a ballast that is built into the reflector for the 175- and 250-watt sizes, or they come pre-wired in their own separate metal box for the 400- and 1000-watt sizes. This box is referred to as the remote ballast. Ballasts contain the capacitor, which provides a quick, strong charge of electricity to light the bulb, and the transformer, which transforms the electric current from one voltage to the next. Be careful if buying used parts, because each wattage ballast must match the wattage of the

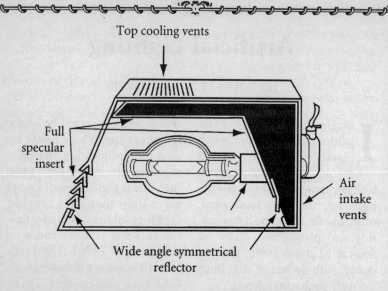

Top cooling vents

Full
specular
insert

Air
intake
vents

Wide angle symmetrical
reflector

*Super Grow Wing HID light with full specular insert, wide angle
symmetrical reflector, top cooling vents and air intake vents*

HID bulb. Each type of bulb must also match the same ballast type.

To get more light for your money, shop for light systems with horizontally-mounted bulbs. HID bulbs do not emit light from the end opposite the socket. Therefore, in vertically aligned systems, light must travel to the reflector first and then down to the plant. Horizontally-mounted bulbs take a direct, shorter route, and hence are brighter in both the center and the edges in the field of coverage. The 175-watt covers a 2' x 2' area, the 250-watt covers 3' x 3', 400-watts cover 5' x 5' and the 1000-watts cover a 10' x 10' area. The field of coverage is considered 20 percent greater for seedlings, low light requiring plants, or for all plants when used to supplement the Sun in a greenhouse.

Reflector designs are very critical, since half of the light is directed upward. The best designs are those that use a double parabolic pattern, where a ridge is directly above the bulb. These designs are used by companies such as Hydrofarm, who make the Super Grow Wing and the Sunburst series of light systems. The double arches used in these systems allow light to bounce out and around the bulb and down toward the plant. Light systems that have only a flat surface above the bulb reflect light back to the bulb, blocking some of it from the plants and causing the bulb to run too hot and burn out prematurely.

Vent ports on the side and top of the reflectors allow heat to escape. Cooling fans can be added to these ports on some systems. These fans mount on the reflector and channel heat out of the room during the summer. In the winter, heat from the bulb can be vented down below the plants for additional warmth.

Tempered glass shields, sometimes called lenses, are available for the better reflectors. Tempered glass keeps more of the damaging heat away from the plants, thus making it possible to lower the light source closer to the plants. Lenses are also an important safety feature. They block any moisture from ever reaching the bulb, which could cause the bulb to rupture.

Hydrofarm's light systems have recently come out with a specular finish insert for their reflectors. This textured surface breaks up the reflected light so there isn't any focused light or light streaks in some areas and less light in others. The new surface is also 25–40 percent more reflective than earlier designs.

Types of High Density Discharge Lights

HID light systems are available in three basic types: metal halide, high pressure sodium, and son agro. Which one will work best for you depends on how much area you want to cover and what your

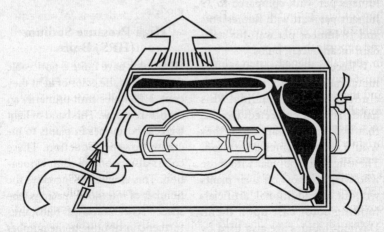

Airflow through Super Grow Wing convection cooling system

plants' needs are. Here is a brief look into each light's uniqueness and its limitations.

Metal Halides

Metal halides produce an abundance of light in the blue spectrum. This color of light is excellent for green leafy growth and keeping plants compact. The average life span is about 10,000 cumulative hours. By this time, the mixture of gases has become ineffective, and the bulb should be replaced. The bulb will light up beyond this time, but due to the gradual decline of light it is not worth your while to wait for the bulb to finally burn out. They are very miserly in their use of power. Compare their lumens (brightness) per unit of energy consumed. Metal halides produce up to 125 lumens per watt, compared to 39 lumens per watt with fluorescents and 18 lumens per watt for standard incandescent bulbs.

Recent developments in the metal halide family of bulbs include the daylight halide. This halide is color corrected. Objects that it illuminates appear as they would on a summer afternoon. These lights are popular with those who want to show off their plants without any additional, artificial-looking color cast upon them. Daylight halides are also used by people with terrariums, and those who need objects illuminated to reveal their "true colors," such as quilters, photographers, painters, and other artists. However, daylight halides are not as bright as the metal halide super bulb. Super metal halides have a noticeable, but slight yellow cast to their light. They are 10 percent brighter than the original metal halide, and require no extra electricity to operate. Of the halides, the super bulb is the best for aggressive growth.

Another new metal halide, which came on the market in 1994, is the Son Agro halide. This bulb has all the brightness of the super metal halide, and the same life span. Its advantage is that it has a wider spectrum than the other metal halides. Its extra 8 percent more orange-red light will induce flowering sooner than the previous models.

High Pressure Sodium (HPS) Bulbs

HPS bulbs have quite a noticeable difference in the color of light they emit. HPS bulbs emit primarily an orange-red glow. This band of light triggers hormones in plants to increase flower production. These colors also promote stem elongation. This elongation increases the number of internode spacings (the space between each leaf bud), thus further contributing to the number of flowering sites.

Not only is this a great flowering light, it has two features that make it a more economical choice. The average life span of HPS bulbs is twice that of metal halides. After 18,000 hours of cumulative use they will actually start to draw more electricity than their rated watts, while gradually producing less light. HPS bulbs are also very efficient. They produce up to 140 lumens per watt. Their disadvantage is they are deficient in the blue spectrum. If a gardener were to start a young plant under a HPS bulb, he would see some impressive vertical growth. In fact, probably too impressive. Most plants grow up thin and lanky, and in no time you will have to prune your plant back before it grows into the light fixture. The exception to this is using a HPS in a greenhouse. Sunlight is high in the blue spectrum, which would offset any stretching caused by HPS bulbs.

Many gardeners start out young plants with a metal halide system (systems include all the essentials: bulb, socket, reflector, cord, and ballast), and as flowering begins they remove the halide bulb and replace it with a HPS "conversion" bulb. Conversion bulbs produce orange-red light, but operate in a halide system. They are available in all sizes for the halide-to-HPS conversion. However, there is only one halide conversion bulb:

the 400-watt halide conversion, which operates in a 400-watt HPS system. It is important to remember to never try mounting a halide bulb in a HPS system or vice-versa. It is guaranteed to burn out the bulb prematurely.

Son Agro

Son agros are somewhat of a hybrid of the halides and HPS bulbs. They are strongest in the orange-red spectrum, with 25 percent more than the HPS bulbs. They also have 30 percent more blue light. This will help offset the stretching one would see using only a high pressure sodium lamp. These are also the brightest and most efficient bulbs. Son agros produce up to 150 lumens per watt. The average life span of a son agro is 16,000 hours. Replacement bulbs should be added after 12,000 hours. Son agros are available in l60-watt, 270-watt, 430-watt, and 1075-watt sizes.

Which Light is Best?

- ✤ For indoors-non greenhouse (mostly non-bloomers): the agro son halide system.

- ✤ For indoors-non greenhouse (flowering/fruiting plants): start with a metal halide system and, at the start of flowering, switch to a HPS conversion bulb. In rooms with limited vertical space this is an especially good path to take. OR use a son agro system for all stages of plant growth.

- For Greenhouse: HPS is considered best for greenhouses. With greenhouse use, the day length can be extended by having the lights come on four hours prior to sunrise and four hours following sunset.

How Much Does It Cost?

A 250-watt agro son halide system costs from about $190.00 to $205.00. HPS systems cost about 12 percent more and son agros cost 25 percent more in their respective size range. Replacement bulbs for the agro son halide cost about $55.00 to $65.00 dollars, electric costs vary from $.04 to $.10 per kilowatt hour, depending on what part of the country you live in. This translates to 3/10 of a cent to $.01 per 100 watts per hour. So a 250-watt light will cost from 1/2 cent to $.02 an hour. This is roughly the same as the cost to run two televisions.

How to Get More Light for Your Dollar

Some utilities offer residents and businesses a choice of rate schedules which can add up to large savings each year. On a peak-off peak schedule, rates are lower after 6 PM and before 12 noon. Rates increase substantially between 12 PM and 6 PM to discourage use during these hours. Grow lights can be successfully run during the off-peak hours at a noticeable savings.

Another rate schedule works on a seasonal basis. This benefits people who use less electricity in the summer and more in the winter. Winter is considered November through April. Many HID gardeners only use these lights in the darker, colder months. This schedule does have a higher monthly meter fee, but still may be worth your while.

An additional drop in hourly rates is available for low-income utility customers.

A free computer rate analysis can be printed up to make the decision easier for you. Decide carefully, as you cannot reverse a schedule change for a full year from the date of the changeover.

Light Movers

Light movers can double, even triple, the coverage that the same stationary light could do with only a negligible increase in energy consumption. Mover motors draw only 10 watts or less. Light movers not only spread the light, but the heat as well. This allows the light to skim over the plants without bleaching the upper leaves. Under a stationary light, the plant closest to the light grows the fastest because it receives the most energy.

1000-watt HPS sodium lights illuminating bean plants on automatic light moving system (Light Rail III) in mid-winter

Eventually the taller plant will shade those toward the perimeter and create a pattern of growth in the shape of a pyramid. Light movers change the sources so plants receive light from different angles.

Light movers come in two basic designs: linear movers that move one light along a track, and the exclusive Sun Circle brand, which spins lights in a 360° rotation. A 400-watt HID light covers a 25 square foot area. On a 9' light track the coverage is rated at 5' x 14', or 70 square feet, nearly three times the coverage area of a stationary light.

Light Rail Three, made by Gualala Robotics, has the fastest and most versatile tracking system. These units carry the light on a very quiet trolley. Light Rail Threes can be shortened or lengthened, unlike the chain-driven models. This system also has the advantage of the Smart Box option. This is a time delay device. which will pause the mover for half a minute at each end of the track. Without it, the light spends more time at the middle, causing plants to grow vigorously at each end. Light Rail Three systems retail for $155.00 to $175.00, and $195.00 to $205.00 for the faster hyper-drive units, which include a built in Smart Box.

The Sun Circle brand light movers cover a square pattern, as opposed to the rectangular coverage you get from a linear mover.

Sun Circles have the advantage of carrying two or three lights. This allows indoor gardeners to blend the metal halide and/or HPS-son agros for the best of each in all stages of plant growth. Sun Circles range in price from $215.00 for a single light mover to $430.00 for one that covers up to a 17' x 17' area.

Covering surfaces in the grow room with mylar is strongly recommended for indoor growers. This is the most reflective material. It keeps usable light from being wasted by absorbing into the walls.

Hours of Light and Dark

There are general guidelines for plants and how they internally track time, or photoperiodism. Most vegetables can use up to eighteen hours of light per day and flower more abundantly when the light is cut back to twelve hours on and twelve hours off. Plants that flower predominately in the spring or summer are long-day plants. They need sixteen hours of light or more to initiate flowering. Day neutral plants are activated by factors other than light, such as temperature or a chronological time tracking. These plants can be illuminated 14–18 hours per day.

A Few Safety Tips

Keep remote ballasts elevated on a cinder block or shelf in case you end up with a lot of water on the floor. Do not use extension cords with the 250-, 400-, or 1000-watt lights, and be sure to use a three-prong, grounded timer. To protect your investment from power surges and spikes, use a surge suppresser. As is the case with sunlight, avoid looking into the bulb or you are sure to see stars. Make sure there is adequate air intake, as plants will need fresh air. Exhaust fans both remove the stale air and bring in fresh, CO_2-rich air. Small plants are more prone to heat damage from your light system. Keep lights at least 3' away, and more for the larger lights. As plants get older, they can handle the extra heat and the plant-to-light distance can be decreased.

❧c❧

GILBERT SCHOENSTEIN is a freelance garden magazine writer who has devoted many hours to hydro-organic experimentation. He is the owner of Gilby's farm, America's first certified organic hydroponic farm.

Harvesting Organic Data from the Internet

By Steven McFadden

As high technology spreads its influence further and further, and as more and more people boot up computers and go on-line, the digital imperative is sinking its roots firmly into agriculture as well. Organic farming and gardening have staked out their own acreage on the vast global web of information known as the Internet. The forecast is for an increasingly large supply of relevant data for all, including people specifically interested in sustainable approaches to growing and processing food.

As writer Lori Pottinger once put it, "Silicon chips are not about to replace cow chips on the farm, but their impact is growing. (Some) farmers have discovered that the computer can be as powerful a farming tool as some they keep in the barn." That may overstate the case a bit, but there is no denying that computers and the Internet are becoming increasingly useful for people who grow and process food.

The Internet connects people with interests in farming and gardening in a way that could never happen in a small-town coffee shop. There are well over twenty million users, and the numbers multiply like weeds each day. The range of facts, ideas, opinions, and personalities is vast. This is the richness and the reward of monitoring Organic Ag on the Net.

More than just another source of information, the Internet is also a web that links people of both similar and divergent interests in ways that were previously unthinkable. People connect with people from around the world and share information and viewpoints. You can listen in on other people's public discussions and learn, ask questions, contact experts, and discover announcements on a host of relevant issues and concerns.

The character of Internet discussions is usually informative, sometimes whimsical, and occasionally idiotic or hostile. In scientifically-oriented agricultural forums, undocumented organic claims are from time to time trashed, or flamed, with a fury approaching fundamentalism—

chemical-industrial fundamentalism, that is. But generally, in all forums, you will encounter sincere debate, polite requests for information, and helpful responses about techniques, tools, timing, and a host of other issues important to farmers and gardeners.

Nowadays some agricultural conferences feature lectures and panels on cyber topics that our grandparents could not have imagined in their wildest dreams: fuzzy decision making in dairy cattle management; use of single-chip micro-controllers in farm data collection systems; or even an object-oriented simulation model of a pig herd with emphasis on information. Those who scout around diligently online will from time to time encounter other equally arcane topics.

This is hardly the kind of talk that characterizes farmer-to-farmer chit-chat sessions at local feed and grain stores, and it may be marginally, if at all, relevant to organic growers, but it is indicative of a growing trend to sharing information via the network of computer connections linking farmers, researchers, and government agencies. To be sure, there is no shortage of information relevant to people with an interest in organic or sustainable agricultural systems.

Don't expect to find answers to all your questions, or even your way around the Internet, in one day. A rhythmic monitoring of key sites, however, will yield insight, and oodles of potentially useful information. As veterans of the Internet will surely attest, though, you run the risk of information overload—more than you need, want, or can cope with. If you are not both prepared and restrained, the Internet can waste a lot of your time and money.

Some valuable features that farmers and gardeners will find on-line are: the Agricultural Market News Database, the Agriculture Decision Support System, the Cooperative Extension Service, the Food and Agriculture Organization of the United Nations, the National Agricultural Library, and the U.S.D.A.'s Current Research Data Base. Up until now, such information could only be accessed at great expense and effort. Now they are available in the comfort of your own home or office via the click of a mouse button.

Searches and requests for specific software, or for specific enterprises such as a cattle operation, are common; and apparently many developers in the private and academic worlds are at work on software that will help farmers manage their operations more efficiently. The Internet is a good way to stay on top of the latest software development news.

Farmers and gardeners will be pleased to discover that many helpful newsletters are regularly posted in newsgroups such as alt.agriculture, and alt.sustainable.agriculture. A quick cybercruise, for example, may net a harvest of the latest offerings from The Nebraska Sustainable Agriculture Society, the Alternative Agriculture News, The Practical Farmer, Farm Aid News, and Sustainable Agriculture Week. These newsletters provide an invaluable source of up-to-date information and announcements.

Getting On-line

To gain access to all this information, one needs a computer, a modem, and some software. If you've got that, you can access the Net via a direct service provider, which is often the lowest-cost option, or through a commercial on-line service such as Compuserve, America OnLine, Prodigy, or Delphi. These commercial services make it easy. Once on-line in such a service, search under key words such as *agriculture, farming,* or *organic* to see what the service itself offers. In most instances, you will be both surprised and initially overwhelmed at the range and quantity of information.

To go further afield, hasten to the service's Internet connection. That's where the widest diversity of action is, for on the Internet anyone with a computer and a modem—no matter where they are in the world, or what service they use—can get connected.

Those who do not own computers, or who deem it a dubious expense, may be able to log onto and explore the Net from public libraries or college campuses. More and more, as public demand builds, schools and libraries are offering computer stations with Internet access.

Getting Oriented

The Internet is the world's largest computer network, having evolved from a federal research program. It is a large community of people all over the world using computers to interact with one another, and a way to get information on a wide range of topics from government, academic research, corporations, and individuals.

Around 1988 and 1989, the number of computers connected to the Internet grew dramatically. In 1981 there were only about 200 host computers on Internet. By the autumn of 1994 the estimate was 3.3 million host computers, and growing rapidly. Here is a synopsis of the major realms available for exploration:

Note: In this article, for the sake of typographical clarity, all Internet addresses are printed enclosed in parentheses. When you are entering these addresses in your computer, omit the parentheses. They are not necessary, and, in fact, will be regarded as invalid addresses. If you use them, you won't get to where you want to go.

Usenet Newsgroups

Usenet is the set of machines that exchange articles tagged with one or more universally-recognized labels, called newsgroups ("groups," for short). Addresses made up of words separated by periods, such as (alt.agriculture) are Internet discussion groups. They are essentially electronic bulletin boards, generally grouped by subject matter, where people post messages and articles.

Usenet is not an organization, and thus has no central authority. In fact, it has no central anything. Usenet is not a public utility. Some Usenet sites are publicly funded or subsidized, but most are not. There is no government monopoly on Usenet, and little or no control.

FTP

FTP stands for File Transfer Protocol. It is a way to download files of software, text, and graphics from the Internet. It is one of the most basic tools used on the Internet. Early users of the Internet developed FTP so people could copy files from one place to another across the Internet. So if there is a piece of software that you know will solve your problem, you can copy it from the source computer, known as an FTP site. FTP sites also contain text and graphics files and some even sound and video files.

Files on the Internet are organized by FTP sites. Finding an FTP site with useful information is the first step to making FTP a useful tool.

Gopher

Gopher is a way of browsing lots of information. It is a huge menu system for the Internet. Organizations or sometimes individuals from all over the world have set up Gopher "servers" with menus of items. Double clicking on a menu retrieves the item. Sometimes the item is text, sometimes it is another set of menus. The next menu item might point to yet another set of menus, and so on. The magical and sometimes mystifying part of Gopher is the ability for a menu to point to an entirely different Gopher server. That server could be in the next room or halfway around the world, but all you do to get there is double click on a menu item.

Mailing Lists

Mailing lists are electronic mail discussion groups that are exchanged through the Internet among groups of people who share similar interests. You can participate in ongoing, interactive discussions with people from all around the world using electronic mail. Thousands of mailing lists exist, and they cover every imaginable topic, including esoteric subjects such as growing ginger or Jerusalem artichokes, or establishing your garden as a sacred site.

When you sign up for a mailing list, follow the instructions precisely. Most mailing lists are automated; rather than a human being, the host computer will be scanning your message for instructions on what to do. If you have entered text different from, or other than the instructions, you won't get onto the mailing list.

World Wide Web

The World Wide Web (WWW), or more simply, the Web, allows even computer novices to easily search the global Internet for text, pictures, and—in some cases—sounds. It is rapidly emerging as the point-and-click prototype for the information superhighway, and will likely be the facet that turns the Internet into a truly mass medium.

An address that begins http:// is a site on the Internet's World Wide Web, a place where information is displayed in graphic form and may include photos, artwork, sound files, and highlighted words that connect you to related information via the click of a mouse button. The highlighted words are called "hypertext," and the http in the address stands for hypertext transfer protocol.These addresses are sometimes referred to as "URLs," which stands for Universal Resource Locator.

The Web works through a process called hyper-linking, a technology that permits a publisher to create links among related documents, regardless of where they physically reside on the computer network. For example, someone reading an article on composting that was located on a computer in Minneapolis might click on a highlighted phrase referring to worms, and be automatically connected to a computer in Australia that offers the latest research information on worms.

You can use the WWW to access gopher, ftp, and telnet sites (the addresses that have gopher:// or ftp:// or telnet:// prefixes) as well as WWW sites (the ones that have http:// prefixes). Just type the entire address as it's shown when using Mosaic, Netscape, WWW, or Lynx—all programs that access the WWW system. To use these addresses when ftp-ing, gopher-ing, or telneting directly, omit the appropriate prefix when typing an address.

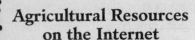

Agricultural Resources on the Internet

The following list will guide you to some key agricultural resources on the Internet, with an emphasis on organic and sustainable approaches. The list is not comprehensive, but it is a start. If you are interested, and you find the Internet helpful, you can always post requests for more information on the aspects of farming, gardening, and sustainability that are important to you.

Mailing Groups

SANET-MG is an electronic mailing group, from the Sustainable Agriculture Network (SAN), and is perhaps the most popular Internet conference on sustainable agriculture. It offers news, calendar listings and magazines, and is also a good place to post your queries on sustainable ag topics. Besides the mailing group, SAN also offers searchable databases on the Internet, including research reports, a directory of individuals and organizations willing to share expertise, and a guide to cover crops. For an information sheet, Getting Started Electronically with SAN, e-mail Gabriel Hegyes at (ghegyes@nalusda.gov) or write to SAN c/o Alternative Farming Systems Information Center, Rm. 304, National Agricultural Library, 10301 Baltimore Blvd., Beltsville, MD 20705.

If you already have an online service and e-mail address, you can subscribe to SANET by sending the message "Subscribe SANET-MG" to the following address: (Al-MANAC@CES.NCSU.EDU).

You can subscribe to sustag-l, another sustainable agriculture mailing list, by sending a message to (listserv@wsuvml.sc.wsu.edu) with a blank subject line and with text that reads: subscribe sustag-l Your Name. Example: subscribe sustag-l John Doe.

The mailing list sustag-principles is a fascinating forum for discussing philosophical concepts that inform gardening and sustainable agriculture. Discussions cover a wide array of topics, including latent geometrical order in the biological world; sacred geometry; symbolic and religious considerations in agriculture, such as culture-specific astro-calendrical beliefs about planting times, and surveys of ancient and contemporary harvest festivals and ceremonies; the geometric principles underlying permaculture, bio-dynamic, biointensive, and organic gardening design; sacred architecture; the history of religious iconography in architecture and garden design; the history and construction of labyrinths, garden grottoes, topiary, and other forms of symbolic landscaping; geomancy; feng shui; celestial observatory sites; and sacred site tourism. The thrust of the mailing list is to integrate agriculture into the wider sphere of cultural life. To subscribe, send e-mail to (almanac @.ces.ncsu.edu) with the message: subscribe sustag-princlples. If this doesn't work, send e-mail to (london@sunSITE.unc.edu) and ask for help.

Rural development issues are regularly raised and discussed though the Community and Rural Economic Development Interests List. For information, send e-mail to (listserv@ksuvm. ksu.edu). In the body of your message type: subscribe RURALDFV your name. For information send e-mail to (majordomo@csn.org) with the following text: subscribe econ-dev Your Name.

The Pesticide Action Network North America Updates Service (PANNUPS) regularly posts online resource pointers with directions on how to obtain specific resources that may be of use. To subscribe to PANNUPS, send e-mail to (MAJORDOMO@igc.apc.org) with the following text on one line: subscribe panups. For general inquiries you can send e-mail to: (panna@econet.apc.org) or gopher to: (gopher.econet.apc.orgl). Failing all that, try the phone: (415) 541-9140.

The International Ag-Sieve is a bimonthly gleaning of the latest and most applicable information in the field of sustainable agriculture in the tropics. Various editions have covered the latest in tropical forest products, training opportunities, seeds, biodiversity, urban gardening, and vegetable systems, women in agriculture, and so forth. To subscribe by e-mail, send a request to: (agsievefb.inbox@parti.inforum.org).

Newsgroups and Bulletin Boards

Some commonly consulted news groups and bulletin boards are: alt.agriculture; alt.agriculture.fruit; alt.agriculture.misc; alt.sci.agriculture; alt.sustainable.agriculture; sci.agriculture; misc.rural; rec.gardens; and tradenet.com.

Fresno State's Advanced Technology Information Network (ATIet) is a bulletin board specializing in agricultural technology and marketing news and information. Its Automated Trade Library is a rich resouce of trade leads. The service is free, and the phone charges are local if you're near any state university. Call (209) 278-4872.

Web Pages

There is a fascinating agriculture conference available at the on line service known as the WELL (Whole Earth 'Lectronic Link), an outgrowth of the Whole-Earth-

Catalog-Whole-Earth-Review-Point-Foundation. The conference is the Well's agriculture discussion area and it now has a Web page describing the conference and showing some of the resources available through it. To access, point your web browser at (http://www. well.com), then scroll to "The Well Itself" and select "conference." On the conferences page select "business and livelihood," and on the B&L section page that follows select "agriculture," and you're there. You can also go there directly by pointing your browser at: (http:// www.well.com/Conferences/agri/).

The Texas Agricultural Extension Service has a gopher or web page. Point your gopher to (gopher://leviathan.tamu.edu:70) or web to (http://leviathan.tamu. edu: 70. Both of these offer a software catalog in browsable, searchable, and downloadable versions.

The Agricultural Economics Department at the University of Nebraska has a WWW home page. The URL is (http://unlvm.unl. edu/agecon.htm). The page contains a description of the department, links to agriculture information in the Internet, other departments of agricultural economics, and a "fun stuff" section.

The Consortium for International Crop Protection (CICP) and the National Biological Impact Assessment Program (NBIAP) jointly offer "IPMnet," a 24-hour free on-line source of international Integrated Pest Management information, which includes IPM special reports, the "IPMnet NEWS," issues of "Resistant Pest Management" newsletters, technical information resources, an IPM forum, and IPM databases. To connect with IPMnet via the Internet, use a communication program or link and: (1) select or key in (telnet), (2) then, at the prompt, key in (cicp. biochem.vt.edu), (3) and follow the on-screen prompts. To receive the latest issue of IPMnet News, address your e-mail to the FTP server (ftpmail@sunsite. unc.edu) or (ftpmail@ftp.uu.net).

A WWW homepage on permaculture can be accessed at: (http://www.latrobe.edu.au/nexus /Permaculture/permaculture.htm) and at (href="http://www.latrobe.edu.au/nexus/Permaculture/sust ag.html">sustainableagriculture</a>).

As of January 1995, IPMnet is linked to the National IPM Network, a group of government, education, and other organizations dedicated to development and implementation of integrated pest management. As a result of this linkage, the IPMnet NEWS can be accessed on the National IPM Network's WWW system. The URL address is: (http://ipm_www .ncsu.edu). The specific address for the IPMnet NEWS is: (http://ipm_www.ncsu.edu/current_ipm/current_ipm.html). You can send E-mail to the editor, A. E. Deutsch, at (deutscha@bcc.orst.edu), or write via "snail mail" to IPMnet NEWS c/o Integrated Plant Protection Center, 2040 Cordley Hall, Oregon State University, Corvallis, OR 97331-2915, USA. The phone is (503) 737-6275.

You may access U.S.D.A. Extension Service Information via: (gopher://zeus.esusda.gov) or (gopher://ra.esusda.gov).

The Computer Network of the Institute of Food and Agricultural Sciences, at the University of Florida, offers the server "AgriGator"at (http://GNV.IFAS.UFL.EDU/WWW/AGATOR_HOME.HTM).

The EnviroWeb claims to be the world's largest environmental information archive on-line, and the clearinghouse of all on-line environmental information: (http://envirolink.org).

The U.S. Environmental Protection Agency (EPA) gives access to the EPA Public Information at: (http://www.epa.gov/).

You may access Solstice (the Center for Renewable Energy and Sustainable Technology) via gopher at: (//gopher.crest.org) or (http://solstice.crest.org/).

Thematic Guides on the human dimensions of global environmental change are available on-line from CIESIN (pronounced "season"), the Consortium for International Earth Science Information Network. Thematic Guides provide on-line overviews and access to the full tens of hundreds of journal articles, book chapters, conference papers, research reports, and other materials. To access these try (http://www.ciesin.org) or gopher: (//gopher.ciesin.org).

Computer/Internet Resources

A worthwhile resource for beginners and veterans alike is a ten-page booklet by Mark Campidonica entitled *A Guide to Agriculture in the Internet*. This explains in plain English how the Internet works and how to access agricultural information. Sections include step-by-step instructions, good explanations of the jargon that can make the Internet appear intimidating, and what each of the main ag services offer. The Guide is $10.00 from UC SAREP; call (916) 752-8664 for more information.

One newsgroup in particular is a helpful resource for those getting started: (comp.infosystems.interpedia). This is essentially an on-line intern encyclopedia. Once connected, check out (comp.internet.net-happenings). It is the source for new offerings on the Internet.

The Online World Resources Handbook tells how to find information on the World Wide Web, WAIS databases, gopher menus, Usenet, etc. To access the handbook, try (http://login.eunet.no/cpresno/index.html) or (gopher://cosn.org) and then select (Networking Information/Reference/The Online World).

To keep abreast of the latest developments in useful computer technology for farms and farmers, try a monthly newsletter called ag/INNOVATOR, which is a division of *Successful Farming Magazine*. Edited by Grant Mangold, the newsletter covers all aspects of agricultural computing, and has a regular column called "ag OnLine," which highlights information available through the Internet, and also gives examples of how farmers apply this information. The newsletter is expensive at $96.00 a year, but offers a guarantee that if it doesn't save readers at least the price of the subscription, they will refund your money, no questions asked. ag INNOVATOR can be contacted at 1716 Locust, Des Moines, IA 50309-3023. Or you can call 1-800-564-4005 for a free sample issue.

The *Electronic Green Journal* is a general, but useful resource that some organic farmers and gardeners may wish to check out. To subscribe, send an e-mail message to (MAJORDOMO@UIDAHO.ED) with the following in the body of the message: subscribe egj your_email_address. Alternatively, gopher to: (//gopher.uidaho.edu). Select (University of Idaho Electronic Publications).

Steven McFadden is director of the Wisdom Conservancy at Merriam Hill Education Center, 148 Merriam Hill Rd., Greenville, NH, 03048 USA, tel. (603) 878-1818. His e-mail address is (wisdomkeep@aol.com). With Trauger Groh, Steven is producer of a one-hour audiotape entitled *The Critical Connection: Families, Food, and Farms* ($10.00) available from The Wisdom Conservancy. Trauger and Steven are also the co-authors of the widely acclaimed book, *Farms of Tomorrow: Community Supported Farms, Farm Supported Communities* (available from the BioDynamic Farming and Gardening Association, tel. 1-800-516-7797.

Indoor Air Pollution: Problems and Solutions

BY ROALD GUNDERSEN

We Americans spend the vast majority of our lives inside buildings. The 1930 U.S. census revealed 80 percent of Americans lived on farms. By 1950, 80 percent of Americans were in cities. Implicit in this urbanization is a large and rapid shift from working in fields to working indoors: the segregation of humans from the natural environment into artificial, machine-operated, fossil-fuel-run environments. Development of such segregating shells is unprecedented in the history of life on Earth. Today, people living in industrialized countries spend over 90 percent of their lives inside of buildings over the average life span of sixty-five years. Many of us spend more time in our cars than we do outside. So when we talk about air pollution, air quality, and people's health, we must talk about indoor air pollution. This is not to say outdoor air quality is unimportant; rather its fate is integrally connected with that of indoor air quality.

The indoor air story begins with the energy crisis of the seventies. A large increase in building energy efficiency resulted in more air-tight construction. An unintended effect of this improved energy efficiency was "sick building syndrome." By plugging the flow of air, we trapped a Pandora's box of airborne toxins inside our buildings. We've since come to the rather humbling realization that fresh air (cleaned complements of the Earth's biosphere) is needed for people to be healthy in buildings. We've also discovered that the things we make buildings out of, and the things we put in and use in buildings, can pollute the interior air and affect the inhabitants' health.

Building a Model of Clean Air

Like most architects in the seventies and eighties, I had not given much thought to the air inside buildings except to keep it at a comfortable temperature and humidity, and to exchange it to keep it from getting stale (whatever that meant). I came to the issue of indoor air quality while designing and supervising construction on Biosphere 2, near Tucson, Arizona. Biosphere 2 is conceived as a closed-system experiment, modeling some of Earth's complex ecological systems as a tool toward understanding them. The 3 ½-acre, high-tech greenhouse is by far the tightest structure of its size on Earth, exchanging one atmosphere every twenty years. We went to extreme efforts to make sure building materials and electro-mechanical equipment would not adversely effect the plant and animal life inside. When I began working on Bio 2 in 1988, the indoor air field was still in its infancy. Building material sales representatives, and even their technical support personnel, were perplexed by our rigid requirements for non-toxic materials, and the accompanying clean air lingo, like "material off-gassing," "MSD sheets," and "low VOCs." Most of their customers were only interested in the latest designer colors and the bottom line costs.

The Birth of Awareness

In the late eighties Americans began awakening to the issue of indoor air pollution. Two Environmental Protection Agency (EPA) reports helped with this awareness. In its *1989 Report to Congress on Indoor Air Quality*, the EPA study showed that indoor air is often more polluted than outside air, and it estimated health and productivity costs to be in the tens of billions of dollars. The second study charged radon gas leaking into buildings from the ground with being the second leading cause of lung cancer in America after cigarettes. In some regions of the country, buildings were found to have radon levels equivalent to the damage caused by smoking twenty packs of cigarettes a day. The EPA recommended that all buildings be tested for radon. Several well publicized cases of sick building syndrome and a Surgeon General's report on second hand cigarette smoke compounded the public's concern for indoor air.

Since the late eighties, the field of indoor air has exploded. Consultants have become overnight experts in low-toxic environments. Manufacturers have begun producing low toxic building materials. Now that we have yet another culprit to blame and new things to agonize over with regard to our health, just how concerned should we be? What are the health risks? How do we know if a building is polluted? What can we do if it is? And, if you're planning to build, how can you build clean? I hope to shed some light on these and other questions with the understanding that this has already become a large and complex field.

Just how concerned should you be about the indoor air you breathe? To be blunt, it is a real problem, certainly with regard to the quality of our lives, and it is something we can all improve. For most of us, however, indoor air pollution is not something to hyperventilate about or to blame all of our health problems on. The EPA has quantified the problem in the worst cases. Little or nothing, however, has been done to quantify the more subtle, long-term changes in our health caused by our artificial indoor air. Chances are we all suffer some minor health effects of indoor air: We are more likely to get colds in winter when we close buildings up; we may suffer weakened immune systems, fatigue, headaches, and sore eyes as a result of polluted indoor air. It is hard to determine the more subtle, long-term effects of indoor air because of the vast array of variables, and the difficulty of creating a controlled experiment. We have chosen to live inside artificial environments without first understanding how they impact our health. This is a vast experiment with ourselves as guinea pigs. Before you start holding your breath, though, there are things you can do about indoor air.

Judging Our Risks

Most people in industrial countries spend nearly 90 percent of their lives in two buildings: their homes and their work places. These are the two buildings we need to focus on, since the health risks of indoor air pollution are most dependent on the duration of our exposure. There are exceptional cases of brief exposures to intense toxins, but these cases exclude the vast majority of us. Fortunately, home and work are also the two places where we have some power to improve indoor air quality. Here are basic criteria to judge your own risks:

1. Are the buildings you are in relatively airtight? Drafty buildings, while energy inefficient, nevertheless provide lots of air changes and are not as prone to indoor air problems. Tight buildings are usually those that have been built or remodeled since the late 1970s, and these pose a substantially increased risk of having polluted air.

2. Do the buildings you're in have inadequate ventilation? In poorly-ventilated buildings the air may seem stale and uncomfortable to breathe. Humidity may build up and contribute to the growth of molds and mildew.

3. Are strong cleaners, glues, sprays, paints, or solvents being used frequently? Any number of toxic substances

may be a regular part of your indoor environment, particularly at work. The Occupational Safety and Health Agency (OSHA) has set stringent guidelines to govern exposures to workplace toxins.

4. Do you notice any symptoms such as burning eyes, headaches, or a feeling of malaise associated with a building? A stressful job or one you don't like can cause these symptoms, but so can bad indoor air.

5. Do you smell things burning? Poorly vented furnaces, wood stoves, and gas appliances can usually be sniffed out. They should be serviced at least once a year.

6. Is your area at high risk for radon? If you don't know, it's a good idea to get your buildings tested, especially if your county health department suspects the area to be at risk.

7. Does your building have that fresh-built smell? Newly built or remodeled buildings are very likely to have polluted air, at least for a period after construction.

8. Do you notice an odor of mold or mildew? Moisture condensing on windows and walls can cause the growth of microbes and become a health hazard.

9. Do you live with polluted *outside* air? People in urban areas may need to clean the air coming into buildings.

If you have answered "yes" to any of these questions, it would be worthwhile for your health to investigate the situation further.

Indoor Pollution

Apart from external pollutants like smog and radon leaking into buildings, the other big factors affecting indoor air quality are internal to the building. These sources fall into categories:

1. Off-gassing building materials.
2. Pollution from mechanical equipment and appliances, air conditioners, copiers, and computers.
3. Biological sources, including molds, mildew, microbes, pet dandruff, etc.
4. Combustion from furnaces, fireplaces, cigarettes, cooking, etc.
5. Cleaning and maintenance compounds.
6. Radon gas.

Off-gassing Building Materials

New buildings often have the worst air. Not only are they tightly constructed so there is less air exchange, but they are the worst offenders with regard to material off-gassing—unless the owners want to pay to build a clean building. A clean building can be expensive, but it doesn't have to be an elitist's pursuit.

The cleanest building materials tend to be organic, and, as with food, the less processed materials tend to be better for you. Good materials include solid, untreated woods, straw (as in straw bale construction), wool and cotton rugs and carpets, cellulose insulation, gypsum wall board, plaster, tile, glass, concrete, and stone.

Some stones used in masonry and aggregates for concrete, like granite, may be a source of radon gas and its progeny. Metals, as a whole, are not an off-gassing concern, but rather can be a water quality concern, as with copper, which can kill aquatic systems at parts per billion, and aluminum pots and pans, which may contribute to arthritis and senility.

When selecting materials for Biosphere 2, the problems we had most frequently were of four types:

1. Materials containing binders: fiberglass insulation, chip board, plywood, and particle board.

2. Materials made from petro-chemicals: foam insulation, gaskets, furniture padding, carpet pads, and softer plastics

3. Paints and coatings: oil-based paints, oil-based stains, and solvents.

4. Glues, adhesives, and solvents: PVC and CPVC glues, vinyl tile adhesives, and caulks.

A good rule of thumb is: if you can smell it, it's off-gassing. Get on your knees and sniff your Dupont Dacron™ carpet with 3M Scotch Guard™ anti-stain protection and you'll know what material off-gassing is. Construction materials are loaded with a chemical candy store of compounds. You need not learn a litany of chemical names to master the basic concerns.

1. How much of a given toxic material is being used in a building? Often this will govern one's primary focus. An example is formaldehyde and mobile homes. Practically everything in a mobile home except the kitchen sink has formaldehyde in it.

2. Another criteria is the duration of off-gassing for toxic chemicals. Again, formaldehyde can off-gas for years, whereas a more toxic compound like xylene, a solvent, might be 99 percent gone in a few days.

3. Where is this material between uses? Where material is

used will also determine its interaction and off-gassing. For instance, a properly installed vapor barrier between you and your fiberglass insulation will allow few, if any, formaldehyde or particulates to enter your environment. By focusing efforts on the primary culprits to clean indoor air, one will not get bogged down with numerous minor offenders.

Binders are often nasty and are, of course, used to hold materials together. Phenyl formaldehyde is used in most chip board, plywood, wall paneling, and fiberglass insulation. Ever wonder why you get a headache and burning eyes shopping in a builders' supply store? When you walk into a building center, that sweet odor is formaldehyde. It's notorious due

to its abundance and the longevity of off-gassing.

Glues and adhesives used to set vinyl tiles or carpeting contain long-term solvents which serve as vehicles in oil-based paints, stains, and caulks, and are often extremely toxic. Most evaporate during the first few weeks after use, contributing to atmospheric pollution. Water-based latex paints avoid most of these VCs (volitile compounds). There are special environmentally-friendly formulations designed by Gliddon and other manufacturers with reduced VOC (volitile organic compound) contents.

In constructing Biosphere 2, most of the common palette of building materials had to be eliminated on their toxicity alone. If a paint had a heavy metal in its pigment, as most do, we couldn't use it for fear it might leach into the marine systems and wreak havoc on algae. If a material like carpeting gave off too much of a volatile organic compound, it might build up and make the crew sick. Granted, Biosphere 2 is an extreme indoor air case, but it illustrates the problems with creating an atmosphere inside a building, which modern buildings do to some extent.

Before a sales representative got past the front door on the site of Biosphere 2, they had to be equipped with Material Safety Data

(MSD) sheets on their products. MSD sheets list a litany of aspects of a product: its flammability, handling, chemical contents, etc. From this EPA-required registrar we could deduce its compatibility with our delicate mini-world. Few reps even knew what MSD sheets were. Today they probably do, and so do many architects.

A Burning Issue

For many of us, the path to energy independence in the late seventies was buying a wood stove. While still a viable renewable heat source for many, burning wood produces its share of pollution, and more than its share of smoke and dust. Any form of combustion, whether smoking a cigarette or burning toast, will produce unhealthy byproducts like carbon monoxide and nitric oxide. Again, we're after the biggest household offenders—usually a wood stove, poorly maintained furnace, or a leaky chimney. Generally the more complete the combustion, the cleaner the burning, so annual maintenance of furnaces, wood stoves, and chimneys is a good indoor air and planet-friendly habit. A carbon monoxide (CO) detector, which detects below ten parts per million or less, is a good investment for anyone who burns things. Carbon monoxide is the most lethal product of poor combustion and poor venting, and

CO detection equipment is reasonably affordable.

Improving the Quality of Indoor Air

Five ways to manage indoor pollution are listed below, in order of easiest to most difficult to implement:

1. Increase ventilation.
2. Clean or condition the air.
3. Protect against the polluting source.
4. Remove the polluting source.
5. Build clean.

Ventilating Pollutants: A Building's Breath

Like people, buildings must breathe. This is achieved actively by windows, doors, fans, and vents, and passively by infiltration of air through walls, roofs, and floors. Most people have good control over ventilation at home, but little if any control over ventilation at work. By code, buildings are required to have multiple air changes every day, one air change being a turnover of air equivalent to the building's volume. The number of air changes varies depending on the building's use (house, factory, school, etc.) and local codes.

A widely accepted value is half an air change per hour. That's twelve times the size of your building daily. Biosphere 2 has one air change in twenty years. Tight, energy-efficient homes or office buildings can achieve as few as two or three air changes a day. Local codes may require such buildings to exchange additional volumes of air. Implied in these codes is that outdoor air is fresher and healthier than indoor air. A disadvantage to exchanging this air is that we need to heat or cool the so-called "fresh" incoming air. This usually requires burning fossil fuels, further polluting the outside air. It's a positive feedback loop with a very negative outcome. Over fifty major cities in the U.S. have dirty air, failing EPA standards, particularly on ozone levels. We are exchanging dirty indoor air with dirty outdoor air.

How do we get out of this pervasive urban smog? The conventional wisdom is to add some more machines to the increasingly electro-mechanical environments we've come to depend upon. Air-to-air heat exchangers can recapture over 80 percent of the heat, and filters can take out the particulates, but each adds initial expense, and requires energy and regular maintenance to operate. Even with these techno-fixes we haven't addressed the deadliest urban offenders—ozone, nitrous oxide, and volatile organic compounds—which pose the greatest health hazards in urban indoor air. Clearly we need tight, energy efficient buildings, made with clean materials and ways of internally refreshing the air inside. This is where Biosphere 2 has some proven applications.

Cleaning and Conditioning the Air

The conventional ways to clean and ventilate indoor air are the air-to-air heat exchangers and the use of filters. Besides the drawback mentioned above, neither eliminates VOCs, the most noxious pollutants in most urban "fresh" incoming air. Biosphere 2 used plants and soils to clean and freshen indoor air. We don't need a rocket scientist to tell us that plants and their symbiotic bacteria in soils are good companions for us animals.

In *A Study of Interior Landscape Plants*, Dr. Roy Wolverton, under a grant from NASA, attempted to quantify the effectiveness of different plants as air cleaners. NASA was interested in alternatives to cleaning space station air during long trips in space.

The space shuttles have extremely polluted air. On short trips, NASA isn't as concerned about polluted air's effects on the astronauts' health as it is about those effects during trips of longer duration (although I'd bet the astronauts' performance suffers). NASA wanted to see if plants could be designed into the space station to perform multiple roles of air cleaning, oxygen production, and a small amount of food production. Wolverton's group tested ten varieties of house plants for their various abilities to remove commonly used chemicals such as trichloroethylene (TCE), Benzene, and formaldehyde. The results of the study were impressive. Plant species varied in their uptake of different chemicals, but were found to be, as a whole, very effective at uptake of each of these VOCs. The report also calculated the number of plants required in an average 1,800 square foot, energy efficient home with 0.2 air changes per hour for the cleaning of formaldehyde. They estimated fifteen average sized mother-in-law tongues (*Sansevieria laurentii*) or six large bamboo palms (*Chamaedorea seifritzii*) would maintain a formaldehyde-free air. A surprisingly small number of plants can perform a huge service.

We used Wolverton as a consultant to design Biosphere 2's biological air-cleaning systems. Apart from the passive benefit of the plants and soils inside Bio 2, we designed a so-called soil bed reactor which drew air off the human habitat and pushed it through the soil bed of the intensive agriculture building. This simple technology can be used in solar greenhouses to force air through soil beds, serving to store heat and clean the air at the same time. If building codes are to reflect health and well-being realities, they should require an established number of plants per square foot of building. If we embraced plants and soils as a regular component of clean indoor air with the same enthusiasm with which we embraced mechanical systems, we could reduce the number of air exchanges, energy consumption, and its resulting pollution, while substantially improving indoor air quality. Most would agree, the aesthetics of plants are a tad more appealing than mechanical equipment. The cost of plants

and their care, while time consuming and expensive, could be well offset by energy savings alone, let alone the potential productivity improvements of their human companions. Like mechanical systems, plants require room. Buildings could be retrofit or designed from the start with attached greenhouses, solariums, atriums, or greenways which, if properly designed, could provide solar heat and food, as well as waste water and air cleaning. Added together, the result could be large savings and environmental benefits. The wholesale embracing of living systems inside our buildings would revolutionize our inside and outside environments for the better. By cleaning indoor air with plants, our buildings can be tighter, saving energy and money and preventing the pollution of the environment while keeping us healthier.

Protecting against the Polluting Source

Another effective way of improving your indoor air is to isolate or segregate the offending sources from exposure to interior air. The most common way this is done is with a vapor barrier at the time of construction, or during a major interior remodeling. A vapor barrier is most often a six millimeter polyethylene plastic sheet. If prop-

erly designed and installed, a vapor barrier can protect indoor air from most, if not all, of the formaldehyde used as a binder in fiberglass insulation, oriented strand board (chipboard), and plywood. Used outside foundations and below poured concrete floors, one can almost eliminate radon gas problems. Other, less effective methods are to use coatings, sealers, and caulks over the offending surfaces and cracks, preventing some of the off-gassing while creating a temporary problem with the off-gassing of the applied product.

Removing the Polluting Sources: Remodeling Your Air

We can improve indoor air quality by removing the biggest offending materials and selecting clean replacement materials. Suspect materials might be carpet and carpet pads, wall paneling, chipboard cabinets, and foam padded furniture. A significant quantity of any given material must be present before it poses a potential health hazard. However, you may have a little paneling, chipboard, and plywood, which all use phenyl formaldehyde as a binder, and when added together constitute a harmful amount of formaldehyde. If you live in a mobile home, it may be impractical to remove all the offending sources. If one has an allergy to an indoor pollutant, careful scrutiny of suspects is important before remodeling time and dollars are spent ineffectually .

Furniture, while usually a minor indoor air pollutant, is easily replaced. Asbestos is still found in buildings, and should be carefully removed by a licensed professional. Another technique for removal of short lived off-gassing toxins in new buildings (usually solvents used in paints and adhesives) is the so-called "bake-off." This is not a bake sale, but it might involve turning on your oven. The idea is to get the new building as hot as possible, which accelerates the release of gasses from materials. This works well with short term pollutants. The best long term way is to avoid indoor air pollution altogether, and, (if you are fortunate enough to be able to) build clean.

Building Clean: Organic Buildings

As I have already mentioned, organic building materials tend to be safe for indoor air. In our strenuous pursuit to find acceptable building materials and interior finishes to use in Biosphere 2, two distinct categories emerged: high-tech materials, coatings and finishes, and low-tech organic materials

The high-tech finishes we used were specialty stainless steels and coated glass, epoxy coatings and caulking, and silicon foams. The organic materials we used were solid woods in furniture, finish trim, doors, and cabinetry; wool carpeting and wool fabric walls and ceilings; wool upholstery and crimped wool batting; jute carpet pads; ceramic tile floorings; and stone pavers. We did use materials which are quite conventional and safe, such as gypsum wall board (sheet rock), concrete (without any heavy metal fly ash), and hard plastics like PVC and CPVC.

Coatings presented one of our largest stumbling blocks. With the advent of low VOC paints since building Biosphere 2, our job would have been much easier.

Two good manufacturers with a wide range of coatings are American Formulating and Manufacturing, and Miller Paint Company.

If you can afford the extra cost of hiring an indoor air specialist, it is a good idea which will pay off in the long run. If you're in my position, however, you'll build organic.

One organic approach which is gaining acceptance is straw bale construction. Unless the bales get wet and turn to mold, straw bale construction is environmentally very safe. Since indoor air pollution is particularly bad in cold climates, straw is particularly attractive for its highly insulative characteristics (R3 per inch).

My wife and I have built perhaps the first A frame straw bale house, using straw in the roofs, walls, and floor as insulation. Most straw bale homes still have conventional roofs with conventional insulation. We have used a minimum of fiberglass and foam insulation, and our other finishes are solid wood, plaster, gypsum board with latex paint, stone, and glass. While we've had a very stressful nine-month adjustment to our new home and a new baby, we've each only gotten sick once, while our family and friends cycle through numerous illnesses. We have some major culprits yet to contend with (i.e., wood stove, propane refrigerator and range), and we look forward to our new attached solar greenhouse to reduce some of these emissions.

❖c౨❖

ROALD GUNDERSEN is an architect who has built his own straw bale home and adjoining solar greenhouse. His previous work with solar greenhouses includes the design of a greenhouse for the cultivation of seedling trees at Badgersett Research Farm. In addition to working on a variety of other architectural projects, Mr. Gundersen was also the Project Architect on the human habitat portion of Biosphere 2.

Health and Alternative Medicine

Naturopathic Medicine

Apitherapy

Kombucha Tea

Your Pet's Health— Holistically

The Old-Time Cold Cure

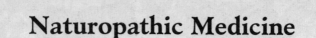

Naturopathic Medicine

By Walter Crinnion, N.D.

I like things simple. I especially like to find simple solutions to problems that seem complex. Maybe that is why I like naturopathic medicine so much. For most of my patients, the simple solutions often work the best, like the time Mr. A. came to see me. This high-powered insurance executive showed up in my office with his wife, wanting help with his heart. For the past year and a half he had been experiencing "ventricular tachycardia" (a fancy word that means his heart would beat *very* rapidly, and *very* inefficiently). He had been put on four different medications to keep his heart working properly, but they didn't solve the problem. In addition he was experiencing dizziness, diarrhea, and depression. As a result of all this, his ability to work was slipping and he feared for his job.

His complex problem turned out to be rather simple. First, I looked up the four heart medications he was on and found that every one of them listed dizziness, depression, and diarrhea as side effects. So we knew what was causing those problems. Then I checked him for food reactions and found

that he was eating several foods that his body was sensitive to. After taking him off of those foods, his ventricular tachycardia stopped. This made it easy for him to stop the heart meds, so his dizziness, diarrhea, and depression stopped. A simple solution to a seemingly complex problem.

Simple, effective, natural solutions that go to the source of the problem are what naturopathic medicine is all about.

Even though most Americans have never heard of naturopathic medicine, it is almost 100 years old. It was built upon centuries of healing wisdom from across the world and blended together in a fashion that could only happen in North America—the world's melting pot. It became a distinct American medical profession in 1902, and by the 1920s, its medical conventions had attracted more than 10,000 practitioners. At one point there were more than twenty naturopathic medical colleges in the United States and naturopathic physicians were licensed in a majority of the states.

Unfortunately, we are constantly pulled to what is new and

glitzy (organic gardeners excepted). The awe inspired by "new scientific discoveries," and "experimental drugs that look promising," has kept us on the edge of our seats for years, knowing that if we stayed tuned we would eventually see the unveiling of "The wonder drug that cures cancer and anything else that ails you." But we haven't and we won't.

This constant parade of medical breakthroughs with pharmaceutical drugs, surgical techniques, and other procedures was one of the factors that ushered in the decline of naturopathic medicine in this country. The rest of the job was done by the Rockefeller funded Flexnor Report, issued in 1922 which set the standards for "acceptable" medical education in the U.S. After this report was put into effect, many of the naturopathic medical colleges closed their doors, so that by the 1950s there was only one remaining, the National College of Naturopathic Medicine. Still active today in Portland, Oregon, it has been joined by Bastyr University of Natural Health Sciences in Seattle, Washington, and the Southwest College of Naturopathic Medicine in Scottsdale, Arizona. There is also the Ontario College of Naturopathic Medicine in Ontario, Canada.

These are all four-year medical colleges that require the equivalent of a bachelor's degree to be considered for acceptance. During their course of study, naturopathic medical students are trained in all of the basic "-ologies," just as they would in a standard medical school. In addition, they are extensively trained in nutrition, botanical medicines, homeopathy, acupuncture, natural childbirth, hydrotherapy, physical therapy, naturopathic manipulation techniques, Ayurvedic medicine, and other therapies. The aim of these programs is to produce trained family/general practice naturopathic physicians. While many of the graduates will practice this eclectic approach, some will specialize in natural childbirth, acupuncture, or homeopathy. There are currently ten states that have licensing laws for naturopathic physicians.

Basic Principles

The basic principles of naturopathic medicine are: The healing power of nature; first do no harm; find the cause; and treat the whole person. As a trained naturopath I believe that the body is designed to heal itself. All that I need to do to help is to identify what is causing the body to malfunction, then to find natural ways to deal with the cause and to stimulate the healing power of nature. In looking at the whole person, I always keep in mind the power of mental and

emotional stressors to impact the health of each person. Sometimes the only way for the subconscious to tell them that something needs to be dealt with is to cause an illness. Most people want their doctor to do away with the messages that their bodies are giving them. I think it is my duty to help them see the message for what it is, so that they have the option to respond to it. After all, if I help them ignore the message, then they will just become ill again when the message returns.

Here is my favorite analogy to describe how emotional issues cause physical problems: I think of these emotional stressors as someone on top of a mountain making very large snowballs (snow boulders actually) and then rolling them down the hill. After the boulder gets rolling it picks up more snow and more speed, smashing into anything that stands in its way (causing physical problems). Once the ball gets rolling, that person may leave the top of the mountain, or they may stay up there making more snowballs to roll down. Once the stress starts a physical problem, you need to deal with the physical consequences (the rolling boulder). Simply dealing

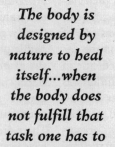

The body is designed by nature to heal itself...when the body does not fulfill that task one has to ask why

with the stress will not make the physical problem go away, any more than removing the person from the top of the mountain will stop the boulder once it has begun to move. But, in order to stop any more boulders from starting, you need to deal with the stress.

The body is designed by nature to heal itself. So when the body does not fulfill that task one has to ask why. What is the body telling us? What is it asking for? In very basic terms, the body should run right if it has the necessary nutrients and if nothing is present to cause malfunction. Toxins are the primary items causing malfunction. These can be physical, emotional, or chemical toxins. It would be impossible to help someone whose body was malfuntioning because of toxins to attain health if these toxins are not identified and eliminated. This is why naturopathic physicians want to look for the cause of the problem. If we only deal with the symptoms, instead of the cause, the problems will return. Any gardener knows this principle. For long lasting results against weeds, you need to get the root out, not just pull off the leaves!

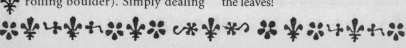

All of the organic gardeners that I have met are concerned with the health of soil, the health of plants, and the interaction of man and nature. They find that the more they understand and abide by the natural laws, the better their results. They see the chemical intrusion on agriculture as swapping short-term yields for long-term problems. Many are following the old Iroquois maxim of weighing each decision according to the effects on the seventh generation hence, and acting accordingly. If you replace the concept of the soil and plants for the body, you end up with the classic naturopathic approach. The chemical onslaught and short-sighted approach that has devastated our soils and food sources have simultaneously been devastating our health. If you believe that synthetic fertilizers and pesticides should *not* be used on the soil, why should synthetic medicines be used on your body when safe and effective natural alternatives are available?

Nature has many lessons to teach those who are willing to learn. While this country likes to cling to the notion that we have conquered nature, we are really just deluded. The first lesson nature teaches is to respect its power. Nature continues to show us that our technology and insistence that it do what we want it to do are re-

ally ineffective after a point. It teaches us to work with it rather than against it. If one can get the immense power of nature working with them, things go much better. This is one of the main differences between naturopathy and conventional medicine. While conventional medicine seeks to alter pain and suffering with medicines and technologies, we seek to realign the body to proper functioning so that the pain and suffering will cease. We do not believe that a headache is due to an aspirin deficiency!

As a naturopathic physician in practice for thirteen years, I have rarely had to rely on synthetic medications to help. Instead I have been amazed at the power of natural substances, beginning with the foods you eat. Choose a diet of organic whole foods that your body likes and you will be buying the best health insurance policy possible. You will be consuming a diet that numerous medical studies have conclusively shown to greatly reduce your risk of cancer and heart disease (the two major killers in our country). While there has been a recent flap over whether taking a beta carotene supplements has any benefit for heavy smokers, there is no doubt that a diet high in the carotenes helps. There have been over fifty studies looking at the effect of diet on cancer, and they have all shown that a diet high

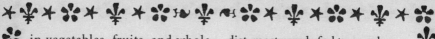

in vegetables, fruits, and whole grains will help prevent cancer.

Organic sources of foods, of course, are very important as there are also recent studies linking pesticides in the body to the development of breast and other cancers. The biggest sources of the pesticides are the air and our foods. While numerous studies have shown links between high fat diets and cancers, it is also clear that pesticides and solvents are concentrated in fats. The possibility exists that at least part of the danger of high fat diets resides in the toxins found in the fat.

In addition to eating organic whole foods, most naturopaths also check to be sure you are not eating foods that you may be sensitive to. There is a very long list of problems that can be attributed to food sensitivities, including: fatigue, sinus troubles, asthma, hives, eczema, arthritis, headaches, migraines, "brain fog," mood swings, diarrhea or constipation, gas and bloating, recurrent ear infections, ADD, etc. Once the offending foods are identified (wheat, milk, and sugar being the three most common) and eliminated from the

The possibility exists that at least part of the danger of high fat diets resides in the toxins found in the fat

diet, most people feel tremendously better in 4–10 days. While this is the most difficult program I have for my patients to follow, it gives the greatest results. Problems that people thought were incurable, or that were just part of "growing old" magically disappear.

In addition to basic dietary concerns, we also are concerned with proper supplementation. I generally recommend a good multivitamin-multimineral with extra vitamin C and whatever nutrients the body may specifically need more of. I can't even count the number of maladies that have been alleviated by simple supplementation. Three of the most dramatic cases were three young women in their thirties who had been unable to conceive after years of trying. After doing nutrient analysis on them I began each of them on the nutrients they were deficient in. Within six months each of them had conceived! That is simple health care. Give the body what it needs and it will run right.

After dietary and supplement support come natural therapies that enhance the ability of your body to function. The most com-

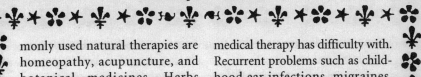

monly used natural therapies are homeopathy, acupuncture, and botanical medicines. Herbs (botanical medicines) exert very powerful actions on the body. There are numerous herbal medicines that do things no drugs can do. While the flood of antibiotics over the past four decades have spawned bacteria that are resistant to all known antibiotics, there are herbs that can come to the rescue. Echinacea is one such herb that is highly effective against both bacteria and viruses, but it functions differently than antibiotics. Instead of killing the invaders directly, it stimulates your own white blood cells to do the killing. There are no bacteria that are resistant to attack by your white blood cells. Echinacea has been a mainstay of my natural armory as long as I have been in practice. There are also herbs that increase blood flow to the brain, that reduce blood pressure, and that protect the liver from such powerful toxins as the death cap mushroom. This just scratches the surface of effective botanical medicines, as there are many more.

While naturopaths are very effective with acute problems such as colds, flus, sore throats, etc., we are also superb with numerous chronic problems. There are many chronic problems that naturopaths are good at helping with that standard medical therapy has difficulty with. Recurrent problems such as childhood ear infections, migraines, arthritis, and other problems are very amenable to the naturopathic care that I have outlined above. We really shine when it comes to stimulating the immune system to take care of chronic infections.

Naturopaths are also trained in preventive medicine. While the current administration views preventive medicine as providing immunizations to all children in the U.S., there is a lot more to it. We are actually trained to spot the "warning signs" of chronic problems before they manifest themselves fully, while standard physicians are trained in the diagnoses of overt disease states. I often tell people that if a N.D. (naturopath) and an M.D. were travelling in a car together and the oil light went on, the N.D. would say "We need oil." The M.D. would say "The engine is fine, just keep driving." Once the engine had frozen up after many more miles the M.D. would do the diagnostic work and say with certainty, "The engine ran out of oil." While this example is kind of silly, I have had numerous patients who have first gone to their regular doctor(s) only to be told that they could find nothing wrong. They did have something wrong, which was fixable with diet and supplementation, but it was

not an overt disease state that the M.D. is trained to spot.

Some of this is merely a difference in training. Medical doctors finish their training with internship and residency in their hospitals, seeing very ill individuals with full blown disease states each day. Naturopaths, on the other hand, cut their teeth seeing ambulatory patients out of the medical school clinic. They are daily seeing people who have not yet gotten to the full blown disease state that required hospitalization. We are better trained to spot these "functional" problems, and we have the natural means at our disposal to effectively treat them. But, both systems of medical care are necessary and complimentary.

In short, naturopathic medicine, the "traditional" form of medicine in this country, provides a safe, natural, simple, and effective alternative and supplement to conventional medical care.

If you would like to know if there is a trained naturopath in your area, or to find out more about naturopathic medical training you can call the American Association of Naturopathic Physicians at (206) 328-8510.

WALTER CRINNION, N.D. is a naturopathic physician in Bellevue, Washington, where he lives with his wife and three daughters. He runs the most comprehensive cleansing protocol in the country for the removal of environmental toxins. He is a faculty member at the Bastyr University School of Naturopathic Medicine. He is also an avid organic gardener.

Apitherapy

By Pamela Spence

According to Christian mythology, human history began when Eve—bless her heart—ate the apple and we all fell out. Clutching ill-fitting garments about our pathetic hides, we humans set off into the wide world beyond the garden gate. This moment was interpreted by many to indicate that nature henceforth stood in opposition and enmity to humankind, and sowed the seeds of our collective alienation. This alienation expresses itself in the obsession we humans seem to have to destroy this planet we call home. Indeed, as we look around at our polluted planet—overpopulated, exhausted, scarred by constant war, violence, and famine—we find plenty of evidence for the human/nature antagonism.

There is, however, one detail of the Garden story, preserved in folk tradition (if not in theology), that belies that antagonism and points to the possibility that we were pushed out into the bigger Garden where creation continues and blessings abound if we can only discover them in time. But where is the wisdom and who are to be our guides? We have been taught repeatedly in many of our religions that the "little ones" of creation will lead us. The honeybee, as any beekeeper will tell you, is the best little guide you could hope to find.

When our paradisical parents went on the lam, a small creature, ignoring the executive order, (or, perhaps, following it) hastened to accompany them. She was winged, snowy white, a giver of sweetness and light—the honeybee. She got her striped and singed coloration, this same legend tells us, from a parting blast of the flaming sword.

As humans struggled to make a go of it, the honeybee quickly set up shop, gathering honey from conspiring flora, constructing waxen honeycomb to hold the golden stores. In time, humans discovered

that honey in a wound fought off bacteria, honey fermented in the Sun fueled their visions; and all they had to do was get past the stings.

As it turns out, the stings as well are a blessing—a powerful medicine is loaded in the venom sac, ready to be delivered through the medium of a highly efficient stinger. Bee Venom Therapy (BVT), which has been used for centuries in the China, is finally gaining long-overdue respect and attention in the United States. Folk medicine has long held that bee stings provided relief from arthritis, but in recent years, BVT has also shown itself to be effective in the treatment of such debilitating conditions as arthritis, MS, and potentially, AIDS.

The Conference

They came in wheelchairs, leaning on canes, and with halting, painful steps, as those seeking the healing waters of Lourdes.

This was not Lourdes, however, but the Ohio State Beekeepers Association annual conference. As the beekeepers were packing up supers and pollen traps, bee veils and smokers, a few of the curious remained behind for the post-conference conference hosted by one of their own, beekeeper/apitherapist Jim Higgins.

A bright, robust young woman handed out pamphlets and guided participants to the meeting hall as Higgins began extolling the benefits of a variety of hive products—honey, beeswax, propolis, and royal jelly; a litany of virtues well-known to the beekeepers present. He launched into a description of bee-venom therapy and its current application in the treatment of arthritis and MS. And then he invited the participants to share their stories.

The first to speak was Kathryn, the young woman I had noticed earlier, handing out pamphlets:

"Two years ago," she began, "I was in the final stages of MS. I had no feeling left in any part of my body except my face. I could no longer hear or speak; all that remained was partial vision in one eye. The doctors told my husband that there was nothing more that they could do and recommended that I be put in a nursing home. They predicted that I would be dead within six months.

"We have two young children," she went on, "and my husband refused to accept it. He had heard about Charlie's (Charlie Mraz) work with bee venom, so he quit his job, packed me and the kids up in the car and drove us all up to Vermont in the dead of winter. We stayed with Charlie for a month. By the time we left, I was walking with a cane. He sent me home with a jar of bees and a hope for a future."

Charles Mraz's—the "father of American Apitherapy"—initial encounter with bee venom therapy came about, as it does for many people, out of sheer desperation. Striken with rheumatic fever in 1934, the twenty-eight-year-old Mraz was left with the permanent, painful affliction of rheumatic arthritis. "The disease attacked a new joint every day," he says. "Finally, after several weeks, I was able to get out of bed again, but I was no longer a young man of twenty-eight. My joints were so painful and stiff that I felt more like an old man of ninety-eight."

Mraz, having chucked big-city life in 1923 for the sanity of rural life and beekeeping, was aware of the "folk wisdom" that bee stings helped relieve the pain of arthritis. A practical man, he dismissed it as an old-wives tale.

"As a youngster," he writes, "I thought arthritis was something old people imagined they had just to get sympathy, and using bee stings for arthritis was utterly ridiculous. If some old-time beekeepers wanted to believe it, that was their business, but I was too intelligent to go for such nonsense. It was the ultimate in superstitious nonesense to a young city-slicker like me."

After six months of crippling pain, however, he was willing to try anything. Enlisting the aid of his bees, he stung himself on his most painful areas—the knee joints. The next morning he awoke free of pain. It was the birth of a quest.

For many years, Mraz promoted apitherapy as a treatment for arthritis, but, by and large, was considered a harmless (or dangerous) eccentric and ignored by the American medical community. "Medical community wasn't interested in it," he says. "There was no money in it for them."

Mraz and his organization, the American Apitherapy Society, had a small following among beekeepers and holistic health buffs for many years. But the accidental discovery that the symptoms of MS also respond to treatment with Bee Venom Therapy has kindled widespread interest in this curious treatment.

"I suspected thirty years ago that bee venom might work for Multiple Sclerosis. No drugs will touch it, and since it had no satisfactory medical treatment, I thought BVT just might help. But as you can imagine, I couldn't find anyone who had been diagnosed with MS who was willing to have me sting them. They all thought I was crazy."

Ten years ago, Mraz got his guinea pig, quite by accident. A young woman came to him with an intriguing story: five years prior, Mraz had administered BVT to relieve her from a painful attack of arthritis. She had been fine for those interceeding five years, but then the tell-tale symptoms returned. She went back to her doctor and he told her that, in fact, the initial diagnosis had been incorrect. She did not have arthritis— rather, she had MS—and had had it for 6–10 years. Since this woman's mother had died with MS, she had no illusions about the prospects for her future.

Encouraged by the results she had received before, the woman returned to Mraz for treatment of her MS. "Again," says Mraz, "she made a dramatic recovery during her five months of treatment. Although I stopped treating her seven years ago, her symptoms have not returned. Here I thought I had been treating her successfully for arthritis, when, in fact I had actually been treating her for MS."

The good news of Mraz's results with MS patients began spreading rapidly. "When I started telling people about my success with MS, it generated an instantaneous interest with victims of MS all over the United States. There is nothing out there that is really helping them, and results with BVT on MS has shown improvement in almost all cases treated."

One of the most dramatic stories of MS and BVT involved a forty-three year old woman, Pat Wagner, who had had MS for more than twenty years. In 1970 she had been diagnosed with chronic progressive MS, one of the most serious varieties of MS. By 1993 she was in the final, terrifying stages of the disease: she was completely bedridden, unable to even roll over without help. Pat reports that she was incontinent, almost totally blind and deaf, waiting for that deadly day—soon to come— when she would no longer be able to breathe or swallow food.

As unbelievable as it may sound, within a few weeks of receiving BVT—a regular application of bee stings—Pat Wagner was up out of her bed and walking again. When she walked into her doctor's office a few weeks later for her check-up, the doctor failed to recognize his "dying" patient. Her dramatic story was picked up by the media and interest in the procedure spread like wildfire. Pat became a "practitioner" herself, using BVT to help others like her.

One woman who read about Pat Wagner's remarkable recovery was acupuncturist Amber Rose. Intrigued, she volunteered to help Pat in her work. Amber noticed immediately that Pat was using a stinging pattern on "trigger points" which roughly corresponded to acupuncture points. Three months later, Amber Rose boarded a plane headed for an apitherapy conference in China and met up with Charlie Mraz.

"It is so uplifting" says Mraz, "that after all this time someone like Amber came along, saw the importance of what I have been trying to do for sixty years and brought it to a whole other level."

Together, they discovered that the Chinese had been using "bee-acupuncture" (bee stings applied to acupuncture points) for over 3,000 years to treat a whole range of afflictions and ailments. They learned that both factors—bee venom itself and the stinging pattern—act in concert to affect treatment and/or cure.

Bee venom is a complex substance, composed of seventy-six different compounds. Some of these compounds, such as melittin and adolapin, produce bacteriocidal and anti-inflammatory effects. Others, like hyaluronidase and phospholipase Al & A2, aid in detoxifying the cells; dopamine is a neurotransmitter that increases motor activity; and mast cell degranulating peptide is believed to stimulate mental alertness and improve concentration. The effect of bee venom in the body, as was discovered by Western medical researchers in the1920s and thirties, is that it stimulates the immune system through the hypothalamus, pituitary, and adrenal glands.

Acupuncture is a form of treatment that also stimulates the body's immune system. (This is an extreme oversimplification of the process, but it is the one thing that mainstream Western medicine will acknowledge.) By applying "pricks" or "stings" along specific nerve pathways, the body's own defenses are activated to engage the disease or affliction.

If bee venom therapy is such a great thing, most people ask, why aren't doctors using it? Why hasn't it been approved as a medical treatment? Charlie Mraz tried for years to get the medical and pharmaceutical industries interested in the potential of BVT. What he discovered, unfortunately, is that health "care" in this country is, by and large,

money driven. Physicians and drug companies make billions of dollars a year treating people with drugs. "We don't need bee venom; we have lots of drugs to take care of arthritis," Charlie was told repeatedly in his early days. To get a substance or treatment approved by the FDA requires extensive, expensive testing. While the big drug companies have the resources to do this, they would not be able to recover their "R & D" investment from a substance that anyone can obtain from her own backyard. Mraz has pointedly observed:

> *Research has so far established that BVT stimulates the activity of the immune system so that the body produces its own healing agents and may result in improved conditions with MS or arthritis. There is much still to learn about immunology but one thing is certain: We cannot cure or control, in the long term, any disease by suppressing or destroying the immune system. Drugs have a great appeal to the medical world because of their potential for high profits. A natural agent such as BVT is easily available, but has little potential for profits by a drug monopoly.*

Since no other funding was available to do research, Charlie Mraz undertook the task himself. Among other things, he established the American Apitherapy Society, which collects data, provides information, contacts, and encouragement for people practicing or seeking apitherapy. Luckily, more and more committed medical people are joining in the effort.

The current president and vice president of the Society are in fact, medical doctors. Secretary for the group is Kate Chatot, a registered nurse who also suffers from MS. "I got involved in the organization after I learned how to sting myself to treat my MS," she says. "I also found that the BVT cleaned up so many other things that were affecting my health."

The Apitherapy Society publishes a newsletter, sponsors conferences and meetings, gathers data, and provides guidelines for practicioners. They insist on attention to safety: no responsible apitherapist stings without testing the client for sensitivity to bee stings or without an emergency bee sting kit (containing an antihistamine and injectabale adrenaline). Most apitherapists avoid legal problems by not charging for their services; maintaining that apitherapy is a treatment, not a cure; and by teaching people or their care-givers how to sting themselves rather than being dependent on the apitherapist for treatment.

BVT is not a panacea—both Charlie and Amber stress a holistic approach to healing that encompasses diet, environment, and attitude. "I pay particular attention to those people who do not respond to treatment," says Amber, who claims a phenomenal 98 percent success rate. "Sometimes there may be scar tissue that is causing the block—either physical or emotional. I had one client who complained that she was not improving even after several months of treatment. After talking to her at some length, I discovered that her husband was beating her up on a regular basis. There is a limit to what apitherapy can do."

But so far, the glowing reports of success, particularly among MS victims, have been gratifying. BVT is also being studied as a potential treatment for AIDS, which is likewise an immune system affliction. "I go to conferences now," says the eighty-nine-year-old Mraz, "and all these young women come up to me throw their arms around me and kiss me. It's great! They tell me over and over again, how my work is responsible for saving their lives."

This past year, Amber Rose, Charles Mraz, and Pat Wagner have written how-to books describing their methods, procedures, and experiences in treating people with BVT. They won't make massive amounts of money for their efforts; they are motivated by a desire to reach and teach as many people as possible. The gratitude they have amassed from the many many people who would otherwise have died a premature, painful death is enormous.

These true healers, with the aid of their honeybees, invite us to discover that the blessings of the Garden are, indeed, all around us. All we have to do is open our eyes that we may finally see and undertake the task of truly caring for one another.

PAMELA SPENCE is an independent writer, currently working on a book about mead.

Kombucha Tea

BY BETTY WOLD

Excerpted from the booklet *Kombucha: Power Drink of the Nineties.*

EDITOR'S NOTE: Kombucha tea has been getting a lot of press lately. Some people call it a wonder cure, others call it an immune booster, and still others say it is potentially harmful if the tea becomes contaminated. To date, the many benefits attributed to drinking kombucha tea have not been scientifically proven or disproven. We are providing this article for the interest of our readers, and not as a statement endorsing the use of kombucha. Should you choose to try kombucha, please make sure (as you would with any fermenting process) that all of your equipment is completely sterile at all times to avoid contamination of the culture.

❧ᑲᑕ❧

It's Friday afternoon and you stop to celebrate TGIF at your best friend's house.

"Hey everybody," she says, "I've got this new drink I want you to try." She passes a tray with glasses of a clear, sparkling, amber-colored beverage, and waits expectantly as you sip your drink.

"Mmm, not bad," you say. After all, she *is* the hostess. A few more sips and you continue, "You know, this is really pretty good, but what is it? Wine, cider, or carbonated apple juice?"

"None of the above," she laughs, "it's called kombucha."

"I've never seen it in the store. Where do you get it?" someone asks.

"Oh, you don't buy it," she replies, "you make it yourself and it only takes a few minutes, some starter, and some sweetened tea. I'll give you the starter and some instructions, but not till you finish your drink. I want to be sure you really like it first."

You all agree that even though it doesn't have the kick of scotch or vodka, it does give a nice lift; if it isn't too much trouble you'll try it. So you troop off to the hot water tank closet. She opens the door, and the aroma immediately takes you back to your last winery tour.

On a shelf above the tank are several gallon-size glass jars. Each is filled to about three-quarters with liquid, some golden amber, some rich russet, and you know at once why she wanted to be sure you really liked it. Floating on the top of each is a malevolent looking white film from ¼"–½" thick. On others, thin strands extend toward the bottom. Shades of high school biology and your jellyfish specimens!

After seeing the jars, a few people lose their enthusiasm, but you and several other adventurers decide to give it a try. As you leave, she gives each one of the daring souls a sheet of instructions and a tightly closed ziplock bag with a cup of starter liquid and the ominous looking film.

"This is the mother, and in 7–10 days she will have produced her first baby. Take good care of it," she says fondly.

All babies have a certain charm, you recall, but it's hard to think you'll develop a real fondness for this offspring.

That evening, feeling like a mad scientist, you assemble your ingredients and utensils, wash your hands, and read the directions.

Kombucha Elixir

- ❖ Remove rings and other jewelry; use only wood, glass, stainless steel, or food grade plastic utensils.
- ❖ Boil 5 cups distilled or pure spring water in a stainless steel pan. When the water is boiling, add ¾–1 cup pure white sugar, stir with wooden spoon if necessary.
- ❖ When water boils again, add 4–5 green or black tea bags, and steep for 15 minutes uncovered.
- ❖ Remove tea bags.
- ❖ Add 5 cups distilled or spring water at room temperature. When mixture is lukewarm, add starter liquid.
- ❖ Pour into (sterilized!) wide-mouth gallon glass jar.
- ❖ Float "jellyfish" on top.
- ❖ Cover with a light cloth that will allow mixture to breathe. Secure tightly with a rubber band. (EDITOR'S NOTE: Be sure to wash these cloths in the washing machine between batches!)
- ❖ Let sit at room temperture away from light for 7–10 days.
- ❖ "Mushroom" will make a "baby." At the end of the fermentation period (7–10 days or when "baby," the one on top, is about ⅛" thick), remove cultures from jar to a glass or china plate.
- ❖ Pour liquid through a non-metal strainer or coffee filter into bottles, reserving 2 cups.
- ❖ Carefully separate the "mother" from the "baby."

- Put the "baby" in a ziplock bag with one cup of starter liquid.

- Leave any sediment in the jar and start the process over with the "mother" and the remaining one cup of liquid. About every four weeks, pour it out, wash the jar with soap and rinse thoroughly with boiling water. EDITOR'S NOTE: To reduce the chances of contamination, you may want to do this between each batch.

- Only use the "mother" four times. For the fifth batch, retire the "mother" and use the "baby."

- Store bottle with finished elixir in the refrigerator.

Begin with 2 ounces (daily), gradually increasing to 6 ounces. Drink in the morning fifteen minutes before eating. If too strong for your taste, dilute with unsweetened tea, seltzer water, or fruit juice.

What Is It?

We do know that kombucha has been around as a refreshing home brew for thousands of years in China, Japan, Manchuria, and through Russia to Eastern Europe. In many cottages, it was the job of the grandmother to keep the brew going—for years and years. You know the conditions were not laboratory sterile and probably the methods, amounts of ingredients and conditions varied, but the culture itself contained the same basic elements. Much research was done on it in Russia, before World War II. The Moscow Central Biological Institute called it tea sponge or tea fungus, and described it as formed from *Bacterius xylinium* (now called *Acetobacter xylinium*), and yeast cells of the genus *Saccharomyces*. It is not a fungus, but that's how it came to be called a mushroom.

Maybe you cringe at the thought of drinking bacteria and yeast. Just remember, they are an essential part of the processes of making cheese, yogurt, wine, vinegar, and leavened breads. Those contained in kombucha are from the same family as those used in making wine and beer. According to research being done in Europe, they have a natural antibiotic effect, and even release a substance in the intestinal tract which combats harmful bacteria. They are said to defend and regulate your digestive system. Research also found that the beverage contained glucoronic acid, many of the B vitamins, folic acid, usnic acid, and L-lactic (+) acid.

What Will It Do for Me?

In Gunther Frank's book *Kombucha*, we read that glucoronic acid is a liver detoxifier which binds up toxins, both metabolic and environmental, and flushes them through the kidneys and out of the system. It is a building block of important polysaccharides necessary for maintaining connective tissue, cartilage, the stomach lining and vitreous humor of the eye.

Folic acid, usually found in leafy green foods, is essential for protein and prevention of anemia.

Lack of L-lactic(+) acid leads to failure of cell respiration and the buildup of DL-lactic acid, which has been linked to cancer.

Usnic acid has a strongly antibacterial effect and can even partly inactivate some viruses.

You don't need to be a dietitian to know the benefits of the B-vitamins: steady nerves, emotional balance, good digestion, disease resistance, healthy skin, and energy.

Folklore has it that kombucha helps with indigestion, constipation, hemorrhoids, and kidney and gallstones. It was also thought to combat the ills of every stage of our lives, from the acne of youth through weight problems, impotence, menopausal symptoms, wrinkles, hair loss, memory loss, and hardening of the arteries.

Since it is not a standardized "medicine" prepared under strictly controlled condition, no scientific claims can be made.

If It's So Great, Why Haven't We Had It Here?

World War II and later political situations halted the research being done on kombucha, and shortages of sugar and tea made it difficult—in many places impossible—to keep the tea going. The growing interest in alternative medicine has sparked a new interest in natural health care, especially preventative and protective measures. Americans who enjoyed its refreshing taste in Europe brought kombucha cultures back to share with friends. In some European countries, it is sold in pharmacies.

Will Every Batch Be Successful?

Yes, if you start with a culture from a beverage you like, use a tea you like, keep hands, work surfaces, and utensils clean, and provide the proper conditions.

What are the proper conditions? Good air and water quality, sufficient warmth (70°F–80°F), and a quiet, dimly lit or dark spot. A wide glass mixing bowl is recommended. The larger the surface, the more air reaches the culture and the faster it grows. Gallon glass jars have proven successful for many.

❧ Do not disturb the bowl or jar once fermentationhas begun;

it may slow the process or produce a misshapen "mushroom."

* Do not smoke while working with the culture or near the fermentation site.

* Avoid having potted plants nearby because of the mold present in the soil, which can be released into the air.

Should I Use Green or Black Tea?

The tea is a source of nitrogen and mineral salts and promotes the growth of organisms. For that reason it should steep longer than is customary for brewed tea. Some directions even call for the tea to be boiled for 3–5 minutes. It is not necessary to use a specific tea; because of local differences in water, results vary even when the same tea is used.

What About Herb Tea?

When you have a backup supply of kombucha culture, you may want to experiment with various herb teas. Remember, you will be introducing different micro-organisms since most herbs grow close to the soil. Herbs with strong volatile oils may inhibit or destroy some of the useful bacteria because they accumulate on the upper surface of the liquid where the new culture floats and growth occurs. While experi-

menting, be sure to add one or two green or black tea bags or equivalent to provide nutrient for the growing culture. The culture will grow, but perhaps not as much, and is not one you would share as kombucha.

How Do I Know My Culture Is the Real Thing?

What do you mean by real? There is no world-wide standard. It is generally agreed that the culture contains *Acetobacter xylinum* and *Schizosaccharomyces pombe*, the same bacteria used in the production of wine and beer. Unless you are a chemist or biologist, you will not be able to identify these substances in your culture.

How Much Can I Drink?

Begin with a small amount, ¼ cup or so, fifteen minutes before breakfast. Gradually increase the amount; again the choice is yours. If the beverage is strongly acid, you will not want much. If you like the flavor, drink it like any refreshing beverage. Taken before meals, it tends to curb the appetite, so it is a good addition to a weight loss program. Drink it after meals to stimulate digestion. Most people report a lift, but without the jitters (of caffeine). Conduct your own test if you feel that it helps you physically or emotionally. Drink it regularly for several months, then stop for one month. Note the difference, if any. Notice any difference in your cholesterol or blood pressure, both of which can be measured precisely. How about your sleep habits, your aches and pains? Keep a record and share your results if you must, but don't expect others to have the same response.

Other Considerations

People addicted to or recovering from addiction to alcohol should not drink kombucha, not because the alcohol content is high, but because even small amounts may stimulate a desire for much stronger drink.

In general, diabetics should avoid kombucha unless they can keep an accurate check on their blood sugar, and regulate their use of the beverage as indicated.

Copies of the complete booklet *Kombucha: Power Drink of the Nineties,* can be ordered from Betty Wold, Route 1, Box 80, Gore, OK 74435. The booklet includes more detailed information on making kombucha, celebrity kombucha stories, recipes using kombucha, a list of references with further information, and a list of other ways to use both the tea and the culture once it is ready to be "retired."

BETTY WOLD, herb grower, author, teacher, and speaker, has been growing and using herbs for more years than she cares to admit. She has been a featured speaker at the International Herb Growers and Marketers Association Convention, Great Lakes Herb Symposium, New Zealand Herb Federation Conference, and many regional herb meetings. She is a member of the Herb Society of America and several local herb groups. Her insatiable curiosity leads her to explore anything having to do with herbs and alternative health care.

Your Pet's Health—Holistically

By Phil Klein

Propylene glycol, BHA, BHT, *Ethoxyquin, dextrose,* maltrose, sucrose, fructose, sodium propionate, titanium dyoside, sodium nitrite, cancerous growths, growth hormones, antibiotics, cortisone, claws, beaks, roadkill, the list is almost endless.

If you were a dog or cat out to hunt for your dinner, it's rather doubtful that you would be attracted to any of the above ingredients, much less eat those same things every day for the rest of your life. But when you, as a pet's caregiver, feed Fluffy or Bowser the canned or dry foods found in the supermarket or in most pet stores, that is exactly what you are doing. We are condemning our pets to the strong potential of contracting diseases and/or conditions that used to be rare, but are now seen by veterinarians in epidemic proportions. Symptoms include excessive scratching, chewing, licking, dermatitis, hot spots, dry flaky skin, oily matted coats, hair loss, eye problems, weight problems, hyperactivity, lethargy, diarrhea, constipation, arthritis, diabetes, epilepsy, heart disease, parasites, and more.

For the same reasons that you may have elected to be not just a vegetarian or vegan, but an organic vegetarian or vegan, and for the same reasons you wouldn't want your children to eat junk food and chemically preserved foods meal after meal after meal, it's important to understand just what's in the food we so injudiciously feed our pets every day for every meal of their lives.

Why do we continue to feed this chemical soup slop to those who don't have a vote, much less a choice? Because we've been told it's okay by the manufacturers, the veterinarians, the shopkeepers, the breeders, etc.

But *why?* Because they want our pets to be harmed? Not likely. Because they want to make a bigger buck? Perhaps. But more likely because they just don't know better. Through our research, we have learned that veterinarians typically receive no more than 4–6 *hours* of nutrition out of four *years* in vet school. Even more surprising, many vets told us that their nutrition courses were taught by representatives of the pet food manufacturers! Self-serving? I'd say so.

Perhaps as readers of this fine, enlightened publication, you have more sense than to just plop drugs and chemicals into or onto your body just because a doctor told you to. But did you ever transfer that "healthy" (excuse the unintentional pun) skepticism to your pet's doctor? Until we were faced with the tragedy of our thirteen-year-old collie-huskie, we didn't either. Tiffany-Anne was the most loved dog in the entire world, according to her mother and father (me). Her illness was the result of blind obedience to a traditional vet who had no clue that his lack of knowledge regarding nutrition and diet could have contributed to her sudden death.

So what can we, as regular folks, do? Simple. Feed your pets what their bodies were meant to eat before we got lazy and let the manufacturers and doctors tell us what's best.

Our paradigm or model is simple. How did Bowser or Fluffy live and eat in the wild 100 years ago? Why 100 years ago? Because 100 years is not enough time to make deep, basic changes to their evolution; nor had we so royally screwed up our land and the fruits of our land yet; and our food animals were not laden with insecticides, pesticides, growth hormones,

antibiotics, acid rain, chemical-spill runoff, toxic waste, radiation, and the whole panoply of insults to good, clean, Earth that exists in and on our farmlands today.

Dogs and cats are really hunters and omnivores, not the strict carnivores that most folks think. As any human hunter will tell you, hunters don't make a kill every time they go out to hunt. Neither did dogs or cats when they went to hunt for their meals. What happened back then? Well, Monday morning Bowser's great-great-great grandfather goes out to hunt for breakfast. After many unsuccessful attempts, he finally catches a rabbit that happens to be at the wrong place at the wrong time. (I know the thought is upsetting, but it *is* real life.) So here's Bowser, proud to have caught his breakfast, although by now, it could be lunch. What does he do? Does he tear off a hunk of shoulder or haunch? No. He goes directly for the belly. He

opens the belly and his first bite, meant for nutritional purposes, is of the contents of the stomach. What is in the stomach of a rabbit and other prey? Greens and grains. That's what rabbits and most other prey of dogs or cats eat—greens and grains. Those greens and grains are already half-digested by the prey's own enzymatic action. Result? Bowser and Fluffy's ancestors breakfast, lunch and dinner usually consisted of greens, grains, and organ meats, all organic. Yep. Heart, liver, and kidneys are the preferred meats, not hard meats from shoulder or haunch, although those parts probably will get eaten. There was little cancer or diabetes in animals of that day—at least not in the epidemic proportions found in every city and town in today's society.

Now, back to us and what we can do. "I work long hours and am out most of the day," you say. "It's difficult enough for me to cook for myself and the family. Do I now have to cook for Fluffy too?" Or,

"My pet is sixteen years old and all we fed him/her was XYZ brand and table scraps. There wasn't any problem." My reply to that is twofold. First and foremost, you both are lucky. Secondly, ten, fifteen, twenty years ago the components and make-up of commercial foods were different, the amount of processing and fast food functions was different, and the origin of the raw materials was different. If the levels of poor animal health were not as high as they are, why would these self-same manufacturers come out with products supposedly formulated for, and marketed as, answers to animal health problems, like uretic formulas for cats with urinary tract diseases, or formulas low in ash and high in bulk? What inevitably occurs? Sell garbage to the unsuspecting caregiver, then sell more garbage to counteract the effects of the original garbage.

Well, there are alternatives.

The first and foremost line of defense is, as always, knowledge. In this case, the acquisition of knowledge is easy. There are a number of excellent books that review the circumstances under which animal foods are produced, the effects these foods have on our beloved pets, and then detail how to produce, quite quickly and easily, a diet that not only provides quality nutrition, but also supports the immune system, turns diseases around, can drastically reduce flea and worm infestation, and save you big bucks as well. Following this article is a short list of top pet resource books available either in your library, from *Whiskers Holistic Pet Products Catalog*, or several other sources. Any of these books listed will give you the tools to effectively and naturally begin the process of alleviating many of the ills that afflict companion animals in today's "modern" society.

Another alternative is the use of top-quality processed foods— not the kind you find in a supermarket or the kind you see on TV. As a matter of fact, it's my personal belief that the more a dog/cat food is advertised on TV, the worse it is—despite and in spite of the claims by the TV vets and/or breeders. My reasoning is simple. As with the now old-fashioned, computer-based acronym GIGO, Garbage In Garbage Out, if the food is made with garbage, then no matter what you do to it in the processing (including the processing itself) you can only get garbage out.

Following the book list at the end of this article is a list of manufacturers whose foods (both dog and cat, canned and dry) when supplemented with fresh, raw, or steamed vegetables, vitamins, and nutritional supplements, can be the base for an excellent, healthy, nutritious, and immune system-supportive diet. These foods are usually not available in most stores, but can be found either by mail order from Whiskers or other local or mail-order sources. Are they more expensive? That is a difficult question to answer, both because of regionality, and the sometimes unscrupulous tactics of some purveyors. For the most part, these foods should not be more expensive than those foods touted by the major manufacturers as "premium" or "super premium" (but which are really just more expensive junk).

The subject of companion animal nutrition is huge and full of controversy, but when you are on the receiving end of a river of sick animals and their distraught owners, the controversy stops the minute a convert to natural feeding and nutritional supplements comes to you with tears of joy and words like, "My dog wouldn't stop chewing/scratching the base of her tail (or paws or neck) and all the vet could do was shoot her with cortisone. But now (four to six weeks later), since I'm feeding her (one of the foods listed below) and the veggies and vitamins, all that has stopped and she's happy and running around like a puppy again." Or: "It cost me a pile of money at the vet and all they did was drug the cat and he still scratches himself to pieces, but once I changed foods and added those veggies and stuff, he seems to be fine again." We hear this and much, much more every day.

Understand, this is not meant to be a blanket condemnation of all vets. As with human doctors, most are as good as their schooling and belief systems allow them to be. But here again, there are alternatives. Give us a call and we'll be happy to refer you to all the holistic vets in your state. Since there are only about 300 holistic vets in the entire U. S., you'll probably end up working with one by phone. Don't be dismayed. This kind of long-distance relationship works very well for thousands and thousands of caregivers. We do stress however, that you find a local vet with at least an open mind, one who will be willing to work under the direction of your long-distance holistic vet. It is not as difficult as it might seem; in the world of human medicine, we get second opinions and have primary, secondary, or specialist doctors all the time. Besides, if your current vet is so stuck in his/her ways that a new technique or thought process wounds his or her sensibilities, I'd want another, more flexible-minded practitioner immediately anyway. The phone number for the President of the American Holistic

Veterinary Association is: (410) 569-7777.

It is very important that you understand that scratching and other aberrant behaviors are often symptoms of a deep-seated medical problem. Very often those problems result from allergies related to food, and natural brands can often resolve the situation, but not always. You should always have your pet checked by a vet. Any vet is better than none, just don't be blinded or bulldozed into letting them do whatever they want just because they are doctors. Use what is inaccurately termed as "common sense" (in my observations, sense is not very common these days). Ask questions. Don't be bullied. If the vet gives you the old "who are you to question me" attitude, find another vet. It's the life and health of your pet and you are entitled to good, sensible, practical answers. Just another reason to be in communication with a holistic vet. One phone call can often resolve a lot of potential problems. At the very least, your holistic vet can answer the questions on a professional level and give you appropriate direction.

How do you feed your pets any of the new foods? It's simple. Let's start with how to change over from what you are currently feeding, to what you now know you should be feeding.

The process is a simple weaning. Wean on and wean off. You are going to need about a week's worth of the old food and a like amount of the new food for the first 9–12 days. It's pretty much a given that the sicker animals are, the more "finicky" they are. Truly healthy pets will eat just about anything you put in front of them. It's the sick or potentially sick pet that won't eat at all, or will only eat one flavor from one maker. Pets get addicted to all the sugar and salt in the junk foods, just as people do. The better a food is, the less junk (like sugars and salts) are in it, therefore it is less palatable to our pet junk-food junkies.

Take the total amount of food you would feed your pet in a day. Of that total, 75 percent would be the "old" food and 25 percent the new food—physically mix them together. (By the way, you should not feed a pet just dry, or just canned food. There are nutrients in each that are not available in the other.) Give this 75–25 percent mixture for three meals a day. Follow the premise of the old Polish general's proverb: feed your loved ones a big breakfast, your friends a large lunch, and your enemies a huge dinner. Give your pets a big breakfast, a large lunch and a small dinner.

Keep the 75-25 percent ratio every meal for four days. Then change to 50 percent old and 50 percent new for four days, and finally, change to 75 percent new and 25 percent old for four days. It's just a cross-over process. No big deal. But once your pet is on the new food for a week or two, start to add in the really good stuff: vegetables, grains, and meats.

If you don't have one, a good old-fashioned "knuckle buster" vegetable grater with "teardrop" openings, the kind grandmammas used to use, is an excellent tool. Grate just enough carrot or broccoli, zucchini, or chopped-up sprouts to fit on the end of a teaspoon and mix into the combined wet and dry pet food. Do that every meal, every day, for three or four days. Then switch to the tip of a teaspoon plus a little more at every meal for four days, and so on. Add beans or steamed cauliflower, baked yams, brown (only) rice, organic only raw egg, zucchini, potato, legumes (well, you get the idea).

Observe the result. Does your kitty or pooch eat the veggies or eat around the veggies? If Bowser eats the veggies, great. If not, find veggies he will eat. Remember to increase the amount of veggies slowly, gradually. Ultimately, the goal is to feed 40 percent to 50 percent raw or steamed veggies plus cooked grains to the balance of top quality processed foods. This system provides the nutrition and life force of live foods, as opposed to dead, processed-only foods the big companies push.

This next caveat is mostly for cat households, but can apply to dog households as well. Do not leave food down all day or all night. Repeat: do not leave food down. Do not leave food down. Do not leave food down. Do not leave food down. I hope you get the message. Do not leave food down.

Leaving food down is the best way to starve your cats, while at the same time making them fat and sloppy, with bellies that hang down and swing in the breeze. Fat, starving cats are almost always the result of well-intentioned caregivers riddled with guilt because they had to go to work all day (and maybe part of the night too). But if we harken back to 100 years ago—or even today—a cat that hunts for a living can go days without a meal. All fasting does is sharpen the cat's appetite and reflexes; the cat won't starve. As a matter of fact, most holistic vets recommend you put your animals on a fast one day a week and one weekend a month.

Whether you fast them or not, do not leave food down. The rea-

sons are too long to go into here. Here is a workable feeding method for those who work or are out of the house for long periods of time.

First, get a wide-mouthed glass jar with a good cover and put the food into it. You'll need fifteen minutes to half an hour for the next step, so adjust your schedule accordingly (don't get nervous, this isn't that big a deal). Put a sufficient amount of food down for Bowser to have for a good-sized breakfast. Pick up whatever is left over after 15–30 minutes, put it back in the glass jar, close the lid, wipe the spot on the floor where the food was, and go to work, secure in the knowledge that Bowser won't starve to death in your absence. By the way, don't refrigerate the food in the glass jar. Cats, especially, don't like refrigerated food, and what is in the jar won't go bad in twelve hours or so if it's processed. (Raw meat should be refrigerated immediately.)

Now you come home and Bowser comes to greet you at the door. Kiss and pet Bowser and any other deserving beings in the house and hang up your coat.

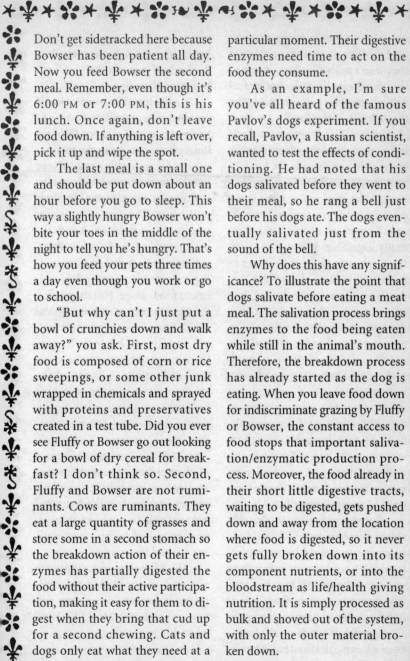

Don't get sidetracked here because Bowser has been patient all day. Now you feed Bowser the second meal. Remember, even though it's 6:00 PM or 7:00 PM, this is his lunch. Once again, don't leave food down. If anything is left over, pick it up and wipe the spot.

The last meal is a small one and should be put down about an hour before you go to sleep. This way a slightly hungry Bowser won't bite your toes in the middle of the night to tell you he's hungry. That's how you feed your pets three times a day even though you work or go to school.

"But why can't I just put a bowl of crunchies down and walk away?" you ask. First, most dry food is composed of corn or rice sweepings, or some other junk wrapped in chemicals and sprayed with proteins and preservatives created in a test tube. Did you ever see Fluffy or Bowser go out looking for a bowl of dry cereal for breakfast? I don't think so. Second, Fluffy and Bowser are not ruminants. Cows are ruminants. They eat a large quantity of grasses and store some in a second stomach so the breakdown action of their enzymes has partially digested the food without their active participation, making it easy for them to digest when they bring that cud up for a second chewing. Cats and dogs only eat what they need at a

particular moment. Their digestive enzymes need time to act on the food they consume.

As an example, I'm sure you've all heard of the famous Pavlov's dogs experiment. If you recall, Pavlov, a Russian scientist, wanted to test the effects of conditioning. He had noted that his dogs salivated before they went to their meal, so he rang a bell just before his dogs ate. The dogs eventually salivated just from the sound of the bell.

Why does this have any significance? To illustrate the point that dogs salivate before eating a meat meal. The salivation process brings enzymes to the food being eaten while still in the animal's mouth. Therefore, the breakdown process has already started as the dog is eating. When you leave food down for indiscriminate grazing by Fluffy or Bowser, the constant access to food stops that important salivation/enzymatic production process. Moreover, the food already in their short little digestive tracts, waiting to be digested, gets pushed down and away from the location where food is digested, so it never gets fully broken down into its component nutrients, or into the bloodstream as life/health giving nutrition. It is simply processed as bulk and shoved out of the system, with only the outer material broken down.

Many manufacturers tout the digestibility of their foods. What they don't tell you is how much of that food can be assimilated and actually used by your animals. The digestibility of the food *is* a primary concern. The government, in its infinite wisdom, mandates that the protein in pet food be at least 12 percent digestible. So when you look at the label and it gives you a protein amount, remember that only 12 percent of that total is actually digestible. If that is the case, then what is the protein made from that is NOT digestible? You don't really want to know, but some of those things are listed at the beginning of this article. The government takes for granted that manufacturers will use such garbage that they, the government, must regulate it to the extent that the food must be at least 12 percent digestible. Pet Guard, for example, is 85 percent digestible. Just think what it would be like for the health and well-being of you and your family if your family's foods were only 12 percent digestible.

Regarding organic foods, what else is there to say? YES. Feed organic meats, vegetables, eggs (particularly), and grains every time you can. I know this may be sacrilege, but *non-organic*, fresh raw or lightly steamed veggies are better than no fresh foods at all. In the case of cats, that is true of even meat. Some non-organic meat is better than no organic meat. Just do the best you can and don't get too crazy about it.

As for humans, your animals are what they assimilate. As long as they are in your care, they no longer have choices in the maintenance of their health. Fresh, raw or lightly steamed vegetables, meats, and grains are essential to their well-being. The cost of fresh veggies, even in combination with the best processed foods listed above, will be significantly less than feeding supermarket or so-called premium foods alone. Not to mention the enormous cost of poor animal health those foods precipitate.

Finally, to be complete, as there are many alternatives to pet food and feeding methods, so too are there alternatives to your pet's medical care. Acupuncture, homeopathy, herbs, Bach Flower Remedies, chiropractic, Tellington Touch, TCM (Traditional Chinese Medicine), behavior modification, and other modalities have all proven extremely efficacious and are available to your pet through the network of holistic veterinarians around the country.

We offer an open invitation to any and all concerned pet caregivers. If you have a problem, give us a call at 1-800-944-7537. We'll assist you in any way we can.

Suggested Readings

Frazier, Anitra, and Norma Eckroate. *The New Natural Cat.* Penguin Books.

Lazarus, Pat. *Keep Your Pet Healthy the Natural Way.* Keats Publishing.

Levy, Juliette de Bairacli. *Cats Naturally.* Faber & Faber Ltd.

McKay, Pat. *Reigning Cats and Dogs.* Oscar Publications.

Pitcairn, Richard, D.V.M., Ph.D. and Susan Hubble. *Dr. Pitcairn's Complete Guide to Natural Health for Dogs and Cats.* Rodale Press.

Plechner, Alfred, D.V.M. and Martin Zucker. *Pet Allergies, Remedies for an Epidemic.*

"Rationale for Animal Nutrition," an interview with Dr. Randy L. Wysong. Inquiry Press.

Stein, Diane. *The Natural Remedy Book for Dogs and Cats.* The Crossing Press.

Suggested Pet Foods

WYNSONG (85–90 percent organic)

PET GUARD (largely organic)

SOLID GOLD (large percentage organic, dry only)

PRECISE

NATURE'S RECIPE

PRO PLAN TURKEY AND BARLEY (from this manufacturer, this particular turkey and barley only)

NATURAL LIFE

ABADY

PHIL KLEIN and his wife Randy are owners of Whiskers, an international mail order company and retail health food store for pets. Following eight months of antibiotics, medications, x-rays, and office visits totalling over $2,000 to cure their dog, Tiffany-Anne, of a "rare" bladder infection, the Kleins changed vets. By changing her diet and putting her on the right mix of vitamins, Tiffany's "rare" condition was completely cured within three weeks. Through Whiskers, the Kleins are committed to helping others find better ways to care for their companion animal friends. For a free catalog, call 1-800-944-7537.

The Old-Time Cold Cure

By Carly Wall

In going through my grand-mother's old recipe books, I stumbled upon this nugget of information and I share it with you here. It's an easy way to make your own vitamin C elixir—at virtually no cost!

Vitamin C plays an important role in the health of teeth and gums, and promotes resistance to infections, allergies, and other diseases. Because of this, my grand-mother put up as much of this extract as she could in the fall, since it contains on average about 1200–1800 milligrams of vitamin C per half cup.

Rose Hip Tonic

1   cup rose hips

1½   cups water

2   tablespoons lemon juice

This fall, gather rose hips (the bright red seed pods which appear on roses, wild or cultivated, after the flowers have faded away).

As soon as you gather the rose hips, make this tonic. You can also keep the rose hips in the refrigerator, but use them soon as possible.

Remove blossom ends, stems, and leaves from one cup rose hips. Bring 1½ cups water to a rolling boil, then add the hips. Cover and simmer 15 minutes. If the rose hips were fresh, mash the contents of the pan with a fork or potato masher after boiling. If they were dried, run the elixir through a blender. Let the mixture stand in a glass bowl, covered, for 24 hours. Strain the mixture, bring it to a rolling boil again, and add 2 tablespoons lemon juice for each pint. Pour into jars, and seal in a water bath canner for 15 minutes. To use, give each family member 1 tablespoon daily (you can add it to fruit juice). If someone has a cold, double their dose.

❖❖

Carly Wall is an aromatherapist, and author of *Flower Secrets Revealed: Using Flowers to Heal, Beautify and Energize Your Life!* A.R.E. Press, $14.95, available in bookstores or by calling 1-800-723-1112.

From Garden to Kitchen

Gourmet Grains

**Herbal Vinegar:
Aromatic Delights
from Your Garden**

Not Milk...Nutmilk!

Super Smoothies

Gourmet Grains

Contemporary Cuisine from the Mountains to the Prairies

By Candia Lea Cole

From the mountains of Peru, where quinoa plants brace sunny cold mountaintops, to the heart of the American midwest, where corn fields embroider the land and shaggy red plots of amaranth stand resurrected, grains speak proudly of our heritage. They have been celebrated in ancient religious rituals, honored in matrimonial ceremonies, revered by goddesses and slaves, relied upon for fodder by livestock and songbirds, and literally been worshipped by the civilizations they once sustained.

Thanks to modern day explorers and agricultural developers, even the most ancient and mystical grains, such as amaranth, quinoa, teff, millet, and spelt, are now available at stores and markets where more common grains, such as rice, are sold. When they bring this variety of hearty, aromatic grasses to the stovetop, cooks often discover that the flavor of cultural diversity is rekindled. A slow-simmering pot of wild rice, for instance, known as *Mahnomen* (precious grain) by many Native Americans, might remind us of a walk in the smoky Canadian woodlands. A pot of fluffy basmati rice may call to mind a rustic picture of the Himalayan mountain people.

The history of grains will, to those who are romantics, fill the dinner hour with intrigue. Consider, for instance, how a platter of "Quinoa Parmesan with Savory Green Beans and Tomatoes" could take the appetite back in time on a Peruvian adventure. The tiny, beige-colored grain featured in this recipe was once a royal mainstay of the pre-Columbian Americas. It was so highly valued by the native culture that Spanish explorers destroyed the crop as a way to squash resistance. Another unusual grain, which built the royal fortunes of the Aztec empire before it, too, was destroyed, is amaranth. A tiny seed which looks like yellow poppy seeds, it makes delicious filling for a rustic supper pie.

If these don't whet your appetite for a dinner that promises something different, there is always spelt, teff, or millet. Spelt is a robust and chewy morsel, grown over 8,000 years ago in medieval Europe. It was used (as indicated in the Old Testament) to remedy ills of the digestive system and to strengthen a weak constitution. Teff, the tiniest grain in the world, was a nutrient-rich part of the Indonesian diet. Millet, a personal favorite of mine, was the mainstay of African and Chinese cultures.

Although the traditional recipes of other cultures have inspired many of America's well-known grain dishes (from oriental rice stir-fry to Middle Eastern bulgur salad), they have yet to be rediscovered by many people. Whether harvested from the mountains or the prairies, ancient grains provide the culinary basis for gourmet soups, stews, stir-frys, non-meat loaves, dinner pies, stuffings, desserts, and even enriched blender drinks!

Millet

Millet, a tiny and pearly yellow colored grain that was once husked, pounded, and mixed with melted fat to feed Africa's poor, is today considered a nutritious breakfast cereal. However, prepared with less water than is necessary for a cereal or pudding, it is a fluffy mouthful of morsels which welcome accents of vegetables, legumes, herbs, and spices. My favorite ways to dress millet are in Morrocan, Mexican, or savory "pilgrim day" style. Herbal (summery) dressings also warm its sweetish, mild flavor. With its high protein, iron, and B complex vitamin content, it has earned its place in my vegetarian menus.

Use approximately 2 cups water to 1 cup millet. Bring to a boil, reducing heat after 3–5 minutes. Cover and gently simmer on very low flame for approximately 20 minutes. Turn flame almost off, and let the grains finish steaming through for another 15 minutes. Grains should appear dry and fluffy on top. Let them rest undisturbed for an hour or more. The grains are easiest to work with when they are cool, because you can flake them apart by rolling them between the palms of your hands. You can also

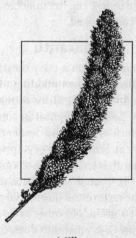

Millet

Amaranth

creamed cereal provides nearly the calcium of one half cup of milk or three cups of broccoli. Its iron content is equally impressive, providing more than four times the amount in brown rice.

Use 2½–3 parts liquid to 1 part amaranth. Bring to a boil, reduce heat, and simmer, stirring occasionally. Cover and cook for about 25 minutes. Grains will bind together like creamed cereal. One cup dry equals 2½ cups cooked.

Quinoa

With its complete protein content, quinoa, the Peruvian-grown "mother grain" of the Inca civilization, promises to be a regular grain on your menu since it cooks quickly. Its delicious and nutty flavor is elegantly complemented by both sweet and savory ingredients. Served with vegetables in a summery garden pilaf, or in a hearty winter soup or stew, it is delightful. Snuck into cookie recipes and muffins it lends nutty sweet flavor and enrichment you can feel good about. Blended into a pudding, it is an elegant dessert. Blending a few tablespoons into a body-building drink enriches the mixture while adding smooth, silky texture and fiber. Quinoa's light, melt-in-your-mouth quality makes it especially easy to digest.

Use approximately 2 parts liquid to 1 part quinoa. Bring to a

break them into individual grains using a fork. 1 cup dry millet equals 3–3½ cups cooked.

Amaranth

Amaranth makes a tasty breakfast porridge or dessert pudding when topped with fruit sauce or maple syrup. I also highlight it in supper fare, such as soups and dinner pies, where it lends a savory appeal. Amaranth is technically not a grain, but it is treated as one because it has the texture and nutritional profile of a grain. No other grain has vitamin C, as amaranth does, or its high calcium count. One cup of the boil and reduce heat to low. Cover and simmer gently until all liquid is absorbed (15–20 minutes) and grains appear fluffy and translucent. One cup dry quinoa equals 4 cups cooked.

Spelt

Spelt is an excellent source of B vitamins, and is higher in protein, fat (the good kind), and fiber than most varieties of wheat. Most people with allergies or sensitivities to gluten do not react to spelt.

Use approximately 4 parts liquid to 1 part spelt. Bring to a boil, reduce heat, and let simmer for about 45 minutes, stirring only occasionally, until all liquid is absorbed and grain is tender.

Teff

Teff, native to Ethiopia, is primarily a bread grain and a creamed cereal, with a sweet flavor. Notwithstanding, it blends nicely with sweetish vegetables (such as squash) and nuts. Containing more nutrient-rich bran than any other grain, it makes delicious "meaty" fritters or meatless burgers that provide a rich source of calcium, iron, zinc and copper.

Use 2 cups liquid to ½ cup teff. Bring to a boil, reduce heat, and simmer over low heat for about 15–20 minutes, stirring often to prevent lumping.

Spelt

Wild Rice

Wild rice, known as *mahnomen* to the Native Americans, is harvested from the aquatic plant known as *Zizania aquatica*. Technically, it is not a grain, but is referred to as one. It is said to have three to four times more protein than plain rice. Wild rice is delicious in stuffings, chilled summer grain salads, and non-meat loaves.

Use–4 parts liquid to 1 part wild rice. Bring to a boil, stir in rice, reduce heat, cover tightly, and simmer for about 45 minutes or until fluffy and tender. One cup wild rice yields about 4 cups cooked.

Long Grain Brown Rice

There are thousands of varieties of rice grown all around the globe.

Brown rice has an earthy appeal, although it is grown in moist conditions. Its plain flavor and color make it ideal for any flavor accents you can imagine.

Use 2 parts liquid to 1 part brown rice. Bring liquid to a boil and stir in brown rice. Reduce heat after a few minutes and simmer, covered, for about 40 minutes. Leave lid on for an additional 10 minutes. Grains will steam through and plump up nicely.

Basmati Rice

Basmati is an aromatic rice native to India and Pakistan. It is a light and nutty flavored rice that adapts deliciously to spices such as curry and cardamon.

Use 2 parts liquid to 1 part Basmati rice. Boil water and add rice. Stir and let boil again. Reduce heat, cover, and simmer for 15 minutes. Let rest 5 minutes and fluff with a fork.

❖c Recipes with Gourmet Grains ɔ❖

Basmati Rice with Szechuan Vegetables and Seitan

4–6   cups Basmati rice

1–1½   cups seitan (wheat meat, or "mock duck"), sliced into strips

Marinade for Seitan

¼–⅓   cup tamari

1½   tablespoon Szechuan sauce

½   cup orange juice

⅛   cup cooking sherry

1   tablespoon grated ginger

⅛   teaspoon ground fennel seed (optional)

1   teaspoon toasted sesame oil

½   cup water

1½   tablespoon arrowroot powder (adjust as needed)

Stir-Fry Ingredients

1   medium onion, sliced in thin crescents

1   garlic clove, crushed

2   cups small broccoli florets

1½   cups pea pods

⅔   cup red bell pepper, cut in thin 1" strips

1   tablespoon freshly grated ginger

⅛–¼ cup canola oil, for sauteeing

few drops hot pepper oil (optional)

toasted cashews for garnish

Prepare grains in advance as indicated in "Basmati Rice" section. Mix marinade ingredients in a bowl, with the exception of the water and arrowroot powder. Soak seitan slices, refrigerated, in marinade for about fifteen minutes. Drain marinade from seitan and transfer marinade to a blender. Add water and arrowroot powder and whiz smooth. Transfer mixture to a non-stick sauce pan. Bring to a gentle boil on the stove and stir constantly, letting it thicken before reducing heat. If mixture is not as thick as you like, simply spoon a small amount from the pan into a cup and mix with an additional one or two teaspoons arrowroot powder. Return to pot and stir. Remove pan from heat and set aside.

Coat a large skillet with canola and pepper oils (as needed). Over medium high heat, stir fry the onions until fragrant and slightly softened. Add seitan and cook briefly. Add a few tablespoons of water to the pan and toss in broccoli. Cook for a minute or so before adding pea pods, red pepper, garlic, and ginger. Mixture should be crisp in color and texture. Drain vegetables if needed.

Stir prepared marinade into vegetable mixture, coating it thoroughly. Warm through on medium low heat. Serve over hot basmati rice. Garnish with cashews. Serves 4–6.

❧୧୦଼

Amaranth Corn Mexican Supper Pie

1 cup amaranth, cooked to resemble Malt-O-Meal

2 tablespoons ghee (clarified butter)

1 cup corn, blended smooth with ½ cup milk (soy or goat)

1 cup zuchini, grated

⅓ cup green bell pepper, chopped fine

⅓ cup red bell pepper, chopped fine

¼ cup scallions, chopped fine

1 tablespoon jalapeno pepper, minced

2 garlic cloves, crushed

2 tablespoons fresh cilantro, minced

½–¾ cup firm tofu, mashed

2 fertile, organic eggs, lightly beaten

1½ teaspoon Spike® vegetable seasoning

1–2¾ teaspoons onion powder

1½ teaspoons Mexican spice blend

1½ cups pinto beans (use canned, whole beans)

½ cup grated cheddar cheese

½ cup grated Monterey jack cheese

¼ cup green olives, sliced

4 tablespoons flour

½ teaspoon baking powder

4–6 tablespoons sunflower seeds, for garnish

Cook amaranth in advance (see "Amaranth" section of this article). Preheat oven to 325°F. Lightly grease a 12" x 8" x 2" baking dish and a small pie plate with the ghee. Set aside.

Blend corn kernels with milk. In a medium-sized mixing bowl, stir together the corn mixture, zuchini, bell peppers, hot peppers, scallions, garlic, and cilantro. Gently beat tofu and eggs into the vegetable mixture. Stir in the Spike, onion powder, and Mexican spice blend. Add pinto beans, cheeses, and green olives. Add flour and baking powder last and stir briefly, mixing smooth.

Pour mixture into both baking dishes about ¾"–1" deep. Sprinkle each with sunflower seeds. Bake for 45 minutes (or more if necessary). Check after 35 minutes. Dish is done when firm in center and lightly golden. Serves 8.

Millet Stuffing with Creamy Cashew Nut Gravy

Stuffing

4 cups millet, cooked fluffy and dry

½ cup fresh pecans or walnuts, chopped

1 medium small white onion, chopped very fine

2 celery stalks, chopped very fine

1½ cups mushrooms, chopped very fine

¼ cup parsley, minced

1 tablespoon canola oil for sauteeing veggies

2 tablespoons ghee

2 teaspoons Spike® herbal seasoning

1 teaspoon onion powder

⅛ teaspoon black pepper

½ teaspoon sage powder

½ teaspoon poultry seasoning

Gravy

2 cups water (adjust as needed)

½ cup fresh, raw cashews, ground to meal

2 tablespoons arrowroot powder

2 tablespoons canola oil

½ teaspoon salt

¼ teaspoon black pepper

½ teaspoon onion powder

2–3 tablespoons tamari

1 teaspoon parsley

Cook grains in advance (see "Millet"). Coat a large skillet with oil and saute′ onions over medium heat until soft and fragrant. Sprinkle a tablespoon or two of water in the pan. Add celery, mushrooms, and seasonings and saute′ briefly. Melt ghee in skillet and add millet morsels. Millet should divide into individual morsels when it is separated with a utensil. Toss in ground nuts and parsley. Let mixture warm through.

Blend gravy ingredients in blender until smooth. Pour into a non-stick saucepan. Stir constantly over high heat until thickened. Set aside. Serve warmed stuffing with gravy. Serves 6.

Cranapple Waldorf Wild Rice Salad

Salad

2 cups wild rice, cooked

3 medium small red skinned apples, chopped fine

2 stalks celery, chopped fine

1 cup soft dates, sliced and pitted

1 cup craisins (dried cranberries)

1 small, ripe banana

1 cup fresh walnuts, chopped

Dressing

¾ cup mayonaise or vanilla flavored yogurt

⅓–½ cup honey or rice syrup

⅓ cup amazake rice milk or pineapple flavored kefir

Curly leaf lettuce (optional)

Prepare grains in advance and chill before chopping fruits and celery. In a medium sized bowl, combine rice with chopped fruits, celery, banana, craisins, and nuts.

Stir dressing ingredients together in separate bowl or whirl in blender for a creamy taste and consistency. Drizzle into salad mixture and toss. Serve salad on curly lettuce in a favorite dish or bowl. Serves 4–6.

Quinoa Tabouli Salad

Tabouli

3 cups quinoa, cooked

1 cup parsley, minced

3 tablespoons fresh mint leaves, minced

½ cup scallions, finely chopped

½–¾ cup green bell pepper, finely chopped

1½ cup cucumber, chopped fine

1½ cups tomatoes, chopped fine

½–¾ cup black olives, sliced

Dressing

⅓ cup light virgin olive oil

½ cup fresh squeezed lemon juice

1 clove garlic, crushed

1½ teaspoon Spike® herbal seasoning

Salt, to taste

Yogurt Sauce

¾–1 cup plain yogurt

⅛ cup light olive oil

3 tablespoons lemon juice

1 small clove garlic

4 curly leaves of lettuce, for garnish

Have grains cooked and chilled in advance of assembling salad (see "Quinoa" section of this article).

Combine parsley, mint leaves, scallions, green pepper, cucumber, tomatoes, and black olives with quinoa. Mix dressing ingredients together and toss with mixture. Taste seasonings and adjust.

Prepare yogurt dressing as an extra. Serve salad on fresh lettuce leaves and top with yogurt sauce if desired. Serves 4–6.

CANDIA LEA COLE is a nutritional artist and whole foods educator living in Minnesota. She is the author of three whole-foods cookbooks, including *Gourmet Grains: Main Dishes Made of Nature*, which is available through Woodbridge Press in Santa Barbara, California, tel. 1-800-237-6053. This book features over seventy-five healthful, meat-free recipes for festive, four-season dining.

Herbal Vinegars: Aromatic Delights from Your Garden

By Susun Weed

S pring is in the air. Buds are swelling, sap is running, the night is alive with sounds after winter's long silence. It's too soon to plant anything in the garden, and there's still deep frost in the ground, but the snow is gone the weeds are green, and my supply of herbal vinegars is low, so I'll spend the morning harvesting herbs to make more vinegars.

A pantry full of herbal vinegars is a constant delight. Preserving fresh herbs and roots in vinegar is an easy way to capture their nourishing goodness. It's easy, too. You don't even have to have an herb garden.

Basic Herbal Vinegar

Takes 5 minutes plus 6 weeks to prepare

1 glass or plastic jar of any size up to one quart/liter
1 plastic lid for jar, or waxed paper and a rubber band
  Fresh herbs, roots, weeds
1 quart apple cider vinegar

Fill any size jar with fresh-cut aromatic herbs (see the accompanying list for suggestions of herbs that extract particularly well in vinegar). For best results and highest mineral content, be sure the jar is well filled with your chosen herb—not just a few springs—and be sure to cut the herbs or roots up into small pieces.

Pour room-temperature apple cider vinegar into the jar until it is full. Cover jar with a plastic screw-on lid, several layers of plastic or wax paper held on with a rubber band, or a cork. Vinegar disintegrates metal lids.

Label the jar with the name of the herb and the date. Put it some place away from direct sunlight (though it doesn't have to be in the dark), and someplace that isn't too hot, but not too cold either. A kitchen cupboard is fine, but choose one that you open a lot so you remember to use your vinegar, which will be ready in six weeks.

Apple Cider Vinegar

Apple cider vinegar has been used as a health-giving agent for centuries. Hippocrates, the father of medicine, is said to have used only two remedies: honey and vinegar. A small book on Vermont folk remedies—primary among them being apple cider vinegar—has sold over five million copies since its publication in the fifties. A current ad in a national health magazine states that vinegar can give us longer, healthier, happier lives. Among the many powers of vinegar: it lowers cholesterol, improves skin tone, moderates high blood pressure, prevents/counters osteoporosis, and improves metabolic functioning. Herbal vinegars are an unstoppable combination: the healing and nutritional properties of vinegar married with the aromatic and health protective effects of green herbs (and a few roots).

How Does It Taste?

Herbal vinegars don't taste like medicine. In fact, they taste so good I use them frequently. I pour a spoonful or more on beans and grains at dinner; I use them in salad dressings; I season stir-fry and soups with them. This regular use boosts the nutrient level of my diet with little effort and expense.

Sometimes I drink my herbal vinegar in a glass of water in the morning, remembering the many older women who've told me that apple cider vinegar prevents and eases their arthritic pains. I aim to ingest a tablespoon or more of mineral-rich herbal vinegar daily. Not just because herbal vinegars taste great (they do!), but because they offer an easy way to keep my calcium levels high (and that's a real concern for a menopausal woman). Herbal vinegars are so rich in nutrients that I never need to take vitamin or mineral pills.

Why Vinegar?

Why vinegar? Water does a poor job of extracting calcium from plants, but calcium and all minerals dissolve into vinegar very easily. You can see this for yourself. Submerge a bone in vinegar for six weeks. What happens? The bone becomes pliable and rubbery. Why? The vinegar extracted the minerals from the bone. (And now the vinegar is loaded with calcium and other bone-building minerals!)

After observing this trick it's not unusual to fear that if you consume vinegar your bones will dissolve. But you'd have to take off your skin and sit in vinegar for weeks in order for that to happen! Adding vinegar to your food actually helps build bones, because it frees up minerals from the vegetables you eat. Adding a splash of vinegar to cooked greens is a classic trick of old ladies who want to be spry and flexible when they're ancient old ladies. (Maybe your granny already taught you this?) In fact, a spoonful of vinegar on your broccoli, kale, or dandelion greens increases the calcium you get from the vegetables by one-third.

Vinegar helps build bones; and when it's combined with mineral-rich herbs, vinegar is better than calcium pills. Some people worry that eating vinegar will contribute to an overgrowth of candida yeast in the intestines. My experience has led me to believe that herbal vinegars do just the opposite, perhaps because they're so mineral-rich. Herbal vinegars are especially useful for anyone who can't (or doesn't want to) drink milk. A tablespoon of herbal vinegar has the same amount of calcium as a glass of milk.

A Walk in the Herb Garden

So out the door I go, taking a basket and a pair of scissors, my warm vest and my gloves, to see what I can harvest for my bone-building vinegars.

The first greens to greet me are the slender spires of garlic grass, or wild chives, common in any soil that hasn't been disturbed too frequently, such as the lawn, the part of the garden where the tiller doesn't go, the rhubarb patch, the asparagus bed, and the comfrey plants. This morning they're all offering me patches of oniony greens. The vinegar I'll make from these tender tops will contain not only minerals, but also allyls, special cancer-preventative compounds found in raw onions, garlic, and the like.

Here, in a sunny corner, is a patch of catnip intermingled with motherwort, two plants especially beloved by women. I use catnip to ease menstrual cramps, relieve colic, and bring on sleep. Motherwort is my favorite remedy for moderating hot flashes and emotional swings. They are both members of the mint family, and like all mints, are exceptionally good sources of calcium and make great-tasting vinegars. Individual mint flavors are magically captured by the vinegar. From now until snow cover next fall, I'll gather the mints of each season and activate their unique tastes and their tonic, nourishing properties by steeping them in vinegar. What a tasty way to build strong bones, a healthy heart, emotional stability, and energetic vitality.

Down here, under the wild rose hedge, is a plant familiar to anyone who has walked the woods and roadsides of the east: garlic mustard. I'll enjoy the leaves in my salad tonight, as I do all winter and spring, but I'll have to wait a bit longer before I can harvest the roots, which produce a vibrant, horseradishy vinegar that's just the thing to brighten a winter salad and keep the sinuses clear.

Chickweed is a good addition to my vinegars, boosting their calcium content, though adding scant flavor. In protected spots, she offers greens year-round.

Look down. The mugwort is sprouting, all fuzzy and grey. I call it *cronewort* to honor the wisdom of grey-haired women. The culinary value of this very wild herb is oft o'erlooked. I was thrilled to find it for sale in little jars in a German supermarket, right next to the dried caraway and rosemary. Mugwort vinegar is one of the tastiest and most beneficial of all the vinegars I make. It is renowned as a general nourishing tonic to circulatory, nervous, urinary, and mental functioning, as well as being a specific aid to those wanting sound sleep and strong bones. Mugwort vinegar is free for the making in most cities, if you know where this invasive weed grows. To mellow mugwort's slightly bitter taste and accent her fragrant, flavorful aspects, I pick her small (under three inches) and add a few of her roots to the jar along with the leaves. I cut the tall, flowering stalks of this aromatic plant in the late summer or early autumn, when they're in full bloom, and dry them.

The Sun is bright and strong and warm. I turn my face toward it and close my eyes, breathing in. I feel the vibrating life-force here. Everything is aquiver. I smile, knowing that that energy will be available to me when I consume the vinegars I'll make from these herbs and weeds. As I relax against the big oak, I breathe out and envision the garden growing and blooming, fruiting and dying, as the seasons slip through my mind's eye.

The air grows chiller at night. The leaves fall more quickly with each breeze. The first mild frosts take the basil, the tomatoes and the squash, freeing me to pay attention once again to the perennial herbs and weeds, and urging me to make

haste before even the hardy herbs drop their leaves and retreat to winter dormancy.

The day dawns sunny. Now's the time to harvest the last of the garden's bounty, the rewards of my work, the gifts of the earth. I dress warmly (remembering to wear red; hunting season's open), stash my red-handled clippers in my back pocket, and take a basket in one hand and a plastic tub in the other.

My gardening friends say the harvest is over for the year, but I know my weeds will keep me at work harvesting until well into the winter. In no time at all my deep basket is full and I'm wishing I'd brought another. Violet leaves push against stalks of lamb's-quarter. Hollyhock, wild malva, and plantain leaves jostle for their own spaces against the last of the comfrey and dandelion leaves. (I think dandelion leaves are much better eating in the fall than in the spring; they seem much less bitter to my taste after they've been frosted a few nights.) The last of the red clover blossoms snuggle in the middle. Though not aromatic or intensely-flavored, a vinegar of these greens will be my super-rich calcium supplement for the dark months of winter.

My baskets are overflowing and I haven't even gotten to the nettles and the raspberry leaves yet. They're superb sources of calcium, too. Ah! The gracious abundance of weeds—or should I say "volunteer herbs?" I actually respect them more than the cultivated herbs—respect their strident life force, their powerful nutritional punch, and their medicinal values that help me stay healthy and filled with energy.

The main work of this frosty fall morning is to harvest roots: dandelion, burdock, yellow dock, and chicory roots. I've been waiting for the frost to bite deep before harvesting the nourishing, medicinal roots of these weeds. With my spading fork (not a shovel, please) I carefully unearth their tender roots, leaving a few to mature and shed seeds so I have a constant supply of young roots. I love the feel of the root sliding free of the soil and into my hands, offering me such gifts of health.

I admire burdock especially, for its strength of character and its healing qualities. I settle down to do some serious digging to unearth its long roots. For peak benefit, I harvest at the end of the first year of growth, when the roots are most tenacious and least willing to leave the ground. Patience is rewarded when I dig burdock. Eaten cooked or turned into a vinegar (and the pickled pieces of the root consumed with the vinegar), burdock root attracts heavy metals and radioactive isotopes and removes them quickly from the body. For several hundred years at least, and in numerous cases that I have witnessed, burdock root has been known to reverse pre-cancerous changes in cells.

Dandelion and chicory are my allies for long life. They support and nourish my liver and improve the production of hydrochloric acid in my stomach, thus insuring that I will be better nourished by any food I eat. I make separate vinegars of each plant, but like to put both their roots and their leaves together in my vinegar. A spoonful of either of these in a glass of water in the morning or before meals can be used to replace coffee. Note that roasted roots used in coffee substitutes do not have the medicinal value of fresh roots eaten cooked or preserved in vinegar.

Yellow dock is the herbalist's classic remedy for building iron in the blood. Like calcium, iron is absorbed better when eaten with an acid, such as vinegar, making yellow dock vinegar an especially good way to utilize the iron-enhancing properties of this weed. (It nourishes the iron in the soil, too, and is said to improve the yield of apple trees it grows under.)

At that thought, I awaken from my reverie and return to spring's sunshine with a smile. A white cat twines my legs and offers to help me carry the basket back inside to the warmth of the fire. The circle has come around again, like the moon in her courses. Autumn memories yield spring richness. The weeds of fall offer tender green magic in the spring. What I harvested last November has been eaten with joy and I return to be gifted yet again by the wild that lives here with me in my garden.

Notes on Making Herbal Vinegars

- ⚜ It is vital to really fill the jar. This may take far more herb or root than you think.

- ⚜ A good selection of jars of different sizes will enable you to fit your jar to the amount of plant you've collected. I especially like baby food, mustard , olive, peanut butter, and juice jars. Plastic is fine, though I prefer glass.

❧ Always fill a jar to the top with plant material; never fill a jar only part way.

❧ Pack the jar full of herb. How much? How tight? Tight enough to make a comfortable mattress for a fairy. Not too tight, and not too loose. With roots, fill jar to within a thumb's width of the top.

❧ For maximum strength herbal vinegars, snip or chop herbs and roots.

❧ For maximum visual delight, leave plants whole.

❧ Regular pasteurized apple cider vinegar from the supermarket is what I use when I make my herbal vinegars.

❧ Rice vinegar, malt vinegar, wine vinegar, or any other natural vinegar can be used, but they are much more expensive than apple cider vinegar and many have tastes which overpower or clash with the taste of the herbs.

❧ I don't use white vinegar, nor do I use umeboshi vinegar (a Japanese condiment).

❧ The reason that most recipes for herbal vinegar tell you to boil the vinegar is to pasteurize it! I do not find it necessary to heat the vinegar, as it is al-ready pasteurized, and the final vinegar tastes better if the herbs are not doused with boiling vinegar.

Exceptionally Good Herbal Vinegars

APPLE MINT leaves, stalks

BEE BALM (*Monarda didyma*) flowers, leaves, stalks

BERGAMOT (*Monarda*) flowers, leaves, stalks

BURDOCK (*Arctium lappa*) roots

CATNIP (*Nepeta cataria*) leaves, stalks

CHICORY (*Cichorium intybus*) leaves, roots

CHIVES and chive blossoms

DANDELION (*Traxacum offinalis*) flower buds, leaves, roots

DILL (*Anethum graveolens*) herb, seeds

FENNEL (*Foeniculum vulgare*) herb, seeds

GARLIC (*Allium sativum*)

GARLIC MUSTARD (*Alliaria officinalis*)

GOLDENROD (*Solidago*) flowers

GINGER (*Zingiber officinalis*) and WILD GINGER (*Asarum canadensis*) roots

LAVENDER (*Lavendula*) flowers, leaves

MUGWORT (*Artemisia vulgaris*) new growth leaves and roots

ORANGE MINT leaves, stalks

ORANGE PEEL, organic only

PEPPERMINT (*Mentha piperata*) leaves, stalks

PERILLA (*Shiso*) leaves, stalks

ROSEMARY (*Rosmarinus officinalis*) leaves, stalks

SPEARMINT (*Mentha spicata*) leaves, stalks

THYME (*Thymus*) leaves, stalks

WHITE PINE (*Pinus strobus*) needles

YARROW (*Achillea millifolium*) flowers and leaves

Calcium Supplements

AMARANTH (*Amaranthus retroflexus*) leaves

CABBAGE leaves

CHICKWEED (*Stellaria media*) all

COMFREY (*Symphytum officinalis*) leaves

DANDELION leaves and root

KALE leaves

LAMB'S-QUARTER (*Chenopodium album*) leaves

MALLOW (*Malva neglecta*) leaves

ALL MINTS, including SAGE, MOTHERWORT, LEMON BALM, LAVENDER, PEPPERMINT, etc.

MUGWORT (cronewort) (*Artemisia vulgaris*)

NETTLE (*Urtica dioica*) leaves

PARSLEY (*Petroselinum sativum*) leaves

PLANTAIN (*Plantago majus*) leaves

RASPBERRY (*Rubus species*) leaves

RED CLOVER (*Trifolium pratense*) blossoms

VIOLET (*Viola ordorata*) leaves

YELLOW DOCK (*Rumex crispus*) roots

Boring Vinegars

BASIL stalks (some color, taste)

MOST FLOWERS, alas ROSEHIPS (no color, no taste)

RASPBERRIES/BLACKBERRIES (nice color, but no taste)

SUSUN WEED is known worldwide for her work in women's health and herbal medicine. Her books *Wise Woman Herbal for the Childbearing Year, Healing Wise,* and *Menopausal Years the Wise Woman Way* are recommended reading in many university courses, and are extremely popular, having sold more than 250,000 copies to date.

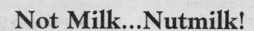

Not Milk...Nutmilk!

A Sip of Elegance from the Orchard

By Candia Lea Cole

Mixed into cake or muffin batter, it creates a moist, "none left for tomorrow" treat. Whisked into a sizzling skillet with scrambled eggs, it transforms standard breakfast fare into the kind of fanciful food that characterizes brunch. Whirled with fresh fruit in the blender, it creates a creamy taste sensation, sans any cholesterol. On its own, highlighted only by a favorite drinking cup, tumbler, or mug, nutmilk is just plain elegant. A delightful dairy-free innovation, nutmilk contains all the romance and intrigue you'd expect to find in the Garden of Eden.

If you can, imagine yourself entering Mother Nature's orchards. Amidst the sweetly scented, flowery boughs, you might also envision yourself blending her fresh nuts, seeds, fruits, spices, and nectars into smooth-sipping, healthful beverages. Banana Coconut Walnut, Orange Apricot Almondine, Mocha Mint Almond, and Apple Fruit Harvest Pecan are but a few of the delightful flavors in my collection of over forty "milk" recipes that can be sipped on their own, or used with many different recipes and menus.

A quart of nutmilk can be easily prepared in ten to fifteen minutes or less with the aid of a standard coffee bean grinder, an electric blender and a hand-held strainer. To make things easy in your kitchen, consider alotting a user-friendly nook of your countertop for these culinary tools. Next, take inventory of any spices, flavoring extracts, and sweetners you've got tucked away in your pantry. Then, pave a place in the refrigerator for a few glass or ceramic mason jars.

Nuts

Raw, unsalted, and preferably organic nuts contain more nutrients than roasted ones, and are certain to leave a more favorable impression on the tastebuds than would stale, dated nuts typically sold in supermarkets. Many whole foods coops carry organic almonds and sunflower seeds. I usually rely on an organic specialties mail order house for unblemished jumbo cashews imported from the rainforest, as well as premium walnuts and pecans which are refrigerated up until the moment they are shipped. Because the importance of freshness can't be overstated, I suggest keeping all nuts and seeds refrigerated until you are ready to use them. Nuts and seeds, I hasten to add, contain "good fats": the kind of healthy monounsaturated fats our bodies need for energy production, growth, tissue repair, immune function, strong nerves, and a healthy heart, to name several benefits substantiated in such widely respected books as *The Nutrition Almanac* (second edition John D. Kirschmann and Lavon J. Dunne). Researchers at Loma Linda University in California have also determined that adults who eat two ounces of walnuts five or more times a week will lower their cholesterol levels by twelve percent!

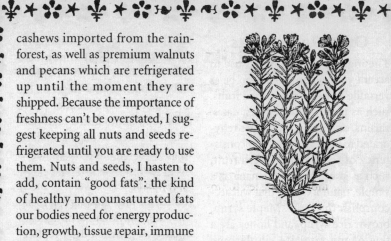

Flax

Flaxseed

In addition to nuts, each of my recipes contain flaxseed, a tiny, glossy brown, sometimes golden, seed; the offspring of beautiful blue flowering field crops known as *Linum usitatissimum,* which can be found in the northern U.S., Canada, and Europe. Painters, weavers, beauticians, and cooks from around the world have used flax for centuries in preparations ranging from hair fixatives to furniture polish. Organically grown flaxseeds can be found at most food coops and health food stores (even in the natural foods department of some mainstream grocers), as it has culinary applications that contribute food and medicinal values to the modern diet. Once the seeds are pulverized and liquid is added to activate their mucilage, flaxseeds contribute a silky texture to nutmilks as well as the nutritionally acclaimed substance known as Omega 3 (an essential fatty acid).

Lecithin

In addition to nuts and seeds, lecithin granules—a moist yellow substance from the soybean, known for its fat and cholesterol digesting ability—enhances my recipes, whose healthy calories (less than 200 per serving) are "made" non-fattening!

Other Ingredients

The ingredients you might use to accent your favorite nuts can be as versatile as you desire. Dried fruits, such as unsulphured apples, dates, raisins, and apricots, can be rehydrated to achieve the velvety consistency of some milks. Fresh fruit, such as sweet, ripened banana, is a simple, natural choice that will accomplish the same. Maple syrup, brown rice syrup, and honey are a few of my favorite wholesome sweeteners, which mingle naturally with the luxurious appeal of nuts.

Finally, fresh liquids (including filtered water or diluted non-acid fruit juice such as pear or apple), and the touch of your finger on the fast pulse of your blender puree these food basics into a high fiber "milk." Poured through a strainer, its consistency is refined to match the appeal of milk or cream. Nutmilks can be served warm or nicely chilled, for four-season enjoyment. They are, individuals of all ages will discover, a gourmet dairy replacement whose preparation invokes the taste of Nature's elegance.

Nutmilk Recipes

See "Guide to Preparing Nutmilks" below for blending instructions.

Orange Apricot Almondine Nutmilk

- ⅓ cup fresh, organic almonds
- 1 tablespoon fresh flaxseed
- 1 teaspoon lecithin granules
- ⅛–¼ cup rehydrated dried apricots (soak overnight in orange juice, or pour boiling water over fruit and let stand for 15 minutes)
- 2½ tablespoons honey
- 1 teaspoon vanilla flavoring
- ¼ teaspoon orange flavoring
- 3¼ cups almost boiling water (adjust as desired)

Banana Pecan Nutmilk

- ⅓ cup fresh, organic pecans
- 1 tablespoon fresh flaxseed
- 1 teaspoon lecithin granules
- 2½ tablespoons maple syrup

½ cup ripe banana

3½ cup almost boiling water

pinch of slippery elm powder, if desired (available at coops)

Creamy Carob Almond Delight Nutmilk

¼ cup fresh, organic almonds

¼ cup fresh, organic cashews

1 tablespoon fresh flaxseeds

1 teaspoon lecithin granules

2 tablespoon carob powder

1 teaspoon cocoa powder

2½ tablespoons honey or maple syrup

1 teaspoon vanilla flavoring or extract

3¼ cups almost boiling water

Guide to Preparing Nutmilks

You will need an electric blender, a coffee bean grinder, a 1-quart pot (to heat water in), a hand-held, fine mesh strainer (4" in diameter), and a stirring spoon.

Keep all nuts and seeds refrigerated and grind before each use for maximum freshness. Organic nuts and seeds will keep for 4 weeks in the refrigerator and up to six weeks in the freezer. For best results, use whole nuts, versus slivered or broken ones. The importance of fresh nuts cannot be overemphasized! Your local food coop may have some organic nuts available, but check the rate of turnover on the supply.

Electric coffee bean grinders and fine mesh strainers can be found in most housewares departments. Reliable brands of grinders include Krups and Moulinex. Be careful not to overload the grinder. It takes only seconds to grind the portion of nuts in each recipe.

If you have never made a nutmilk, allow fifteen minutes of prep time for your introductory acquaintaince with the procedure. When you become familiar with the many choices for preparing nutmilk and have your culinary "essentials" well organized, you can create one in half the time.

Spend time experimenting with your electric seed and nut grinder. Dry nuts and oily nuts grind up somewhat differently. Dry nuts, such as almonds, sunflower seeds, and pumpkin seeds, when finely ground, will shake out of your grinder fairly easily when you tap it upside down. The oilier ground nuts, such as walnuts, pecans, and cashews, will be pastier, and will require a cautious index finger to sweep them out. Most of the oily nuts will grind up completely, but don't be concerned if, occasionally, a few don't.

Specific Blending Procedure

Blending a nutmilk is simple. After grinding nuts and flaxseeds to a fine powder using your electric seed grinder, transfer them to your blender. Add the remaining ingredients (sweeteners, fruits, flavorings, etc.) to your blender with the exception of the water. Heat the water until almost boiling. To begin with, add only ⅓–½ cup of the water to the blender and puree ingredients into a smooth sauce. This way, the fibers in the fruits and nuts will have a better chance to break down and become amenable to one another. Hot water (versus cold) will also help this process. Once you have achieved this consistency, you can slowly add the remaining water and continue blending for about 15–30 seconds on high speed. Although it is a matter of personal preference, straining nutmilks can make the difference between a slightly fibrous beverage that is drunk immediately, and a velvety drink that has the appeal of milk and the capacity to stay fresh longer.

Regarding strainers, the finer the mesh, the smoother the nutmilk will be. I don't recommend cheesecloth, as it is neither easy nor fuss free. To strain nutmilks, put a strainer that is at least 4" in diameter over a medium-sized mixing bowl and pour contents of blender, about a cup at a time, through the strainer, stirring and mashing as you go. Pulp from the nuts and flax may be used to give texture and nutriment to baked goods. Drink nutmilk within 24–72 hours.

❖⊂⊃❖

CANDIA LEA COLE lives in Mahtomedi, Minnesota. with her family. She refers to herself as a "nutritional artist and culinary shaman." She is the author of three whole-foods cookbooks, including *Not Milk...Nutmilks!* which is available through Woodbridge Press, Santa Barbara, CA. Tel: 1-800-237-6053.

Super Smoothies!

By Candia Lea Cole

Someone once suggested that bodies are built when muscles strain under iron and tastebuds concede to heavy, powder puffed milkshakes. They just didn't know. Bodies can be built while we are dancing with nature and sipping on the light and color-rich nectar of life! Rest assured, I'll stretch high and shimmy low to maintain my shape. But let it occur while I'm tugging at the branch of a fruit or nut tree, or digging up the roots in a garden or field. The way Mother Nature herself jazzes up my inspiration simply can't be beat by a pre-packaged milkshake. To learn the improvisation of her seasonal splendor is a cinch. Since discovering the zest and vitality I always feel after sipping "smoothies," which are nature's body-building drink, my kitchen blender has become my favorite partner in fitness. I rely on this simple piece of equipment every day to prepare smoothies (so named for their creamy texture) that are healthier than those vitamin drinks once fashioned from dairy products and fruit.

The exclusion of dairy products in my recipes encourages a healthy body weight from muscle rather than fat. And it gives us a multi-purpose use for the many nutritious, saturate-free (animal free) milk alternatives such as rice, soy, and nutmilks. Malted soy milk for instance, contains barley, which is a great source of iron and thiamine, as well beta glucans—a type of soluble fiber which lowers cholesterol. Plain or malted soymilks give luxurious appeal to smoothies.

Homemade nutmilk, a high protein, smooth-sipping beverage with about 150–200 calories per serving, will do the same. If, like me, you cherish the idea of supporting your immune system and boosting your body's hormonal output naturally, nutmilk, with its essential fatty acids, is for you!

Rice milk, known as amazake in the Orient and available at food co-ops, is another refreshing and naturally sweet milk alternative. By itself, an eight-ounce serving contains 200 replenishing calories.

To sweeten the basic ingredients a blender drink might feature, and provide nourishment in the process, rice syrup, a product made from whole grain brown rice, is unbeatable. Because it is cultured by enzymes which break down its complex carbohydrates into predigested sugars, it requires little or no insulin to digest and provides the body with stable energy. Other sweeteners include maple syrup, honey, malted grain sweeteners and dehydrated, mineral-rich sugar cane juice: all wholesome products of nature.

If you are curious about the quality of protein smoothies can deliver, consider two impressive facts: On their own, vegetables, seeds, and grains provide two to four times the protein anyone would need during any type of physical activity. And they contain all of the same essential amino acids as animal protein. Since my smoothies often combine several different nutritional factors at once, they are a super source of nourishment! Although commercially prepared protein formulas are often the choice of some bodybuilders because they contain an exhaustive formulation of nutrients, many individuals, including myself, cannot tolerate their concentration of protein. Wanda Koszewski, director of the undergraduate dietetics program at Cornell University put my concern into perspective when she said: "The body is a well-organized machine. If you have too much of something, it throws the entire system off. All Americans would look like body builders if the consumption of protein dense foods actually led to the storage of protein in muscles." (The daily percentage of protein required to build muscles is 2½ to 5 percent.) Referring to protein powders, she concluded that "the only way those cans of protein punch will build muscle is if you're lugging them home from the store." Well, I'm going to agree. But not without first inviting you to the taste of body building that works for me!

Smoothie Recipes

Creamy Butterscotch Yam Smoothie

2   medium sized sweet potatoes, baked (about 2 cups)

1   tablespoon maple syrup or rice syrup

1½ tablespoon Sucanat® (organic sugarcane powder) or brown sugar

1   tablespoon sesame tahini

¼–½ teaspoon butterscotch flavoring

1   teaspoon vanilla flavoring

2–2½ cups water or malted vanilla soymilk (adjust as desired)

Bake sweet potatoes in a hot oven until tender. Let cool for fifteen minutes. Peel skins and scoop contents into blender. Pour liquid into blender. Add sweeteners, nut butter, and flavoring. Blend on high speed until creamy and smooth. Add water as desired to achieve either pudding consistency or thinner. Serves 2–4.

Pearly Prune and Sesame Smoothie

- ½ cup rehydrated prunes (plus ½ cup soak water)
- 1 banana, frozen
- ½ cup pearled barley, cooked tender
- 2 teaspoon sesame tahini
- 2 tablespoons brown rice syrup
- 1 tablespoon Sucanat® (organic sugar cane powder) or brown sugar)
- 1 cup water
- ¾ cup malted vanilla soymilk (or use water)

In advance, peel ripe banana and freeze until hard. Have barley cooked and ready (leftovers work well, too). Slice prunes and rehydrate by soaking in almost boiling water for 15 minutes or longer. Remove banana from freezer and break into small chunks. Set aside. Put barley into blender along with tahini and sweetners. Add about ¾ cup water and soak water from prunes and puree to a smooth pudding. Add prunes, flavorings, banana chunks, and remaining liquids. Blend on high speed to a creamy consistency. Serves 4. Drink the same day.

Avocado Pineapple Paradise

- 1 medium-large, fresh ripe avocado, pitted
- 1–¼ cups fresh or canned pineapple
- 1 tablespoon honey
- 1½ cup orange juice (could use part apple also)
- 2 teaspoon lime juice
- ¼ teaspoon coconut flavoring
- 2 ice cubes

Peel and slice avocado and pineapple into small chunks. Combine with sweetener, flavoring, and juices in blender. Add ice cubes and blend on high speed until creamy. Serves 2.

❖c❖

Raspberry Revel

1½ frozen bananas

¾ cup fresh or frozen raspberries

½ cup vanilla flavored frozen amazake (non-dairy "ice cream," available at natural food co-ops or grocery stores)

1–3 teaspoons chocolate fruit sauce*

1 teaspoon slippery elm powder** (opt.)

¼ cup fresh, raw, ground almonds

½ cup (or more) water

*Chocolate Mountain® brand chocolate sauce is naturally sweetened with fruit juices. Your local food coop may carry it. If it doesn't, a sustitute will do. ** Slippery elm powder is derived from the inner bark of the elm tree and has healing properties as well as body building ones. It's generally available at food co-ops and herb stores.

Peel bananas and freeze. Break frosty bananas into small chunks. Add about ½ cup or more water to the blender, followed by frozen amazake, chocolate sauce, elm powder, and ground nuts. Begin blending process. As texture becomes smooth, add bananas and raspberries. Continue blending, adding more water if needed, to achieve a thick and creamy beverage. Serves 2–3. Drink immediately.

❖c❖

Candia Lea Cole is a nutritional artist and whole foods educator living in Minnesota. She is the author of three whole foods cookbooks, including *Super Smoothies: Taste the Nectar of Life*. It is available through Woodbridge Press, Santa Barbara, CA, Tel. 1-800-237-6053.

Conservation
and
Ecology

The Albino Redwood

The Albino Redwood

By Bernyce Barlow

The coast redwood (*Sequoia sempervirens*) grows along the Pacific coastal region from southern Oregon to central California. It is a cousin of the giant sequoia and the dawn redwood of China. These three cousins are the last of their genera on the planet, and are found in extremely restricted regions. The coast redwood has been reduced to less than 4 percent of its original population by careless exploitation, and has stood as a symbol for what can happen to a species when willful neglect presides over environmental respect.

The redwoods are said to be the tallest trees on the earth, their only rival being the Australian eucalyptus. Their average age is 2,500 years old. To experience a redwood grove is truly humbling. They reach heights of nearly 400', with diameters as large as 25', and you cannot help but feel as if you are standing within a living cathedral when among them.

A cut redwood tree can yield a ton or two of timber, and after cutting (given forty years) the tree will reproduce offshoots suitable for another round of lumbering. This, and the fact that redwoods contain high amounts of tannin in their trunks (which protects the tree from insect infestation and bacterial decay) made the tree very popular with the lumber industry.

The branches of the redwood are close together, supporting flat needle-like leaves indicative of its family (Cypress). The flat needles retain moisture from the humid coastal environment, providing the massive amount of water it takes to keep these giants alive. The needles have a dark blue-green hue, giving the forest a feeling of density and darkness even in the brightest of sunlight.

Occasionally, a saprophytic redwood sprouts from a grove. These are commonly referred to as *albino* redwoods because their needles are silver-white instead of green. This redwood cannot manufacture food by photosynthesis. Instead, it derives its nutrients from organic matter (through its root system) by utilizing a unique enzyme found in all saprophytic plants. Some of the most common saprophytes include certain types of mushrooms, bacteria, molds, and fungi. The Indian Pipe plant is saprophytic as well.

At one time, the coast redwoods of the western Pacific were abundant. Their sheer mass was overwhelming. However, out of millions of trees there were only a few albino redwoods. That is why the Native Americans of the region considered them sacred and set them aside as holy trees.

Today, only a handful of these albino trees can be found in the redwood forests. The Big Sur area of central California hosts a few, and others can be found scattered here and there up the coast. All of the albino redwoods living today are in the process of dying out. They are among a group of outshoots from mother grove trees that have fallen, or, more likely, been cut. With no source for photosynthesis, these youngsters will also die in a few years.

The Esselen Indian tribe of central California disappeared around 450 years ago, leaving very little behind in the way of history. Pieces of the Esselen puzzle can be gathered here and there from some of the nearby tribes in the Carmel Valley, but 450 years is a long time to preserve a small pocket of culture that was assimilated by an exacting mission system.

It *is* known, however, that the albino redwood was somehow connected with the burial rituals of the Esselen tribe. They referred to it as the *ghost tree*. When researching the locations of albino redwoods no longer standing, burial grounds are usually found within a quarter of a mile of an albino redwood tree. Burial beneath mounds of dirt was the common practice of the central coastal tribes, and if there was an albino redwood in the area it somehow became incorporated into the burial ceremony.

There is an enchanting legend of a young Indian maiden named Monacca and her experience with an albino redwood. Apparently, Monacca became lost in the dense redwood forest after dark while picking spring berries for her grandmother. After trying in vain to find her way through the pitch black forest she remembered a story told around the campfires of the elders about the albino redwood.

It was said, on a moonlit night, the ghost tree danced with moonbeams and its glow could be seen from the heavens. Monacca figured if the sacred tree could be seen from the heavens, then surely it could be seen from the ridge directly above her. The sacred tree was near Monacca's home and she could use its glow, like a dagger of light, to guide her safely through the forest. Monacca climbed up to the highest point on the ridge. Since it was a Full Moon, once she got above the tree line she could see much better. And there, far in the distance was the albino redwood, shimmering silver-white like a candle in the dark. She followed the illuminated giant until she could see the flicker of the watch fires of her camp.

Once Monacca was safely tucked into her bed, she dreamed of the sacred tree and how it had saved her life. While she was sleeping, the spirit of place of the redwood forest taught her a special melody that was the windtune of the ghost tree. In her dreams Monacca saw the tree from the heavens and soared on the wings of her imagination through its snow white branches.

Unfortunately, this legend is the only story that can be connected to the history of the Esselen and the albino redwood. It is as if the albino is destined to follow the Esselen down the path of extinction.

It is possible for other albino trees to sprout, but not probable. The surviving trees along the coast are literally numbered, and even with a life span of a couple of thousand years, they are running out of time. So, if for no other reason than homage, the albino redwood will remain a noble subject of study, as well as a link (if only by rote and legend) to a people that have all but been forgotten.

❖⊂⊃❖

BERNYCE BARLOW researches and leads seminars on sacred sites of the ten western states. She is currently documenting petroglyphs found at Topaz Lake. Bernyce claims that she is frequently mistaken for Dot from the "Animaniacs" television show, and that Mo'okini, on the island of Hawaii, is her favorite sacred site.

Gardening Tables

Gardening by the Moon

Time Zone Conversions

Moon Tables

Gardening Dates

The Zodiac Garden

Gardening by the Moon
Using the Moon's phases and signs

Today, we still find those who reject the notion of Moon gardening—the usual non-believer is not the scientist, but the city dweller who has never had any real contact with nature and no conscious experience of natural rhythms.

Cato wrote that "fig, apple, olive, and pear trees, as well as vines, should be planted in the dark of the Moon in the afternoon."

Camille Flammarian, the French astronomer, also testifies to Moon planting. "Cucumbers increase at Full Moon, as well as radishes, turnips, leeks, lilies, horseradish, saffron; onions, on the contrary, are much larger and better nourished during the decline and old age of the Moon than at its increase, during its youth and fullness. Herbs gathered while the Moon increases are of great efficiency. If the vines are trimmed at night when the Moon is in the sign of the Lion, Sagittarius, the Scorpion, or the Bull, it will save them from field-rats, moles, snails, flies, and other animals."

Dr. Clark Timmins is one of the few modern scientists to have conducted tests in Moon planting.

The following is a summary of some of his experiments:

- Beets: When sown with the Moon in Scorpio, the germination rate was 71 percent; when sown in Sagittarius, the germination rate was 58 percent.

- Scotch marigold: When sown with the Moon in Cancer, the germination rate was 90 percent; when sown in Leo, the germination rate was 32 percent.

- Carrots: When sown with the Moon in Scorpio, the germination rate was 64 percent; when sown in Sagittarius, the germination rate was 47 percent.

- Tomatoes: When sown with the Moon in Cancer, the germination rate was 90 percent; when sown in Leo, the germination rate was 58 percent.

Two things should be emphasized. First, remember that this is only a summary of the results of the experiments; the experiments themselves were conducted in a scientific manner to eliminate any variation in soil, temperature, moisture, etc., so that only the Moon's sign used in planting varied. Second, note that these astonishing results were obtained without regard to the *phase* of the Moon—the other factor we use in Moon planting, and which presumably would have increased the differential in germination rates.

Further experiments by Dr. Timmins involved transplanting Cancer- and Leo-planted tomato seedlings while the Moon was increasing and in Cancer. The result was 100 percent survival. When the transplanting was done with the Moon decreasing and in Sagittarius, there was 0 percent survival.

The results of Dr. Timmins' tests show that the Cancer-planted tomatoes had first blossoms twelve days earlier than those planted under Leo; the Cancer-planted tomatoes had an average height of 20" at the same age when the Leo plants were only 15" high; the first ripe tomatoes were gathered from the Cancer plantings eleven days ahead of the Leo·plantings; and finally, a count of the hanging fruit and comparison of size and weight shows an advantage to the Cancer plants over the Leo plants of 45 percent.

Dr. Timmins also observed that there have been similar tests that did not indicate results favorable to the Moon planting theory. As a scientist, he asked why one set of experiments indicated a positive verification of Moon planting, and others did not. He checked these other tests and found that the experimenters had not followed the geocentric system for determining the Moon sign positions, but the heliocentric. When the times used in these other tests were converted to the geocentric system, the dates chosen often were found to be in barren rather than fertile signs. Without going into the technical explanations, it is sufficient to point out that geocentric and heliocentric positions often vary by as much as four days. This is a large enough differential to place the Moon in Cancer, for example, in the heliocentric system, and at the same time in Leo by the geocentric system.

Most almanacs and calendars show the Moon's signs heliocentrically—and thus incorrectly for Moon planting—while the *Organic Gardening Almanac* is calculated

correctly for planting purposes, using the geocentric system.

Some readers are also confused because the *Organic Gardening Almanac* talks of first, second, third, and fourth quarters, while some almanacs refer to these same divisions as New Moon, first quarter, Full Moon, and last quarter. Thus, these almanacs say first quarter when the *Organic Gardening Almanac* says second quarter.

There is nothing complicated about using astrology in agriculture and horticulture in order to increase both pleasure and profit, but there is one very important rule that is often neglected—use common sense! Of course this is one rule that should be remembered in every activity we undertake, but in the case of gardening and farming by the Moon it is not always possible to use the best dates for planting or harvesting, and we must select the next best and just try to do the best we can.

This brings up the matter of the other factors to consider in your gardening work. The dates we give as best for a certain activity apply to the entire country (with slight time correction), but in your section of the country you may be buried under three feet of snow on a date we say is good to plant your flowers. So we have factors of weather, season, temperature and moisture variations, soil conditions, your own available time and opportunity, and so forth. Some astrologers like to think it is all a matter of science, but gardening is also an art. In art you develop an instinctive identification with your work so that you influence it with your feelings and visualization of what you want to accomplish.

The *Organic Gardening Almanac* gives you the place of the Moon for every day of the year so that you can select the best times once you have become familiar with the rules and practices of lunar agriculture. We try to give you specific, easy-to-follow directions so that you can get down to work.

We give you the best dates for planting, but we cannot just tell you when it's good to plant at the time. Many of these rules were learned by observation and experience, but as our body of experience grew, we could see various patterns emerging which allowed us to make judgments about new things. Then we tested the new possible applications and learned still more. That's what you should do, too. After you have worked with lunar agriculture for a while and have gained a working background of knowledge, you will probably begin to try new things—and we hope you will share your experiments and findings with us. That's how the science grows.

Here's an example of what we mean. Years ago, Llewellyn George suggested that we try to combine our bits of knowledge about what to expect in planting under each of the Moon signs in order to benefit with several such lunar factors in one plant. From this came our rule for developing "thoroughbred seed." To develop thoroughbred seed, save the seed for three successive years from plants grown by the correct Moon sign and phase. You can plant in the first quarter phase and in the sign of Cancer for fruitfulness; the second year, plant seeds from the first year plants in Libra for beauty; and in the third year, plant the seeds from the second year plants in Taurus to produce hardiness. In a similar manner you can combine the fruitfulness of Cancer, the good root growth of Pisces, and the sturdiness and good vine growth of Scorpio.

Unlike common almanacs, we consider both the Moon's phase and the Moon's sign in making our calculations for the proper timing of our work within nature's rhythm. It is perhaps a little easier to understand this if we remind you that we are all living in the center of a vast electromagnetic field that is the Earth and its environment in space. Everything that occurs within this electromagnetic field has an effect on everything else within the same field, but since we are living on the Earth we must relate these happenings and effects to our own health and happiness. The Moon and the Sun are the most important and dynamic of the rhythmically changing factors affecting the life of the Earth, and it is their relative positions to the Earth that we project for each day of the coming year.

We provide a few basic rules and then give you month-by-month and day-by-day guidance for your farming and gardening work. You will be able to choose the best dates to meet your own needs and opportunities.

Planting by the Moon's Phases

During the increasing light (from New Moon to Full Moon), plant annuals that produce their yield above the ground. (An annual is a plant that completes its entire life cycle within one growing season and has to be re-seeded each year.)

During the decreasing light (from Full Moon to New Moon), plant biennials, perennials, bulbs, and root plants. (Biennials include crops that are planted one season to winter over and produce crops the next, such as winter wheat. Perennials and bulb and root plants include all plants that grow from the same root year after year.)

A simple, though less accurate, rule is to plant crops that produce above the ground during the increase of the Moon, and to plant crops that produce below the ground during its decrease.

Llewellyn George went a step further and divided the lunar month into quarters. He called the first two from New Moon to Full Moon the first and second quarters, and the last two from Full Moon to New Moon the third and fourth quarters.

First Quarter
(Increasing)

Plant annuals producing their yield above the ground, generally those that produce their seed outside the fruit. Examples are asparagus, broccoli, Brussels sprouts, cabbage, cauliflower, celery, cress, endive, kohlrabi, lettuce, parsley, spinach, etc. Cucumbers are an exception, as they do best in the first quarter rather than the second, even though the seeds are inside the fruit. Also plant cereals and grains.

Second Quarter
(Increasing)

Plant annuals producing their yield above the ground, which are generally of the viny kind that produce their seed inside the fruit. Examples include beans, eggplant, melons, peas, peppers, pumpkins, squash, tomatoes, etc. These are not hard and fast divisions. If you can't plant during the first quarter, plant during the second, and vice versa. There are many plants that seem to do equally well planted in either quarter, such as watermelon, garlic, hay, and cereals and grains.

Third Quarter
(Decreasing)

Plant biennials, perennials, and bulb and root plants. Also plant trees, shrubs, berries, beets, carrots, onions, parsnips, peanuts, potatoes, radishes, rhubarb, rutabagas, strawberries, turnips, winter wheat, grapes, etc.

Fourth Quarter
(Decreasing)

This is the best time to cultivate, turn sod, pull weeds, and destroy pests of all kinds, especially when the Moon is in the barren signs of Aries, Leo, Virgo, Gemini, Aquarius and Sagittarius.

Planting by Moon Sign

Moon in Aries

Barren and dry, fiery and masculine. Used for destroying noxious growths, weeds, pests, etc., and for cultivating.

Moon in Taurus

Productive and moist, earthy and feminine. Used for planting many crops, particularly potatoes and root crops, and when hardiness is important. Also used for lettuce, cabbage, and leafy vegetables.

Moon in Gemini

Barren and dry, airy and masculine. Used for destroying noxious growths, weeds and pests, and for cultivation.

Moon in Cancer

Very fruitful and moist, watery and feminine. This is the most productive sign, used extensively for planting and irrigation.

Moon in Leo

Barren and dry, fiery and masculine. This is the most barren sign, used only for killing weeds and for cultivation.

Moon in Virgo

Barren and moist, earthy and feminine. Good for cultivation and destroying weeds and pests.

Moon in Libra

Semi-fruitful and moist, airy and masculine. Used for planting many crops and producing good pulp growth and roots. A very good sign for flowers and vines. Also used for seeding hay, corn fodder, etc.

Moon in Scorpio

Very fruitful and moist, watery and feminine. Nearly as productive as Cancer; used for the same purposes. Especially good for vine growth and sturdiness.

Moon in Sagittarius

Barren and dry, fiery and masculine. Used for planting onions, seeding hay, and for cultivation.

Moon in Capricorn

Productive and dry, earthy and feminine. Used for planting potatoes, tubers, etc.

Moon in Aquarius

Barren and dry, airy and masculine. Used for cultivation and destroying noxious growths, weeds, and pests.

Moon in Pisces

Very fruitful and moist, watery and feminine. Used along with Cancer and Scorpio, especially good for root growth.

World Time Zones

Compared to Eastern Standard Time

(R) EST—Used	(N) Add 4 hours
(A) Add 6 hours	(Z) Add 5 hours
(S) CST—Subtract 1 hour	(B) Add 7 hours
(T) MST—Subtract 2 hours	(C) Add 8 hours
(U) PST—Subtract 3 hours	(D) Add 9 hours
(V) Subtract 4 hours	(E) Add 10 hours
(W) Subtract 5 hours	(F) Add 11 hours
(X) Subtract 6 hours	(G) Add 12 hours
(Y) Subtract 7 hours	(H) Add 13 hours
(Q) Add 1 hour	(I) Add 14 hours
(P) Add 2 hours	(K) Add 15 hours
(O) Add 3 hours	(L) Add 16 hours

WORLD MAP OF TIME ZONES

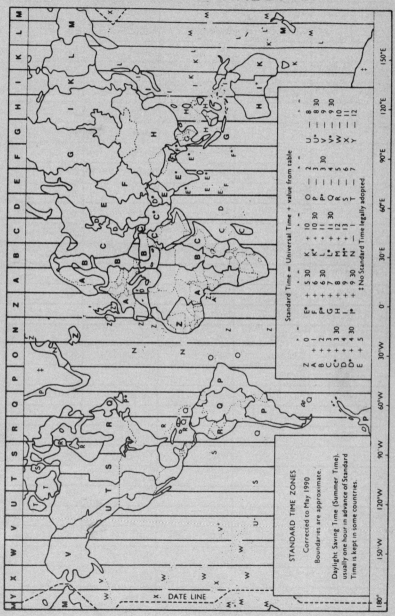

STANDARD TIME ZONES
Corrected to May 1990
Boundaries are approximate.

Daylight Saving Time (Summer Time),
usually one hour in advance of Standard
Time is kept in some countries.

DATE LINE

January Moon Table

Date	Sign	Element	Nature	Phase
1 MON 9:30 pm	Gemini	Air	Barren	2nd
2 TUE	Gemini	Air	Barren	2nd
3 WED	Gemini	Air	Barren	2nd
4 THU 9:56 am	Cancer	Water	Fruitful	2nd
5 FRI	Cancer	Water	Fruitful	Full 3:51 pm
6 SAT 10:31 pm	Leo	Fire	Barren	3rd
7 SUN	Leo	Fire	Barren	3rd
8 MON	Leo	Fire	Barren	3rd
9 TUE 10:29 am	Virgo	Earth	Barren	3rd
10 WED	Virgo	Earth	Barren	3rd
11 THU 8:55 pm	Libra	Air	Semi-fruit	3rd
12 FRI	Libra	Air	Semi-fruit	3rd
13 SAT	Libra	Air	Semi-fruit	4th 3:45 pm
14 SUN 4:30 am	Scorpio	Water	Fruitful	4th
15 MON	Scorpio	Water	Fruitful	4th
16 TUE 8:25 am	Sagittarius	Fire	Barren	4th
17 WED	Sagittarius	Fire	Barren	4th
18 THU 9:07 am	Capricorn	Earth	Semi-fruit	4th
19 FRI	Capricorn	Earth	Semi-fruit	4th
20 SAT 8:15 am	Aquarius	Air	Barren	New 7:51 am
21 SUN	Aquarius	Air	Barren	1st
22 MON 8:02 am	Pisces	Water	Fruitful	1st
23 TUE	Pisces	Water	Fruitful	1st
24 WED 10:37 am	Aries	Fire	Barren	1st
25 THU	Aries	Fire	Barren	1st
26 FRI 5:17 pm	Taurus	Earth	Semi-fruit	1st
27 SAT	Taurus	Earth	Semi-fruit	2nd 6:14 am
28 SUN	Taurus	Earth	Semi-fruit	2nd
29 MON 3:43 am	Gemini	Air	Barren	2nd
30 TUE	Gemini	Air	Barren	2nd
31 WED 4:11 pm	Cancer	Water	Fruitful	2nd

February Moon Table

Date	Sign	Element	Nature	Phase
1 THU	Cancer	Water	Fruitful	2nd
2 FRI	Cancer	Water	Fruitful	2nd
3 SAT 4:46 am	Leo	Fire	Barren	2nd
4 SUN	Leo	Fire	Barren	Full 10:58 am
5 MON 4:22 pm	Virgo	Earth	Barren	3rd
6 TUE	Virgo	Earth	Barren	3rd
7 WED	Virgo	Earth	Barren	3rd
8 THU 2:30 am	Libra	Air	Semi-fruit	3rd
9 FRI	Libra	Air	Semi-fruit	3rd
10 SAT 10:35 am	Scorpio	Water	Fruitful	3rd
11 SUN	Scorpio	Water	Fruitful	3rd
12 MON 3:59 pm	Sagittarius	Fire	Barren	4th 3:38 am
13 TUE	Sagittarius	Fire	Barren	4th
14 WED 6:30 pm	Capricorn	Earth	Semi-fruit	4th
15 THU	Capricorn	Earth	Semi-fruit	4th
16 FRI 7:00 pm	Aquarius	Air	Barren	4th
17 SAT	Aquarius	Air	Barren	4th
18 SUN 7:10 pm	Pisces	Water	Fruitful	New 6:31 pm
19 MON	Pisces	Water	Fruitful	1st
20 TUE 8:58 pm	Aries	Fire	Barren	1st
21 WED	Aries	Fire	Barren	1st
22 THU	Aries	Fire	Barren	1st
23 FRI 2:08 am	Taurus	Earth	Semi-fruit	1st
24 SAT	Taurus	Earth	Semi-fruit	1st
25 SUN 11:14 am	Gemini	Air	Barren	1st
26 MON	Gemini	Air	Barren	2nd 12:52 am
27 TUE 11:10 pm	Cancer	Water	Fruitful	2nd
28 WED	Cancer	Water	Fruitful	2nd
29 THU	Cancer	Water	Fruitful	2nd

March Moon Table

Date	Sign	Element	Nature	Phase
1 FRI 11:47 am	Leo	Fire	Barren	2nd
2 SAT	Leo	Fire	Barren	2nd
3 SUN 11:13 pm	Virgo	Earth	Barren	2nd
4 MON	Virgo	Earth	Barren	2nd
5 TUE	Virgo	Earth	Barren	Full 4:23 am
6 WED 8:41 am	Libra	Air	Semi-fruit	3rd
7 THU	Libra	Air	Semi-fruit	3rd
8 FRI 4:06 pm	Scorpio	Water	Fruitful	3rd
9 SAT	Scorpio	Water	Fruitful	3rd
10 SUN 9:33 pm	Sagittarius	Fire	Barren	3rd
11 MON	Sagittarius	Fire	Barren	3rd
12 TUE	Sagittarius	Fire	Barren	4th 12:15 pm
13 WED 1:08 am	Capricorn	Earth	Semi-fruit	4th
14 THU	Capricorn	Earth	Semi-fruit	4th
15 FRI 3:15 am	Aquarius	Air	Barren	4th
16 SAT	Aquarius	Air	Barren	4th
17 SUN 4:50 am	Pisces	Water	Fruitful	4th
18 MON	Pisces	Water	Fruitful	4th
19 TUE 7:15 am	Aries	Fire	Barren	New 5:45 am
20 WED	Aries	Fire	Barren	1st
21 THU 11:58 am	Taurus	Earth	Semi-fruit	1st
22 FRI	Taurus	Earth	Semi-fruit	1st
23 SAT 7:59 pm	Gemini	Air	Barren	1st
24 SUN	Gemini	Air	Barren	1st
25 MON	Gemini	Air	Barren	1st
26 TUE 7:06 am	Cancer	Water	Fruitful	2nd 8:31 pm
27 WED	Cancer	Water	Fruitful	2nd
28 THU 7:38 pm	Leo	Fire	Barren	2nd
29 FRI	Leo	Fire	Barren	2nd
30 SAT	Leo	Fire	Barren	2nd
31 SUN 7:15 am	Virgo	Earth	Barren	2nd

April Moon Table

Date	Sign	Element	Nature	Phase
1 MON	Virgo	Earth	Barren	2nd
2 TUE 4:27 pm	Libra	Air	Semi-fruit	2nd
3 WED	Libra	Air	Semi-fruit	Full 7:08 pm
4 THU 10:57 pm	Scorpio	Water	Fruitful	3rd
5 FRI	Scorpio	Water	Fruitful	3rd
6 SAT	Scorpio	Water	Fruitful	3rd
7 SUN 3:21 am	Sagittarius	Fire	Barren	3rd
8 MON	Sagittarius	Fire	Barren	3rd
9 TUE 6:30 am	Capricorn	Earth	Semi-fruit	3rd
10 WED	Capricorn	Earth	Semi-fruit	4th 6:36 pm
11 THU 9:09 am	Aquarius	Air	Barren	4th
12 FRI	Aquarius	Air	Barren	4th
13 SAT 11:59 am	Pisces	Water	Fruitful	4th
14 SUN	Pisces	Water	Fruitful	4th
15 MON 3:43 pm	Aries	Fire	Barren	4th
16 TUE	Aries	Fire	Barren	4th
17 WED 9:06 pm	Taurus	Earth	Semi-fruit	New 5:49 pm
18 THU	Taurus	Earth	Semi-fruit	1st
19 FRI	Taurus	Earth	Semi-fruit	1st
20 SAT 4:55 am	Gemini	Air	Barren	1st
21 SUN	Gemini	Air	Barren	1st
22 MON 3:25 pm	Cancer	Water	Fruitful	1st
23 TUE	Cancer	Water	Fruitful	1st
24 WED	Cancer	Water	Fruitful	1st
25 THU 3:45 am	Leo	Fire	Barren	2nd 3:41 pm
26 FRI	Leo	Fire	Barren	2nd
27 SAT 3:49 pm	Virgo	Earth	Barren	2nd
28 SUN	Virgo	Earth	Barren	2nd
29 MON	Libra	Air	Semi-fruit	2nd
30 TUE 1:27 am	Libra	Air	Semi-fruit	2nd

May Moon Table

Date	Sign	Element	Nature	Phase
1 WED	Libra	Air	Semi-fruit	2nd
2 THU 7:43 am	Scorpio	Water	Fruitful	2nd
3 FRI	Scorpio	Water	Fruitful	Full 6:48 am
4 SAT 11:04 am	Sagittarius	Fire	Barren	3rd
5 SUN	Sagittarius	Fire	Barren	3rd
6 MON 12:54 pm	Capricorn	Earth	Semi-fruit	3rd
7 TUE	Capricorn	Earth	Semi-fruit	3rd
8 WED 2:39 pm	Aquarius	Air	Barren	3rd
9 THU	Aquarius	Air	Barren	3rd
10 FRI 5:29 pm	Pisces	Water	Fruitful	4th 12:04 am
11 SAT	Pisces	Water	Fruitful	4th
12 SUN 10:01 pm	Aries	Fire	Barren	4th
13 MON	Aries	Fire	Barren	4th
14 TUE	Aries	Fire	Barren	4th
15 WED 4:25 am	Taurus	Earth	Semi-fruit	4th
16 THU	Taurus	Earth	Semi-fruit	4th
17 FRI 12:48 pm	Gemini	Air	Barren	New 6:47 am
18 SAT	Gemini	Air	Barren	1st
19 SUN 11:17 pm	Cancer	Water	Fruitful	1st
20 MON	Cancer	Water	Fruitful	1st
21 TUE	Cancer	Water	Fruitful	1st
22 WED 11:28 am	Leo	Fire	Barren	1st
23 THU	Leo	Fire	Barren	1st
24 FRI 11:59 pm	Virgo	Earth	Barren	1st
25 SAT	Virgo	Earth	Barren	2nd 9:13 am
26 SUN	Virgo	Earth	Barren	2nd
27 MON 10:33 am	Libra	Air	Semi-fruit	2nd
28 TUE	Libra	Air	Semi-fruit	2nd
29 WED 5:30 pm	Scorpio	Water	Fruitful	2nd
30 THU	Scorpio	Water	Fruitful	2nd
31 FRI 8:43 pm	Sagittarius	Fire	Barren	2nd

June Moon Table

Date	Sign	Element	Nature	Phase
1 SAT	Sagittarius	Fire	Barren	Full 3:47 pm
2 SUN 9:29 pm	Capricorn	Earth	Semi-fruit	3rd
3 MON	Capricorn	Earth	Semi-fruit	3rd
4 TUE 9:45 pm	Aquarius	Air	Barren	3rd
5 WED	Aquarius	Air	Barren	3rd
6 THU 11:20 pm	Pisces	Water	Fruitful	3rd
7 FRI	Pisces	Water	Fruitful	3rd
8 SAT	Pisces	Water	Fruitful	4th 6:06 am
9 SUN 3:24 am	Aries	Fire	Barren	4th
10 MON	Aries	Fire	Barren	4th
11 TUE 10:11 am	Taurus	Earth	Semi-fruit	4th
12 WED	Taurus	Earth	Semi-fruit	4th
13 THU 7:16 pm	Gemini	Air	Barren	4th
14 FRI	Gemini	Air	Barren	4th
15 SAT	Gemini	Air	Barren	New 8:36 pm
16 SUN 6:08 am	Cancer	Water	Fruitful	1st
17 MON	Cancer	Water	Fruitful	1st
18 TUE 6:21 pm	Leo	Fire	Barren	1st
19 WED	Leo	Fire	Barren	1st
20 THU	Leo	Fire	Barren	1st
21 FRI 7:07 am	Virgo	Earth	Barren	1st
22 SAT	Virgo	Earth	Barren	1st
23 SUN 6:38 pm	Libra	Air	Semi-fruit	1st
24 MON	Libra	Air	Semi-fruit	2nd 12:23 am
25 TUE	Libra	Air	Semi-fruit	2nd
26 WED 2:54 am	Scorpio	Water	Fruitful	2nd
27 THU	Scorpio	Water	Fruitful	2nd
28 FRI 7:02 am	Sagittarius	Fire	Barren	2nd
29 SAT	Sagittarius	Fire	Barren	2nd
30 SUN 7:48 am	Capricorn	Earth	Semi-fruit	Full 10:59 pm

July Moon Table

Date	Sign	Element	Nature	Phase
1 MON	Capricorn	Earth	Semi-fruit	3rd
2 TUE 7:06 am	Aquarius	Air	Barren	3rd
3 WED	Aquarius	Air	Barren	3rd
4 THU 7:07 am	Pisces	Water	Fruitful	3rd
5 FRI	Pisces	Water	Fruitful	3rd
6 SAT 9:42 am	Aries	Fire	Barren	3rd
7 SUN	Aries	Fire	Barren	4th 1:55 pm
8 MON 3:43 pm	Taurus	Earth	Semi-fruit	4th
9 TUE	Taurus	Earth	Semi-fruit	4th
10 WED	Taurus	Earth	Semi-fruit	4th
11 THU 12:52 am	Gemini	Air	Barren	4th
12 FRI	Gemini	Air	Barren	4th
13 SAT 12:08 pm	Cancer	Water	Fruitful	4th
14 SUN	Cancer	Water	Fruitful	4th
15 MON	Cancer	Water	Fruitful	New 11:15 am
16 TUE 12:31 am	Leo	Fire	Barren	1st
17 WED	Leo	Fire	Barren	1st
18 THU 1:17 pm	Virgo	Earth	Barren	1st
19 FRI	Virgo	Earth	Barren	1st
20 SAT	Virgo	Earth	Barren	1st
21 SUN 1:14 am	Libra	Air	Semi-fruit	1st
22 MON	Libra	Air	Semi-fruit	1st
23 TUE 10:43 am	Scorpio	Water	Fruitful	2nd 12:50 pm
24 WED	Scorpio	Water	Fruitful	2nd
25 THU 4:24 pm	Sagittarius	Fire	Barren	2nd
26 FRI	Sagittarius	Fire	Barren	2nd
27 SAT 6:18 pm	Capricorn	Earth	Semi-fruit	2nd
28 SUN	Capricorn	Earth	Semi-fruit	2nd
29 MON 5:48 pm	Aquarius	Air	Barren	2nd
30 TUE	Aquarius	Air	Barren	Full 5:36 am
31 WED 5:01 pm	Pisces	Water	Fruitful	3rd

August Moon Table

Date	Sign	Element	Nature	Phase
1 THU	Pisces	Water	Fruitful	3rd
2 FRI 6:05 pm	Aries	Fire	Barren	3rd
3 SAT	Aries	Fire	Barren	3rd
4 SUN 10:33 pm	Taurus	Earth	Semi-fruit	3rd
5 MON	Taurus	Earth	Semi-fruit	3rd
6 TUE	Taurus	Earth	Semi-fruit	4th 12:25 am
7 WED 6:49 am	Gemini	Air	Barren	4th
8 THU	Gemini	Air	Barren	4th
9 FRI 5:58 pm	Cancer	Water	Fruitful	4th
10 SAT	Cancer	Water	Fruitful	4th
11 SUN	Cancer	Water	Fruitful	4th
12 MON 6:29 am	Leo	Fire	Barren	4th
13 TUE	Leo	Fire	Barren	4th
14 WED 7:08 pm	Virgo	Earth	Barren	New 2:35 am
15 THU	Virgo	Earth	Barren	1st
16 FRI	Virgo	Earth	Barren	1st
17 SAT 6:56 am	Libra	Air	Semi-fruit	1st
18 SUN	Libra	Air	Semi-fruit	1st
19 MON 4:51 pm	Scorpio	Water	Fruitful	1st
20 TUE	Scorpio	Water	Fruitful	1st
21 WED 11:48 pm	Sagittarius	Fire	Barren	2nd 10:37 pm
22 THU	Sagittarius	Fire	Barren	2nd
23 FRI	Sagittarius	Fire	Barren	2nd
24 SAT 3:22 am	Capricorn	Earth	Semi-fruit	2nd
25 SUN	Capricorn	Earth	Semi-fruit	2nd
26 MON 4:10 am	Aquarius	Air	Barren	2nd
27 TUE	Aquarius	Air	Barren	2nd
28 WED 3:48 am	Pisces	Water	Fruitful	Full 12:52 pm
29 THU	Pisces	Water	Fruitful	3rd
30 FRI 4:15 am	Aries	Fire	Barren	3rd
31 SAT	Aries	Fire	Barren	3rd

September Moon Table

Date	Sign	Element	Nature	Phase
1 SUN 7:20 am	Taurus	Earth	Semi-fruit	3rd
2 MON	Taurus	Earth	Semi-fruit	3rd
3 TUE 2:09 pm	Gemini	Air	Barren	3rd
4 WED	Gemini	Air	Barren	4th 2:07 pm
5 THU	Gemini	Air	Barren	4th
6 FRI 12:30 am	Cancer	Water	Fruitful	4th
7 SAT	Cancer	Water	Fruitful	4th
8 SUN 12:55 pm	Leo	Fire	Barren	4th
9 MON	Leo	Fire	Barren	4th
10 TUE	Leo	Fire	Barren	4th
11 WED 1:29 am	Virgo	Earth	Barren	4th
12 THU	Virgo	Earth	Barren	New 6:08 pm
13 FRI 12:51 pm	Libra	Air	Semi-fruit	1st
14 SAT	Libra	Air	Semi-fruit	1st
15 SUN 10:20 pm	Scorpio	Water	Fruitful	1st
16 MON	Scorpio	Water	Fruitful	1st
17 TUE	Scorpio	Water	Fruitful	1st
18 WED 5:30 am	Sagittarius	Fire	Barren	1st
19 THU	Sagittarius	Fire	Barren	1st
20 FRI 10:12 am	Capricorn	Earth	Semi-fruit	2nd 6:23 am
21 SAT	Capricorn	Earth	Semi-fruit	2nd
22 SUN 12:39 pm	Aquarius	Air	Barren	2nd
23 MON	Aquarius	Air	Barren	2nd
24 TUE 1:43 pm	Pisces	Water	Fruitful	2nd
25 WED	Pisces	Water	Fruitful	2nd
26 THU 2:46 pm	Aries	Fire	Barren	Full
27 FRI	Aries	Fire	Barren	3rd
28 SAT 5:24 pm	Taurus	Earth	Semi-fruit	3rd
29 SUN	Taurus	Earth	Semi-fruit	3rd
30 MON 11:02 pm	Gemini	Air	Barren	3rd

October Moon Table

Date	Sign	Element	Nature	Phase
1 TUE	Gemini	Air	Barren	3rd
2 WED	Gemini	Air	Barren	3rd
3 THU 8:15 am	Cancer	Water	Fruitful	3rd
4 FRI	Cancer	Water	Fruitful	4th 7:05 am
5 SAT 8:12 pm	Leo	Fire	Barren	4th
6 SUN	Leo	Fire	Barren	4th
7 MON	Leo	Fire	Barren	4th
8 TUE 8:49 am	Virgo	Earth	Barren	4th
9 WED	Virgo	Earth	Barren	4th
10 THU 8:00 pm	Libra	Air	Semi-fruit	4th
11 FRI	Libra	Air	Semi-fruit	4th
12 SAT	Libra	Air	Semi-fruit	New 9:14 am
13 SUN 4:46 am	Scorpio	Water	Fruitful	1st
14 MON	Scorpio	Water	Fruitful	1st
15 TUE 11:07 am	Sagittarius	Fire	Barren	1st
16 WED	Sagittarius	Fire	Barren	1st
17 THU 3:38 pm	Capricorn	Earth	Semi-fruit	1st
18 FRI	Capricorn	Earth	Semi-fruit	1st
19 SAT 6:52 pm	Aquarius	Air	Barren	2nd 1:10 pm
20 SUN	Aquarius	Air	Barren	2nd
21 MON 9:23 pm	Pisces	Water	Fruitful	2nd
22 TUE	Pisces	Water	Fruitful	2nd
23 WED 11:51 pm	Aries	Fire	Barren	2nd
24 THU	Aries	Fire	Barren	2nd
25 FRI	Aries	Fire	Barren	2nd
26 SAT 3:12 am	Taurus	Earth	Semi-fruit	Full 9:12 am
27 SUN	Taurus	Earth	Semi-fruit	3rd
28 MON 8:35 am	Gemini	Air	Barren	3rd
29 TUE	Gemini	Air	Barren	3rd
30 WED 4:57 pm	Cancer	Water	Fruitful	3rd
31 THU	Cancer	Water	Fruitful	3rd

November Moon Table

Date	Sign	Element	Nature	Phase
1 FRI	Cancer	Water	Fruitful	3rd
2 SAT 4:16 am	Leo	Fire	Barren	3rd
3 SUN	Leo	Fire	Barren	4th 2:50 am
4 MON 4:57 pm	Virgo	Earth	Barren	4th
5 TUE	Virgo	Earth	Barren	4th
6 WED	Virgo	Earth	Barren	4th
7 THU 4:29 am	Libra	Air	Semi-fruit	4th
8 FRI	Libra	Air	Semi-fruit	4th
9 SAT 1:02 pm	Scorpio	Water	Fruitful	4th
10 SUN	Scorpio	Water	Fruitful	New 11:17 pm
11 MON 6:27 pm	Sagittarius	Fire	Barren	1st
12 TUE	Sagittarius	Fire	Barren	1st
13 WED 9:44 pm	Capricorn	Earth	Semi-fruit	1st
14 THU	Capricorn	Earth	Semi-fruit	1st
15 FRI	Capricorn	Earth	Semi-fruit	1st
16 SAT 12:15 am	Aquarius	Air	Barren	1st
17 SUN	Aquarius	Air	Barren	2nd 8:10 pm
18 MON 3:00 am	Pisces	Water	Fruitful	2nd
19 TUE	Pisces	Water	Fruitful	2nd
20 WED 6:34 am	Aries	Fire	Barren	2nd
21 THU	Aries	Fire	Barren	2nd
22 FRI 11:12 am	Taurus	Earth	Semi-fruit	2nd
23 SAT	Taurus	Earth	Semi-fruit	2nd
24 SUN 5:19 pm	Gemini	Air	Barren	Full 11:10 pm
25 MON	Gemini	Air	Barren	3rd
26 TUE	Gemini	Air	Barren	3rd
27 WED 1:37 am	Cancer	Water	Fruitful	3rd
28 THU	Cancer	Water	Fruitful	3rd
29 FRI 12:30 pm	Leo	Fire	Barren	3rd
30 SAT	Leo	Fire	Barren	3rd

December Moon Table

Date	Sign	Element	Nature	Phase
1 SUN	Leo	Fire	Barren	3rd
2 MON 1:11 am	Virgo	Earth	Barren	3rd
3 TUE	Virgo	Earth	Barren	4th 12:06 am
4 WED 1:24 pm	Libra	Air	Semi-fruit	4th
5 THU	Libra	Air	Semi-fruit	4th
6 FRI 10:39 pm	Scorpio	Water	Fruitful	4th
7 SAT	Scorpio	Water	Fruitful	4th
8 SUN	Scorpio	Water	Fruitful	4th
9 MON 3:59 am	Sagittarius	Fire	Barren	4th
10 TUE	Sagittarius	Fire	Barren	New 11:57 am
11 WED 6:15 am	Capricorn	Earth	Semi-fruit	1st
12 THU	Capricorn	Earth	Semi-fruit	1st
13 FRI 7:14 am	Aquarius	Air	Barren	1st
14 SAT	Aquarius	Air	Barren	1st
15 SUN 8:44 am	Pisces	Water	Fruitful	1st
16 MON	Pisces	Water	Fruitful	1st
17 TUE 11:55 am	Aries	Fire	Barren	2nd 4:31 am
18 WED	Aries	Fire	Barren	2nd
19 THU 5:09 pm	Taurus	Earth	Semi-fruit	2nd
20 FRI	Taurus	Earth	Semi-fruit	2nd
21 SAT	Taurus	Earth	Semi-fruit	2nd
22 SUN 12:17 am	Gemini	Air	Barren	2nd
23 MON	Gemini	Air	Barren	2nd
24 TUE 9:14 am	Cancer	Water	Fruitful	Full 3:41 pm
25 WED	Cancer	Water	Fruitful	3rd
26 THU 8:09 pm	Leo	Fire	Barren	3rd
27 FRI	Leo	Fire	Barren	3rd
28 SAT	Leo	Fire	Barren	3rd
29 SUN 8:46 am	Virgo	Earth	Barren	3rd
30 MON	Virgo	Earth	Barren	3rd
31 TUE 9:33 pm	Libra	Air	Semi-fruit	3rd

Gardening Dates

Dates	Qtr	Sign	Activity
Jan. 4, 9:56 am - Jan. 5, 3:51 pm	2nd	Cancer	Plant grains, leafy annuals. Fertilize. Graft or bud plants. Irrigate. Trim to increase growth.
Jan. 5, 3:51 pm - Jan. 6, 10:31 pm	3rd	Cancer	Plant biennials, perennials, bulbs and roots. Prune. Irrigate. Fertilize (organic).
Jan. 6, 10:31 pm - Jan. 9, 10:29 am	3rd	Leo	Cultivate. Destroy weeds and pests.
Jan. 9, 10:29 am - Jan. 11, 8:55 pm	3rd	Virgo	Cultivate, especially medicinal plants. Destroy weeds and pests. Trim to retard growth.
Jan. 14, 4:30 am - Jan. 16, 8:25 am	4th	Scorpio	Plant biennials, perennials, bulbs and roots. Prune. Irrigate. Fertilize (organic).
Jan. 16, 8:25 am - Jan. 18, 9:07 am	4th	Sagittarius	Cultivate. Destroy weeds and pests. Harvest fruits and root crops. Trim to retard growth.
Jan. 18, 9:07 am - Jan. 20, 7:51 am	4th	Capricorn	Plant potatos and tubers. Trim to retard growth.
Jan. 20, 7:51 am - Jan. 20, 8:15 am	1st	Capricorn	Graft or bud plants. Trim to increase growth.
Jan. 22, 8:02 am - Jan. 24, 10:37 am	1st	Pisces	Plant grains, leafy annuals. Fertilize. Graft or bud plants. Irrigate. Trim to increase growth.
Jan. 26, 5:17 pm - Jan. 27, 6:14 am	1st	Taurus	Plant annuals for hardiness. Trim to increase growth.
Jan. 27, 6:14 am - Jan. 29, 3:43 am	2nd	Taurus	Plant annuals for hardiness. Trim to increase growth.
Jan. 31, 4:11 pm - Feb. 3, 4:46 am	2nd	Cancer	Plant grains, leafy annuals. Fertilize. Graft or bud plants. Irrigate. Trim to increase growth.
Feb. 4, 10:58 am - Feb. 5, 4:22 pm	3rd	Leo	Cultivate. Destroy weeds and pests. Harvest fruits and root crops. Trim to retard growth.
Feb. 5, 4:22 pm - Feb. 8, 2:30 am	3rd	Virgo	Cultivate, especially medicinal plants. Destroy weeds and pests. Trim to retard growth.
Feb. 10, 10:35 am - Feb. 12, 3:38 am	3rd	Scorpio	Plant biennials, perennials, bulbs and roots. Prune. Irrigate. Fertilize (organic).
Feb. 12, 3:38 am - Feb. 12, 3:59 am	4th	Scorpio	Plant biennials, perennials, bulbs and roots. Prune. Irrigate. Fertilize (organic).
Feb. 12, 3:59 pm - Feb. 14, 6:30 pm	4th	Sagittarius	Cultivate. Destroy weeds and pests. Harvest fruits and root crops. Trim to retard growth.
Feb. 14, 6:30 pm - Feb. 16, 7:00 pm	4th	Capricorn	Plant potatos and tubers. Trim to retard growth.
Feb. 16, 7:00 pm - Feb. 18, 6:31 pm	4th	Aquarius	Cultivate. Destroy weeds and pests. Harvest fruits and root crops. Trim to retard growth.

Gardening Dates

Dates	Qtr	Sign	Activity
Feb. 18, 7:10 pm - Feb. 20, 8:58 pm	1st	Pisces	Plant grains, leafy annuals. Fertilize (chemical). Graft orbud plants. Irrigate. Trim to increase growth.
Feb. 23, 2:08 am - Feb. 25, 11:14 am	1st	Taurus	Plant annuals for hardiness. Trim to increase growth.
Feb. 27, 11:10 pm - Mar. 1, 11:47 am	2nd	Cancer	Plant grains, leafy annuals. Fertilize. Graft or bud plants. Irrigate. Trim to increase growth.
Mar. 5, 4:23 am - Mar. 6, 8:41 am	3rd	Virgo	Cultivate, especially medicinal plants. Destroy weeds and pests. Trim to retard growth.
Mar. 8, 4:06 pm - Mar. 10, 9:33 pm	3rd	Scorpio	Plant biennials, perennials, bulbs and roots. Prune. Irrigate. Fertilize (organic).
Mar. 10, 9:33 pm - Mar. 12, 12:15 pm	3rd	Sagittarius	Cultivate. Destroy weeds and pests. Harvest fruits and root crops. Trim to retard growth.
Mar. 12, 12:15 pm - Mar. 13, 1:08 am	4th	Sagittarius	Cultivate. Destroy weeds and pests. Harvest fruits and root crops. Trim to retard growth.
Mar. 13, 1:08 am - Mar. 15, 3:15 am	4th	Capricorn	Plant potatos and tubers. Trim to retard growth.
Mar. 15, 3:15 am - Mar. 17, 4:50 am	4th	Aquarius	Cultivate. Destroy weeds and pests. Harvest fruits and root crops. Trim to retard growth.
Mar. 17, 4:50 am - Mar. 19, 5:45 am	4th	Pisces	Plant biennials, perennials, bulbs and roots. Prune. Irrigate. Fertilize (organic).
Mar. 19, 5:45 am - Mar. 19, 7:15 am	1st	Pisces	Plant grains, leafy annuals. Fertilize. Graft or bud plants. Irrigate. Trim to increase growth.
Mar. 21, 11:58 am - Mar. 23, 7:59 pm	1st	Taurus	Plant annuals for hardiness. Trim to increase growth.
Mar. 26, 7:06 am - Mar. 26, 8:31 pm	1st	Cancer	Plant grains, leafy annuals. Fertilize. Graft or bud plants. Irrigate. Trim to increase growth.
Mar. 26, 8:31 pm - Mar. 28, 7:38 pm	2nd	Cancer	Plant grains, leafy annuals. Fertilize. Graft or bud plants. Irrigate. Trim to increase growth.
Apr. 2, 4:27 pm - Apr. 3, 7:08 pm	2nd	Libra	Plant annuals for fragrance and beauty. Trim to increase growth.
Apr. 4, 10:57 pm - Apr. 7, 3:21 am	3rd	Scorpio	Plant biennials, perennials, bulbs and roots. Prune. Irrigate. Fertilize (organic).
Apr. 7, 3:21 am - Apr. 9, 6:30 am	3rd	Sagittarius	Cultivate. Destroy weeds and pests. Harvest fruits and root crops. Trim to retard growth.
Apr. 9, 6:30 am - Apr. 10, 6:36 pm	3rd	Capricorn	Plant potatos and tubers. Trim to retard growth.
Apr. 10, 6:36 pm - Apr. 11, 9:09 am	4th	Capricorn	Plant potatos and tubers. Trim to retard growth.

Gardening Dates

Dates	Qtr	Sign	Activity
Apr. 11, 9:09 am - Apr. 13, 11:59 am	4th	Aquarius	Cultivate. Destroy weeds and pests. Harvest fruits and root crops. Trim to retard growth.
Apr. 13, 11:59 am - Apr. 15, 3:43 pm	4th	Pisces	Plant biennials, perennials, bulbs and roots. Prune. Irrigate. Fertilize (organic).
Apr. 15, 3:43 pm - Apr. 17, 5:49 pm	4th	Aries	Cultivate. Destroy weeds and pests. Harvest fruits and root crops. Trim to retard growth.
Apr. 17, 9:06 pm - Apr. 20, 4:55 am	1st	Taurus	Plant annuals for hardiness. Trim to increase growth.
Apr. 22, 3:25 pm - Apr. 25, 3:45 am	1st	Cancer	Plant grains, leafy annuals. Fertilize). Graft or bud plants. Irrigate. Trim to increase growth.
Apr. 30, 1:27 am - May 2, 7:43 am	2nd	Libra	Plant annuals for fragrance and beauty. Trim to increase growth.
May 2, 7:43 am - May 3, 6:48 am	2nd	Scorpio	Plant grains, leafy annuals. Fertilize. Graft or bud plants. Irrigate. Trim to increase growth.
May 3, 6:48 am - May 4, 11:04 am	3rd	Scorpio	Plant biennials, perennials, bulbs and roots. Prune. Irrigate. Fertilize (organic).
May 4, 11:04 am - May 6, 12:54 pm	3rd	Sagittarius	Cultivate. Destroy weeds and pests. Harvest fruits and root crops. Trim to retard growth.
May 6, 12:54 pm - May 8, 2:39 pm	3rd	Capricorn	Plant potatoes and tubers. Trim to retard growth.
May 8, 2:39 pm - May 10, 12:04 am	3rd	Aquarius	Cultivate. Destroy weeds and pests. Harvest fruits and root crops. Trim to retard growth.
May 10, 12:04 am - May 10, 5:29 pm	4th	Aquarius	Cultivate. Destroy weeds and pests. Harvest fruits and root crops. Trim to retard growth.
May 10, 5:29 pm - May 12, 10:01 pm	4th	Pisces	Plant biennials, perennials, bulbs and roots. Prune. Irrigate. Fertilize (organic).
May 12, 10:01 pm - May 15, 4:25 am	4th	Aries	Cultivate. Destroy weeds and pests. Harvest fruits and root crops. Trim to retard growth.
May 15, 4:25 am - May 17, 6:47 am	4th	Taurus	Plant potatoes and tubers. Trim to retard growth.
May 17, 6:47 am - May 17, 12:48 pm	1st	Taurus	Plant annuals for hardiness. Trim to increase growth.
May 19, 11:17 pm - May 22, 11:28 am	1st	Cancer	Plant grains, leafy annuals. Fertilize. Graft or bud plants. Irrigate. Trim to increase growth.
May 27, 10:33 am - May 29, 5:30 pm	2nd	Libra	Plant annuals for fragrance and beauty. Trim to increase growth.
May 29, 5:30 pm - May 31, 8:43 pm	2nd	Scorpio	Plant grains, leafy annuals. Fertilize. Graft or bud plants. Irrigate. Trim to increase growth.

Gardening Dates

Dates	Qtr	Sign	Activity
Jun. 1, 3:47 pm - Jun. 2, 9:29 pm	3rd	Sagittarius	Cultivate. Destroy weeds and pests. Harvest fruits and root crops. Trim to retard growth.
Jun. 2, 9:29 pm - Jun. 4, 9:45 pm	3rd	Capricorn	Plant potatoes and tubers. Trim to retard growth.
Jun. 4, 9:45 pm - Jun. 6, 11:20 pm	3rd	Aquarius	Cultivate. Destroy weeds and pests. Harvest fruits and root crops. Trim to retard growth.
Jun. 6, 11:20 pm - Jun. 8, 6:06 am	3rd	Pisces	Plant biennials, perennials, bulbs and roots. Prune. Irrigate. Fertilize (organic).
Jun. 8, 6:06 am - Jun. 9, 3:24 am	4th	Pisces	Plant biennials, perennials, bulbs and roots. Prune. Irrigate. Fertilize (organic).
Jun. 9, 3:24 am - Jun. 11, 10:11 am	4th	Aries	Cultivate. Destroy weeds and pests. Harvest fruits and root crops. Trim to retard growth.
Jun. 11, 10:11 am - Jun. 13, 7:16 pm	4th	Taurus	Plant potatoes and tubers. Trim to retard growth.
Jun. 16, 6:08 am - Jun. 18, 6:21 pm	1st	Cancer	Plant grains, leafy annuals. Fertilize. Graft or bud plants. Irrigate. Trim to increase growth.
Jun. 23, 6:38 pm - Jun. 24, 12:23 am	1st	Libra	Plant annuals for fragrance and beauty. Trim to increase growth.
Jun. 24, 12:23 am - Jun. 26, 2:54 am	2nd	Libra	Plant annuals for fragrance and beauty. Trim to increase growth.
Jun. 26, 2:54 am - Jun. 28, 7:02 am	2nd	Scorpio	Plant grains, leafy annuals. Fertilize. Graft or bud plants. Irrigate. Trim to increase growth.
Jun. 30, 7:48 am - Jun. 30, 10:59 pm	2nd	Capricorn	Graft or bud plants. Trim to increase growth.
Jun. 30, 10:59 pm - Jul. 2, 7:06 am	3rd	Capricorn	Plant potatoes and tubers. Trim to retard growth.
Jul. 2, 7:06 am - Jul. 4, 7:07 am	3rd	Aquarius	Cultivate. Destroy weeds and pests. Harvest fruits and root crops. Trim to retard growth.
Jul. 4, 7:07 am - Jul. 6, 9:42 am	3rd	Pisces	Plant biennials, perennials, bulbs and roots. Prune. Irrigate. Fertilize (organic).
Jul. 6, 9:42 am - Jul. 7, 1:55 pm	3rd	Aries	Cultivate. Destroy weeds and pests. Harvest fruits and root crops . Trim to retard growth.
Jul. 7, 1:55 pm - Jul. 8, 3:43 pm	4th	Aries	Cultivate. Destroy weeds and pests. Harvest fruits and root crops. Trim to retard growth.
Jul. 8, 3:43 pm - Jul. 11, 12:52 am	4th	Taurus	Plant potatoes and tubers. Trim to retard growth.
Jul. 13, 12:08 pm - Jul. 15, 11:15 am	4th	Cancer	Plant biennials, perennials, bulbs and roots. Prune. Irrigate. Fertilize (organic).

Gardening Dates

Dates	Qtr	Sign	Activity
Jul. 15, 11:15 am - Jul. 16, 12:31 am	1st	Cancer	Plant grains, leafy annuals. Fertilize. Graft or bud plants. Irrigate. Trim to increase growth.
Jul. 21, 1:14 am - Jul. 23, 10:43 am	1st	Libra	Plant annuals for fragrance and beauty. Trim to increase growth.
Jul. 23, 10:43 am - Jul. 23, 12:50 pm	1st	Scorpio	Plant grains, leafy annuals. Fertilize. Graft or bud plants. Irrigate. Trim to increase growth.
Jul. 23, 12:50 pm - Jul. 25, 4:24 pm	2nd	Scorpio	Plant grains, leafy annuals. Fertilize. Graft or bud plants. Irrigate. Trim to increase growth.
Jul. 27, 6:18 pm - Jul. 29, 5:48 pm	2nd	Capricorn	Graft or bud plants. Trim to increase growth.
Jul. 30, 5:36 am - Jul. 31, 5:01 pm	3rd	Aquarius	Cultivate. Destroy weeds and pests. Harvest fruits and root crops. Trim to retard growth.
Jul. 31, 5:01 pm - Aug 2, 6:05 pm	3rd	Pisces	Plant biennials, perennials, bulbs and roots. Prune. Irrigate. Fertilize (organic).
Aug 2, 6:05 pm - Aug 4, 10:33 pm	3rd	Aries	Cultivate. Destroy weeds and pests. Harvest fruits and root crops. Trim to retard growth.
Aug 4, 10:33 pm - Aug 6, 12:25 am	3rd	Taurus	Plant potatos and tubers. Trim to retard growth.
Aug 6, 12:25 am - Aug 7, 6:49 am	4th	Taurus	Plant potatos and tubers. Trim to retard growth.
Aug 9, 5:58 pm - Aug 12, 6:29 am	4th	Cancer	Plant biennials, perennials, bulbs and roots. Prune. Irrigate. Fertilize (organic).
Aug 12, 6:29 am - Aug 14, 2:35 am	4th	Leo	Cultivate. Destroy weeds and pests. Harvest fruits and root crops. Trim to retard growth.
Aug 17, 6:56 am - Aug 19, 4:51 pm	1st	Libra	Plant annuals for fragrance and beauty. Trim to increase growth.
Aug 19, 4:51 pm - Aug 21, 10:37 pm	1st	Scorpio	Plant grains, leafy annuals. Fertilize. Graft or bud plants. Irrigate. Trim to increase growth.
Aug 21, 10:37 pm - Aug 21, 11:48 pm	2nd	Scorpio	Plant grains, leafy annuals. Fertilize. Graft or bud plants. Irrigate. Trim to increase growth.
Aug 24, 3:22 am - Aug 26, 4:10 am	2nd	Capricorn	Graft or bud plants. Trim to increase growth.
Aug 28, 3:48 am - Aug 28, 12:52 pm	2nd	Pisces	Plant grains, leafy annuals. Fertilize. Graft or bud plants. Irrigate. Trim to increase growth.
Aug 28, 12:52 pm - Aug 30, 4:15 am	3rd	Pisces	Plant biennials, perennials, bulbs and roots. Prune. Irrigate. Fertilize (organic).
Aug. 30, 4:15 am - Sept. 1, 7:20 am	3rd	Aries	Cultivate. Destroy weeds and pests. Harvest fruits and root crops. Trim to retard growth.

Gardening Dates

Dates	Qtr	Sign	Activity
Sept. 1, 7:20 am - Sept. 3, 2:09 pm	3rd	Taurus	Plant potatos and tubers. Trim to retard growth.
Sept. 6, 12:30 am - Sept. 8, 12:55 pm	4th	Cancer	Plant biennials, perennials, bulbs and roots. Prune. Irrigate. Fertilize (organic).
Sept. 8, 12:55 pm - Sept. 11, 1:29 am	4th	Leo	Cultivate. Destroy weeds and pests. Harvest fruits and root crops. Trim to retard growth.
Sept. 11, 1:29 am - Sept. 12, 6:08 pm	4th	Virgo	Cultivate, especially medicinal plants. Destroy weeds and pests. Trim to retard growth.
Sept. 13, 12:51 pm - Sept. 15, 10:20 pm	1st	Libra	Plant annuals for fragrance and beauty. Trim to increase growth.
Sept. 15, 10:20 pm - Sept. 18, 5:30 am	1st	Scorpio	Plant grains, leafy annuals. Fertilize. Graft or bud plants. Irrigate. Trim to increase growth.
Sept. 20, 10:12 am - Sept. 22, 12:39 pm	2nd	Capricorn	Graft or bud plants. Trim to increase growth.
Sept. 24, 1:43 pm - Sept. 26, 2:46 pm	2nd	Pisces	Plant grains, leafy annuals. Fertilize. Graft or bud plants. Irrigate. Trim to increase growth.
Sept. 26, 9:51 pm - Sept. 28, 5:24 pm	3rd	Aries	Cultivate. Destroy weeds and pests. Harvest fruits and root crops. Trim to retard growth.
Sept. 28, 5:24 pm - Sept. 30, 11:02 pm	3rd	Taurus	Plant potatos and tubers. Trim to retard growth.
Oct. 3, 8:15 am - Oct. 4, 7:05 am	3rd	Cancer	Plant biennials, perennials, bulbs and roots. Prune. Irrigate. Fertilize (organic).
Oct. 4, 7:05 am - Oct. 5, 8:12 pm	4th	Cancer	Plant biennials, perennials, bulbs and roots. Prune. Irrigate. Fertilize (organic).
Oct. 5, 8:12 pm - Oct. 8, 8:49 am	4th	Leo	Cultivate. Destroy weeds and pests. Harvest fruits and root crops. Trim to retard growth.
Oct. 8, 8:49 am - Oct. 10, 8:00 pm	4th	Virgo	Cultivate, especially medicinal plants. Destroy weeds and pests. Trim to retard growth.
Oct. 12, 9:14 am - Oct. 13, 4:46 am	1st	Libra	Plant annuals for fragrance and beauty. Trim to increase growth.
Oct. 13, 4:46 am - Oct. 15, 11:07 am	1st	Scorpio	Plant grains, leafy annuals. Fertilize. Graft or bud plants. Irrigate. Trim to increase growth.
Oct. 17, 3:38 pm - Oct. 19, 1:10 pm	1st	Capricorn	Graft or bud plants. Trim to increase growth.
Oct. 19, 1:10 pm - Oct. 19, 6:52 pm	2nd	Capricorn	Graft or bud plants. Trim to increase growth.
Oct. 21, 9:23 pm - Oct. 23, 11:51 pm	2nd	Pisces	Plant grains, leafy annuals. Fertilize. Graft or bud plants. Irrigate. Trim to increase growth.

Gardening Dates

Dates	Qtr	Sign	Activity
Oct. 26, 3:12 am - Oct. 26, 9:12 am	2nd	Taurus	Plant annuals for hardiness. Trim to increase growth.
Oct. 26, 9:12 am - Oct. 28, 8:35 am	3rd	Taurus	Plant potatos and tubers. Trim to retard growth
Oct. 30, 4:57 pm - Nov. 2, 4:16 am	3rd	Cancer	Plant biennials, perennials, bulbs and roots. Prune. Irrigate. Fertilize (organic).
Nov. 2, 4:16 am - Nov. 3, 2:50 am	3rd	Leo	Cultivate. Destroy weeds and pests. Harvest fruits and root crops. Trim to retard growth.
Nov. 3, 2:50 am - Nov. 4, 4:57 pm	4th	Leo	Cultivate. Destroy weeds and pests. Harvest fruits and root crops. Trim to retard growth.
Nov. 4, 4:57 pm - Nov. 7, 4:29	4th	Virgo	Cultivate, especially medicinal plants. Destroy weeds and pests. Trim to retard growth.
Nov. 9, 1:02 pm - Nov. 10, 11:17 pm	4th	Scorpio	Plant biennials, perennials, bulbs and roots. Prune. Irrigate. Fertilize (organic).
Nov. 10, 11:17 pm - Nov. 11, 6:27 pm	1st	Scorpio	Plant grains, leafy annuals. Fertilize. Graft or bud plants. Irrigate. Trim to increase growth.
Nov. 13, 9:44 pm - Nov. 16, 12:15 am	1st	Capricorn	Graft or bud plants. Trim to increase growth.
Nov. 18, 3:00 am - Nov. 20, 6:34 am	2nd	Pisces	Plant grains, leafy annuals. Fertilize. Graft or bud plants. Irrigate. Trim to increase growth.
Nov. 22, 11:12 am - Nov. 24, 5:19 pm	2nd	Taurus	Plant annuals for hardiness. Trim to increase growth.
Nov. 27, 1:37 am - Nov. 29, 12:30 pm	3rd	Cancer	Plant biennials, perennials, bulbs and roots. Prune. Irrigate. Fertilize (organic).
Nov. 29, 12:30 pm - Dec. 2, 1:11 am	3rd	Leo	Cultivate. Destroy weeds and pests. Harvest fruits and root crops. Trim to retard growth.
Dec. 2, 1:11 am - Dec. 3, 12:06 am	3rd	Virgo	Cultivate, especially medicinal plants. Destroy weeds and pests. Trim to retard growth.
Dec. 3, 12:06 am - Dec. 4, 1:24 pm	4th	Virgo	Cultivate, especially medicinal plants. Destroy weeds and pests. Trim to retard growth.
Dec. 6, 10:39 pm - Dec. 9, 3:59 am	4th	Scorpio	Plant biennials, perennials, bulbs and roots. Prune. Irrigate. Fertilize (organic).
Dec. 9, 3:59 am - Dec. 10, 11:57 am	4th	Sagittarius	Cultivate. Destroy weeds and pests. Harvest fruits and root crops. Trim to retard growth.
Dec. 11, 6:15 am - Dec. 13, 7:14 am	1st	Capricorn	Graft or bud plants. Trim to increase growth.
Dec. 15, 8:44 am - Dec. 17, 4:31 am	1st	Pisces	Plant grains, leafy annuals. Fertilize. Graft or bud plants. Irrigate. Trim to increase growth.

Gardening Dates

Dates	Qtr	Sign	Activity
Dec. 17, 4:31 am - Dec. 17, 11:55 am	2nd	Pisces	Plant grains, leafy annuals. Fertilize. Graft or bud plants. Irrigate. Trim to increase growth.
Dec. 19, 5:09 pm - Dec. 22, 12:17 am	2nd	Taurus	Plant annuals for hardiness. Trim to increase growth.
Dec. 24, 9:14 am - Dec. 26, 8:09 pm	3rd	Cancer	Plant biennials, perennials, bulbs and roots. Prune. Irrigate. Fertilize (organic).
Dec. 26, 8:09 pm - Dec. 29, 8:46 am	3rd	Leo	Cultivate. Destroy weeds and pests. Harvest fruits and root crops. Trim to retard growth.
Dec. 29, 8:46 am - Dec. 31, 9:33 pm	3rd	Virgo	Cultivate, especially medicinal plants. Destroy weeds and pests. Trim to retard growth.

The Zodiac Garden

Although the plants below are ruled by the signs listed, they should not necessarily be planted while the Moon is in that sign. For planting information, please read the "Gardening by the Moon" section of this book.

ARIES (MARS): aloe, arum, bayberry, cayenne, cowslip, crowfoot, garlic, hemp, holly, hops, juniper, leeks, marjoram, mustard, onions, peppermint, thistle.

TAURUS (VENUS): alder, asparagus, beans, coltsfoot, lovage, mint, poppy, sage, spearmint, tansy, thyme, yarrow.

GEMINI (MERCURY): anise, bittersweet, cabbage, caraway, celery, fern, lily of the valley, parsley, valerian.

CANCER (MOON): chickweed, cucumbers, flax, geraniums, honeysuckle, hyssop, jasmine, lemon balm, lettuce, melons, mushrooms, pumpkins, turnips, wintergreen.

LEO (SUN): almond, angelica, bay, borage, bugloss, celandine, chamomile, citrus, cowslip, heliotrope, marigold, mistletoe, olive, peony, poppy, rue, saffron, St.-John's-wort, sunflower.

VIRGO (MERCURY): artemisia, cabbage, caraway, carrots, celery, cornflower, fennel, hazelnut, lavender, myrtle.

LIBRA (VENUS): asparagus, beans, cloves, daisies, feverfew, orchids, pennyroyal, thyme, violets.

SCORPIO (PLUTO): basil, blackberry, heather, horehound, horseradish, witch hazel, wormwood.

SAGITTARIUS (JUPITER): agrimony, balm, borage, carnations, clover, dandelions, dock, pinks, sage, tomatoes, wallflowers.

CAPRICORN (SATURN): aconite, beets, comfrey, flaxseed, heartsease, horsetail grass, ivy, pansies, plantain, shepherd's purse, spinach, wintergreen.

AQUARIUS (URANUS): coltsfoot, grapes, marigold, marsh mallow, pears, primrose, snakeroot, sorrel, southernwood, valerian.

PISCES (NEPTUNE): chamomile, Irish moss, liverwort, mint, sea mosses and other water plants, verbena, wormwood.

Directory of
Products and
Services

The Daily Astro-Planner
for Serious Astrologers

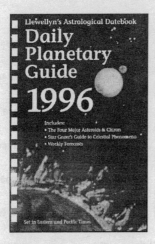

Llewellyn's Computerized Astrological Services

Llewellyn has been a leading authority in astrological chart readings for more than 30 years. We feature a wide variety of readings with the intent to satisfy the needs of any astrological enthusiast. Our goal is to give you the best possible service so that you can achieve your goals and live your life successfully. **Be sure to give accurate and complete birth data on the order form. This includes exact time (A.M. or P.M.), date, year, city, county and country of birth. Note: Noon will be used as your birthtime if you don't provide an exact time. Check your birth certificate for this information! Llewellyn will not be responsible for mistakes made by you.** An order form follows these listings.

SIMPLE NATAL CHART
Learn the locations of your midpoints and aspects, elements, and more. Discover your planets and house cusps, retrogrades, and other valuable data necessary to make a complete interpretation. Matrix Software programs and designs The Simple Natal Chart printout.
APS03-119 .... $5.00

PERSONALITY PROFILE
Our most popular reading also makes the perfect gift! This 10-part profile depicts your "natal imprint" and how the planets mark your destiny. Examine emotional needs and inner feelings. Explore your imagination and read about your general characteristics and life patterns.
APS03-503 .... $20.00

LIFE PROGRESSION
Progressions are a special system astrologers use to map how the "natal you" develops through specified periods of your present and future life. With this report you can discover the "now you!" This incredible reading covers a year's time and is designed to complement the Personality Profile Reading. **Specify present residence.**
APS03-507 .... $20.00

COMPATIBILITY PROFILE
Are you compatible with your lover, spouse, friend, or business partner? Find out with this in-depth look at each person's approach to the relationship. Evaluate goals, values, potential conflicts. This service includes planetary placements for both individuals, so send birth data for both. **Indicate each person's gender and the type of relationship involved** (romance, business, etc.).
APS03-504 .... $30.00

PERSONAL RELATIONSHIP INTERPRETATION

If you've just called it quits on one relationship and know you need to understand more about yourself before testing the waters again, then this is the report for you! This reading will tell you how you approach relationships in general, what kind of people you look for and what kind of people might rub you the wrong way. Important for anyone!

APS03-506 ....$20.00

TRANSIT REPORT

Keep abreast of positive trends and challenging periods in your life. Transits are the relationships between the planets today and their positions at your birth. They are an invaluable timing and decision-making aid. This report starts on the first day of the month, devotes a paragraph to each of your transit aspects and their effective dates. *Be sure to specify present residence for all getting this report!*

APS03-500 – 3-month report $12.00
APS03-501 – 6-month report $20.00
APS03-502 – 1-year report $30.00

BIORHYTHM REPORT

Some days you have unlimited energy, then the next day you feel sluggish and awkward. These cycles are called biorhythms. This individual report accurately maps your daily biorhythms and thoroughly discusses each day. Now you can plan your days to the fullest!

APS03-515 – 3-month report $12.00
APS03-516 – 6-month report $18.00
APS03-517 – 1-year report $25.00

TAROT READING

Find out what the cards have in store for you with this 12-page report that features a 10-card "Celtic Cross" spread shuffled and selected especially for you. For every card that turns up there is a detailed corresponding explanation of what each means for you. Order this tarot reading today! *Indicate the number of shuffles you want.*

APS03-120 ....$10.00

LUCKY LOTTO REPORT (State Lottery Report)

Do you play the state lotteries? This report will determine your luckiest sequence of numbers for each day based on specific planets, degrees, and other indicators in your own chart. Give your full birth data and middle name. *Tell us how many numbers your state lottery requires in sequence, and the highest possible numeral. Indicate the month you want to start.*

APS03-512 – 3-month report $10.00
APS03-513 – 6-month report $15.00
APS03-514 – 1-year report $25.00

NUMEROLOGY REPORT

Find out which numbers are right for you with this insightful report. This report uses an ancient form of numerology invented by Pythagoras to determine the significant numbers in your life. Using both your name and date of birth, this report will calculate those numbers that stand out as yours. With these numbers, you can tell when the important periods of your life will occur. *Please indicate your full birth name.*

APS03-508 – 3-month report $12.00
APS03-509 – 6-month report $18.00
APS03-510 – 1-year report $25.00

ULTIMATE ASTRO-PROFILE

More than 40 pages of insightful descriptions of your qualities and talents. Read about your burn rate (thirst for change). Explore your personal patterns (inside and outside). The Astro-Profile doesn't repeat what you've already learned from other personality profiles, but considers the natal influence of the lunar nodes, plus much more.

APS03-505 ....$40.00

Special Combo Offer!

Personality Profile & Life Progression

This powerful combination of readings will help you understand what challenges lie ahead for you and what resources you have to achieve the success you want.

Special Combo Price!

APS03-216 $30.00

ASTROLOGICAL SERVICES ORDER FORM

SERVICE NAME & NUMBER _____

_____

Provide the following data on all persons receiving a service:

1ST PERSON'S FULL NAME, including current middle & last name(s)

_____

Birthplace (city, county, state, country) _____

_____

Birthtime _____ ☐ A.M. ☐ P.M. Month _____ Day _____ Year _____

2ND PERSON'S FULL NAME (if ordering for more than one person)

_____

Birthplace (city, county, state, country) _____

_____

Birthtime _____ ☐ A.M. ☐ P.M. Month _____ Day _____ Year _____

BILLING INFORMATION

Name _____

Address _____

_____

City _____ State _____ Zip _____

Country _____ Day phone: _____

Make check or money order payable to Llewellyn Publications, or charge it!
Check one: ☐ Visa ☐ MasterCard ☐ American Express

Acct. No. _____ Exp. Date _____

Cardholder Signature _____

Mail this form and payment to:

LLEWELLYN'S PERSONAL SERVICES
P.O. BOX 64383-K915 • ST. PAUL, MN 55164-0383
Allow 4-6 weeks for delivery.

SUPER DISCOUNTS ON
LLEWELLYN DATEBOOKS AND CALENDARS!

Llewellyn offers several ways to save money on our almanacs and calendars. With a four-year subscription you receive your books as soon as they are published. The price remains the same for four years even if there is a price increase! Llewellyn pays postage and handling. *Buy any 2 subscriptions and take $2 off! Buy 3 and take $3 off! Buy 4 and take an additional $5 off the cost!*

Subscriptions (4 years, 1997-2000) Available on these annuals only:

❐	Astrological Calendar	$48.00
❐	Sun Sign Book	$27.80
❐	Moon Sign Book	$27.80
❐	Daily Planetary Guide	$39.80
❐	Organic Gardening Almanac	$27.80

Dozen Orders: 40% Off

Order *by the dozen* and save 40%! Sell them to your friends or give them as gifts. Llewellyn pays all postage and handling on dozen orders.

1996	1997		
❐	❐	Astrological Calendar	$86.40
❐	❐	Sun Sign Book	$50.04
❐	❐	Moon Sign Book	$50.04
❐	❐	Daily Planetary Guide	$71.64
❐	❐	Magical Almanac	$50.04
❐	❐	Organic Gardening Almanac	$50.04
❐		Myths of the Gods & Goddesses Calendar	$86.40
❐		Pocket Planner: Daily Ephemeris & Aspectarian	$57.24

Individual Copies of Llewellyn Almanacs and Calendars

When ordering individual copies, include $4 postage for orders $15 & under and $5 for orders over $15. Llewellyn pays postage for all orders over $100.

1996	1997		
❐	❐	Astrological Calendar	$12.00
❐	❐	Sun Sign Book	$6.95
❐	❐	Moon Sign Book	$6.95
❐	❐	Daily Planetary Guide	$9.95
❐	❐	Magical Almanac	$6.95
❐	❐	Organic Gardening Almanac	$6.95
❐		Myths of the Gods & Goddesses Calendar	$12.00
❐		Pocket Planner: Daily Ephemeris & Aspectarian	$7.95

PLEASE USE ORDER FORM ON LAST PAGE.

LLEWELLYN ORDER FORM

Llewellyn Publications
P.O. Box 64383-K915, St. Paul, MN 55164-0383

You may use this form to order any of the Llewellyn books or services listed in this publication.

GIVE TITLE OF BOOK, AUTHOR OF BOOK, ORDER NUMBER AND PRICE.

_____

_____

_____

_____

_____

Shipping and Handling: Include $4 for orders $15 & under; $5 for orders over $15. Llewellyn pays postage for all orders over $100. We ship UPS when possible. Please give street address (UPS cannot deliver to P.O. Boxes). **Now Available — Second Day Air! Cost is $8/one book; add $1 for each additional book.**

Credit Card Orders: In the U.S. and Canada call 1-800-THE-MOON. In Minnesota call 612-291-1970. Or, send credit card order by mail. Any questions can be directed to customer service 612-291-1970.

❑ VISA ❑ MasterCard ❑ American Express ❑ Check/M.O.

Account No. _____

Expiration Date _____ Phone _____

Cardholder Signature _____

Name_____

Address_____

City _____

State _____ Zip _____

MN residents add 7% sales tax to cost of book(s)